Published by ParentMap
Distributed by Ingram Publisher Services

Cover photographs: Sandra Lamb, Megan Lee
Cover design: Amy Chinn
Interior design and composition: Amy Chinn
Illustrations: Alli Arnold/*alliarnold.com*
Copy editor: Sunny Parsons
Library of Congress Cataloging-in-Publication Data is available.

ISBN-13: 978-0-9904306-6-7
ISBN-10: 0-9904306-6-9

ParentMap dba Gracie Enterprises
7683 SE 27th St. PMB#190
Mercer Island, WA 98040
206-709-9026

ParentMap books are available at special discounts when purchased in bulk for premiums and sales promotions as well as for fundraisers or educational use. Place book orders at *parentmap.com* or 206-709-9026.

le of Contents

52 Seatt[le]
Adventu[res]
With Ki[ds]

A four-season g[uide]

ParentMap
'cause parenting is a trip!

ParentMap is a Seattle-based resource for award-winning p[arents]
parentmap.com

Why 52 Adventures?

When my son was 2, my job (and life) changed. I became an editor at ParentMap, trading an office at a downtown Seattle nonprofit for my laptop and cluttered dining room table. For the next five years, I had the fortunate, home-based situation of assigning, editing and writing hundreds of stories about exploring the Puget Sound region — and the Northwest — with kids in tow.

This was not quite as fun as it sounds. It was, in fact, a tiny bit excruciating to be editing a story on "best beaches" while my child was in day care and my only dose of the outdoors was a 10-minute walk.

Nevertheless, I knew how lucky I was, not only because the work was interesting, but also because when I did have time, it was immediately useful. I had learned early on that the key to my parenting sanity was to get out and explore, and this job rewarded my family with a pipeline of inspired ideas for where to go around our glorious, green, gray, sunny, muddy, cosmopolitan Cascadian region.

What I discovered along the way was — no surprise — that the most rewarding excursions were often the simplest: mini adventures that helped us uncover the natural and cultural beauty of the Puget Sound area on kid time.

JULIE NIMMERGUT/THE HIDDEN LENS

The editor's family

FOR EXAMPLE: Although I had lived in Seattle for almost 15 years before becoming a parent, it wasn't until after editing a ParentMap article on secret gardens that I visited the Rainier Beach neighborhood's spectacular Kubota Garden, which remains one of my favorite Seattle places. Via my work, my family also discovered the Mountain Loop Highway's Boulder River trail, which my son still refers to as "the castle hike"; Guemes Island, a small San Juan island that's only a five-minute ferry ride from Anacortes; and the log pile at Magnuson Park's Children's Garden, which facilitated our first foray into fort building.

This book came about because I wanted to share. With much help from ParentMap writers and staff, I've compiled some of ParentMap's most unexpected, engaging and useful content for nearby adventures with kids into this slim, bookmark-ready guidebook. (I say "some of" because we had to make hard choices and couldn't come close to including everything.)

Instead of tourist-path highlights, you'll find a bucket list of experiences that are off the beaten path and will help you make the most of this extraordinary region we live in.

We also have a subversive goal: connectedness. Our kids are busy. We are all plugged in. Taking time as a family to hike to a waterfall, get on island time and explore a museum fosters family bonding that pays off, over and over.

How to use "52"

➤ Each season includes a dozen or more adventures that fit multiple ages of kids. Each adventure spotlights 4–10 places so you can find a good fit for your family.

➤ Most adventures are free or affordable and almost all are within a two-hour drive of Seattle (the "farther afield" icon ▬▬➤ marks those excursions that entail a longer drive).

➤ The season is just a suggestion, of course. Mix and match.

➤ Some adventures are epic. Many are extraordinarily ordinary, in that Northwest way. What they all have in common: They're worth the drive (or the bus ride).

➤ Because we focused on adventures that aren't date-specific, we excluded whole categories of wonderful things to do, such as music and theater. (Find tons of information on those activities at *parentmap.com*.)

➤ Similarly, we also only lightly covered well-known sites — as worthy as they are — because they are well-known.

➤ We did not include comprehensive information for each adventure (go online for that), but focused on insider tips that you won't find everywhere.

➤ And finally … y'all know this: Everything changes. Check hours and prices for attractions; check status of trails for hikes. Be safe, be smart, have fun.

A word about our writers

Each adventure was written by a Seattle-area writer who knows her stuff. Several have written their own books on local travel, such as Linnea Westerlind's "Discovering Seattle Parks" and Fiona Cohen's "Curious Kids Nature Guide"; and/or have fantastic blogs that you should bookmark right now (examples include Maegen Blue's "Sounds Fun Mom," Lauren Braden's "Northwest TripFinder" and Jennifer Johnson's "The Hiker Mama").

A FINAL NOTE: Much of this content has appeared in an earlier version on *parentmap. com*. When you're ready for more (and what's new), go there.

Happy adventuring.

—*Elisa Murray*

Help us keep this guide up to date

While we've made every effort to ensure that the information in this guide is as accurate as possible, things change quickly around here (as you know). Please email us at *editor@parentmap.com* about updates you're aware of, and let us know of your suggestions for adventures and outings to include in future editions.

ParentMap books are available at special discounts when purchased in bulk for premiums and sales promotions, as well as for fundraisers or educational use. Contact *books@parentmap.com* for more information.

About ParentMap

ParentMap is Seattle's largest parenting media brand (*ParentMap.com*) providing trusted, innovative and award-winning content that supports and inspires families across the greater Puget Sound and beyond. We bring you a full menu of parenting nourishment, from the most fascinating research and important news (what we like to call the broccoli) to get-out-of-the-house-now ideas for adventure and enrichment (the popcorn!). Our deep community connections, family advocacy and unique partnerships allow you to build the best village for your children. Sign up to get our weekly picks for family fun and the latest parenting buzz delivered to your inbox at *ParentMap.com/enews*.

Other ParentMap Titles

"Ready, Set, Sleep: 50 Ways to Help Your Child Sleep, So You Can Sleep Too"
By Malia Jacobson

"Getting to Calm: Cool Headed Strategies for Parenting Tweens and Teens"
By Laura S. Kastner, Ph.D., and Jennifer Wyatt

"Getting to Calm, The Early Years: Cool-Headed Strategies for Raising Happy, Caring, and Independent Three- to Seven-Year-Olds"
By Laura S. Kastner, Ph.D.

"Spare Me 'The Talk'!: A Girl's Guide to Sex, Relationships and Growing Up"
By Jo Langford, M.A.

"Spare Me 'The Talk'!: A Guy's Guide to Sex, Relationships and Growing Up"
By Jo Langford, M.A.

"Wise-Minded Parenting: 7 Essentials for Raising Successful Tweens and Teens"
By Laura S. Kastner, Ph.D. with Kristen A. Russell

"Beyond Smart: Boosting Your Child's Social, Emotional and Academic Potential"
By Linda Morgan

"Northwest Kid Trips: Portland, Seattle, Victoria, Vancouver"
By Lora Shinn

Ready, Set, $ave

Ah, kids. They make ordinary living way more expensive while simultaneously taking away the time necessary to look for ways to save. Add in the soaring cost of everything else and it can be hard to justify funds for fun.

Luckily, we Seattle-area parents are not only experts at stretching our fun-designated dollars, but we're more than happy to share our hard-earned tips. So, before you find an adventure in the pages that follow, peruse this list of reader-tested hacks.

PLAYING TOURIST

1. Museum passes, check! Local libraries including the Seattle Public Library, the Pierce County Library System and the King County Library System allow patrons to check out passes to many museums and attractions, including Seattle Aquarium, the Museum of Pop Culture, Northwest African American Museum, Tacoma Art Museum and even Woodland Park Zoo. Go online and reserve early!

2. Members only: Become a member of a museum or zoo, which brings down your cost per visit and usually has reciprocal membership privileges with other institutions.

3. Free museum days: Many museums have one or two free days per month (see *parentmap.com/museumsfree*). Many Seattle museums offer free admission on first Thursdays, and several Tacoma museums offer free admission on third Thursdays (usually in the evening, check hours).

4. Free museums: A number of excellent small museums in the area don't charge admission, including the Gates Foundation Discovery Center, Frye Art Museum, the Seattle unit of the Klondike Gold Rush National Historical Park in Pioneer Square, the Harbor History Museum in Gig Harbor and the Duwamish Longhouse and Cultural Center in West Seattle. Donations, of course, are always welcome.

5. BOA bennies: If you have a Bank of America debit or credit card, you are eligible for one free admission to several local museums (including Seattle Art Museum) on the first weekend of every month, through the Museums On Us program. *bankofamerica.com/museumsonus*

6. More museum discounts: Other discount programs include Museums for All (for

EBT cardholders) and Blue Star Museums (for families with active-duty service members). Local residents also sometimes get deals (King County residents pay less at Chihuly Garden and Glass, for example).

7. T-Town rocks: Downtown Tacoma museums are located within blocks of each other and offer bundled discounts, such as the Tacoma Museum Pass (one price gets you into six museums over a one-year period). *traveltacoma.com/things-to-do/museum-district*

8. Borrow instead of buy: Ask members of your local Buy Nothing group for coupons and passes that they're not using (and offer your unused coupons, too).

9. Be happy (hour): Especially in the summer, when bedtimes are later, happy-hour deals are a restaurant-loving family's best friend.

10. Kids eat free: Many local restaurants have a "kids eat free" night of the week; check out ParentMap's "Kids Eat Free" guide. *parentmap.com/kidseatfree*

11. #Sundayfunday: In Seattle, metered street parking is (still) free on Sundays, which makes Sunday the best weekend day for sightseeing in the city.

12. See Seattle with CityPass: This discounted combo pass lets you pay one price for tickets to five downtown Seattle attractions, a savings of 45 percent. Buy online. *citypass.com/seattle*

13. Group think: Organize a group outing to a show or museum and get a discount as well as the fun of a shared experience.

14. Coupon cool: Check for discounts that come with a AAA card or Microsoft Prime card or airline or hotel loyalty memberships. Chinook Book and the Seattle Entertainment Coupon Book have many "experience" discounts. In downtown Seattle, look for coupon- and info-packed publications from Seattle Premier Attractions and Visit Seattle.

15. Sporting fun: No budget for Seahawks or Sounders tickets? No matter: Get even closer to the excitement at matches featuring Seattle Reign FC, Seattle Sounders FC2, UW women's volleyball and other local teams.

16. Minor league magic: And in the spring and summer, cheer on the Everett AquaSox in the team's open-air stadium or the Tacoma Rainiers, with its Wiffle ball field and family deals.

NATURE AND OUTDOORS

17. Free hiking days: National and state parks have more than a dozen fee-free days every year. *wta.org/go-outside/passes/fee-free-days*

18. Free hiking every day: Many nearby hikes (Mercer Slough, Cougar or Tiger Mountain, city parks such as Discovery Park or Point Defiance) don't require a parking pass.

19. Free for fourth-graders: If you have a fourth-grader in your house, your family can get a free pass to national parks and historic sites (don't forget these!) through the Every Kid in a Park program. *everykidinapark.gov*

20. Owl right! Many nature centers, such as Lewis Creek Park Visitor Center in Bellevue, Seward Park Audubon Center, Tacoma Nature Center and Magnuson Nature Programs, offer free or very affordable programming for families.

21. Beach it: During low tide on summer days, get on-beach tutoring at many local beaches through programs such as Seattle Aquarium's beach naturalist program or Tacoma's Explore the Shore program.

22. Transit rules: In our crowded metropolis, taking transit can be fun, affordable and climate-friendly. Kids only pay $1.50 for King County Metro bus fare (5 and younger are free). Some attractions offer discounts to transit riders.

23. Starry nights: Peer up at the sky through a telescope at the Seattle Astronomical Society's monthly star parties at Green Lake in Seattle, Paramount School Park in Shoreline, Kent's Green River Natural Resource Area and other locations. The Tacoma Astronomical Society hosts free star parties at Pierce College.

ARTS SMARTS

24. Community centered: Your local community center is a hot spot for affordable (sometimes free) classes, camps and drop-in programs.

25. TeenTix: This amazing nonprofit allows teens to get $5 day-of-show tickets at dozens of Seattle-area arts venues. And on select days, TeenTix tickets are two for $10, meaning you can accompany your kid for next to nothing. *teentix.org*

26. Subscribe and save: A family subscription to a season of theater or music cuts costs per show and helps you plan ahead. Many subscriptions provide steep discounts and flexible options for exchanging tickets.

27. Teen artists alert! Gage Academy of Art runs two awesome sessions of Teen Art Studios — a free, weekly drop-in studio art program — at locations in Bellevue and Seattle.

28. SAM teens: Seattle Art Museum's programs let teens study art, lead programs (Teen Arts Group) and even take over the museum (Teen Night Out).

29. Free and fearless: Bureau of Fearless Ideas, located in Seattle's Greenwood neighborhood, offers free writing camps, classes and tutoring for kids. *fearlessideas.org*

30. Stage right: Seattle Public Theater's student productions are always free to everyone (though donations are welcome). Kids ages 12 and younger are free at Town Hall Seattle's Saturday Family Concert series. (Accompanying adults pay only $5.)

31. Classical on the cheap: For every adult ticket purchased for the Meany Center President's Piano or International Chamber Music series at the University of Washington, you can add two free youth tickets (ages 5–17). *meanycenter.org/tickets/ways-save*

32. Symphony smarts: Both the Seattle Symphony and Symphony Tacoma have affordable family series. And the Seattle Symphony's Family Connections Program offers two free tickets for kids ages 8–18 with the purchase of one adult ticket, for select concerts.

33. High school chops: Bring the kids to a concert or show at a local high school, or a student production by a professional theater, whose productions are often very good and affordable.

34. Social savings: Sign up for the email newsletter or "like" the Facebook page of arts organizations, which is where they often advertise giveaways and discounts.

35. In real time: ParentMap's online calendar (*parentmap.com/calendar*) lists hundreds of events a month and allows you to search for those that are free.

Getting to the Places You'll Go

As anyone who has watched a 4-year-old waiting for a train knows, the journey is absolutely the destination with kids. And given our region's increasing traffic challenges, taking the bus or light rail, biking or even car-sharing often makes practical and environmental sense. After all, wouldn't you rather skip traffic and parking hassles in favor of watching the city roll by with your kids?

Here are tips and apps for car-free adventuring, from A to W.

Amtrak. Amtrak runs trains south to Portland and destinations beyond; and north to Edmonds, Bellingham and Vancouver, British Columbia. For a fun overnight escape, ride the rails north to Fairhaven, or south to Centralia, where you can stay at the McMenamins Olympic Club Hotel.

Bolt Bus. Fifteen-dollar fare to Portland? Yes, please. The Bolt might not be as fun as Amtrak for kids, but it's quicker and cheaper. Take it to pedestrian-friendly Vancouver, B.C., or Portland, and book early (as always) for the best fares. *boltbus.com*

Bus Chick. Seattleite Carla Saulter, a mom of two, hasn't owned a car for more than a decade; she shares stories, inspiration, transit tips and more on her blog. *buschick.com*

Cascade Bicycle Club. One of the nation's largest bicycle nonprofits, Cascade Bicycle Club, has maps, camps, workshops and more to help your family get pedal empowered. *cascade.org*

King County Water Taxi. This passenger-only ferry whisks you from downtown Seattle to Seacrest Park in West Seattle and back. (It also goes to Vashon Island.) Bring bikes!

Link light rail. Seattle's slowly expanding light rail line runs from Seattle-Tacoma International Airport to Seattle destinations such as Beacon Hill, Columbia City, Westlake Center, Capitol Hill and the University of Washington's Husky Stadium. There is also a small Link line in downtown Tacoma, currently free to ride.

OneBusAway. Download this app to keep you up to date on bus arrivals in real time. *onebusaway.org*

ORCA card. ORCA is a regional fare system that makes it possible to use the same card to pay fares on buses, ferries, the Sounder train and light rail. Add funds and tap before and after your ride.

Pedalheads. Legions of Seattle kids have ditched their training wheels with the help of Pedalheads, which runs biking camps all over the region. *pedalheads.com*

Pogo. This Seattle-based company, which uses technology to help parents find car pool matches, serves a unique niche for drive-weary parents. *pogorides.com*

RapidRide buses. With well-lit shelters, free Wi-Fi, accessible design and such frequent service you don't need a schedule, King County Metro's RapidRide buses feel like light rail.

Seattle Center Monorail. Built for the 1962 World's Fair, the monorail connects downtown Seattle's Westlake Center to Seattle Center. It's a thrilling 1-mile, two-minute ride for kids.

Seattle Family Biking. This Facebook group shares tons of information about family biking, from routes to gear to meetups. *facebook.com/groups/seattlefamilybiking*

Seattle Streetcar. Seattle has a nascent streetcar system, with two lines (South Lake Union and First Hill) that shuttle passengers to many downtown attractions.

Seattle Transit Blog. This super-active blog has mapped out many useful transit-based tourist itineraries and offers the latest in area transit news. *seattletransitblog.com*

Sounder. This commuter train system runs north to Edmonds and south to Tacoma, and works well for a one-way trip to those destinations (take a bus the other way).

Trailhead Direct. A free shuttle bus system takes hikers to popular trails in the Issaquah/North Bend region. Can you say "sleep in"? *parentmap.com/trailhead*

Transit app. This useful app shows you nearby departure times for transit, and you don't even have to tap. *transitapp.com*

Trip Planner. Another indispensable app (it's also available on the web), Trip Planner will help you plan transit trips around Greater Seattle or beyond. *m.tripplanner.kingcounty.gov*

Washington State Ferries. See ferry wait times, make reservations to the San Juan Islands and plan your trip.

SPRING

Break out the bikes, the trikes, the skateboards and the fishing rods. Every day until June 21, we get an extra two minutes and eight seconds of daylight. Have rain boots at the ready, though.

Twin Falls

1.

Roaring Waterfall Hikes

By Lauren Braden

The Cascade Mountain Range is named for the hundreds of waterfalls, big and small, that cascade over cliffs, carrying huge amounts of water from winter rains and melting snow. It adds up to a five-senses hiking experience at (almost) any time of the year, but especially in the spring. Here are five of the best waterfall hikes for families within a two-hour drive of Seattle; find more at *parentmap.com/waterfall*.

IMPORTANT: Be safe. Be especially careful with kids around waterfall trails (see sidebar "Safety First"), and always check conditions of trails and roads before your hike.

Wallace Falls   *70 MIN DRIVE*

Gold Bar

One of the most stunning waterfalls in Washington state, Wallace Falls is composed of upper, middle and lower falls, first plunging a dramatic 265 vertical feet onto the first tier, then churning and tumbling two more times. The trail starts under hissing power lines, but you'll finish this stretch soon enough if you take a right on the Woody Trail and wind down to the lower falls, through stairs and switchbacks. Traverse up more switchbacks to get a better look at the middle falls viewpoint, a good turnaround spot. Important: As with all waterfalls, be safe and don't let kids (or adults!) climb anywhere near the falls.

GOOD TO KNOW: Tell your kids this fun fact: Many of the steps, turnpikes and switchbacks along the trail were built by high school students who volunteered with the Washington Trails Association (WTA).

FINE PRINT: Hike as far as 5.6 miles round-trip, 1,300 feet elevation gain. Wallace Falls State Park, 14503 Wallace Lake Rd., Gold Bar. Find directions and trip reports at WTA.org. *Discover Pass needed.* parks.state.wa.us/289/Wallace-Falls

Boulder River   FREE   / hR 45 mIN DRIVE
Mountain Loop Highway

Winding through one of the few remaining low-elevation, old-growth forests in the Cascades, this lush hike passes sword ferns, cedars and several cliffside waterfalls that plunge into the trail's namesake river. At just 1.25 miles is the trail's highlight, a massive twin curtain waterfall that streams down a moss-laden cliff wall. Just beyond, hike (carefully) down to the river for a perfect lunch and wading spot. Turn around or continue through the verdant wonderland to the trail's end.

GOOD TO KNOW: Kids will love crossing the log bridges, wading in the chilly river, climbing rocks and staying cool on a hot day.

FINE PRINT: Hike as far as 8.5 miles round-trip, 700 feet elevation gain. Mount Baker-Snoqualmie National Forest, Boulder River Trail 734. Find directions and trip reports at WTA.org. *No parking pass required. No restrooms at the trailhead.* fs.usda.gov

Franklin Falls
Snoqualmie Pass

This short, easy historical hike runs alongside an old wagon track that led early settlers over the Cascades to lower Puget Sound. The falls are 1 mile in, but the whole path is scenic as it hugs the South Fork of the Snoqualmie River. The trail steepens as you near the falls. Be wary of the drop-off on one side of the trail. Hold tight to little ones. The hike finishes with a short, rocky descent to the river bank and base of the impressive falls, which spill from the top of a sheer rock face. Be especially careful here (rocks can be slippery) and watch safely from the edge of the waterfall's pool.

GOOD TO KNOW: Have kids look for the actual ruts of pioneer-era wagon wheels near the beginning of the hike.

SPRING

NATURE

FINE PRINT: 2 miles round-trip, 400 feet elevation gain. Mount Baker-Snoqualmie National Forest, Denny Creek Trail, North Bend. Find directions and trip reports on WTA.org. Northwest Forest Pass needed. No restrooms at the trailhead (though reportedly there is one at the Denny Creek trailhead). fs.usda.gov

Twin Falls / hR DRIVE
North Bend

Just an hour's drive from Seattle, Twin Falls is one of the most popular family hikes in our region for a great reason — the falls are beautiful year-round. Kids love the trail from the get-go, as moss-draped trees flank the South Fork of the Snoqualmie River over ground filled with nurse logs and spring wildflowers. The first viewpoint is about .75 mile into the hike, and there are benches; this a great turnaround spot for younger children. One more mile of trail brings you to the payoff, a high footbridge over the river between the two waterfalls.

NEARBY BONUS: Another post-hike payoff: In North Bend, stop for milkshakes at Twede's Cafe of "Twin Peaks" fame.

FINE PRINT: 3 miles round-trip, 500 feet elevation gain. Olallie State Park, North Bend. Find directions and trip reports at WTA.org. Discover Pass needed. parks.state.wa.us/555/Olallie

SAFETY FIRST

Waterfalls are beautiful but can be dangerous, especially in spring conditions. Never venture into the direct stream, as loose rocks often tumble down with the water. Never climb up waterfalls, don't let children jump from rocks into a pool, and make sure kids are closely supervised and wearing sturdy shoes.

Follow basic hiking safety, too. Always check conditions of trails and roads before your hike; a great resource is Washington Trails Association's trip reports (*WTA.org*). Bring the 10 Essentials and be sure kids know how to be safe on the trail. Find out more at *parentmap.com/outdoorsafety.*

Murhut Falls
Olympic National Forest

Short and sweet, the trail to Murhut Falls delivers its reward — an enchanting 130-foot tiered waterfall — in just under a mile of easy walking, likely in solitude. Although the hike is not well-known, it is maintained, and the ascent is gentle enough for small children as the trail is a converted logging road. Use caution and hold small hands in the final ascent to the falls as the trail gets narrow and there's a drop-off to one side.

GOOD TO KNOW: This fern-fringed forest is pretty any time of year, but late spring offers a special enticement — blooming pink Pacific rhododendrons.

FINE PRINT: *1.6 miles round-trip, 300 feet elevation gain. Olympic National Forest, Murhut Falls Trail #828. Find directions and trip reports at WTA.org. Northwest Forest Pass required.* fs.usda.gov

More like this:
- ➤ Hikes With a Prize (Adventure 16)
- ➤ Secret Urban Hikes (Adventure 42)
- ➤ Rainy-Day Playgrounds (Adventure 50)

2.

Forts and Tree Houses

By Nancy Schatz Alton

Try this trick: Tell your kids you're going for a hike. Then follow with the phrase "and there's a tree house to explore." Watch their interest level shoot up. Because, as we all know, although inspiration always lies outside our front doors, if there happens to be a tree house, fort or stump house woven into an outing, inspiration quadruples.

COURTESY MERCER SLOUGH

Mercer Slough tree house

Magnuson Park Children's Garden   FREE

Sand Point, Seattle

Next time you're at Magnuson Park's beloved Junior League Playground, save time to explore the Children's Garden, just across the street and next to the Magnuson Community Garden. The garden, lovingly designed and maintained by Magnuson Nature Programs, has an unexpected delight known as the "wood pile," a 75-square-foot area of splinter-free wood that kids can pull apart to see the decomposition process, or use to build small piles, forts and other structures. Kids will also enjoy the mosaic art scattered around the garden.

GOOD TO KNOW: Dress to get dirty; some children might want gloves if they are first-time users. Magnuson Nature Programs hosts many affordable classes and events; check the schedule.

FINE PRINT: The wood pile is accessible during the hours that Magnuson Park is open. Magnuson Park Children's Garden, 7400 Sand Point Way N.E., Seattle. magnusonnatureprograms.com

Mercer Slough tree house   FREE

Bellevue

Mercer Slough Nature Park, tucked away in Bellevue near Interstate 405, is one of the Eastside's largest and most wildlife-rich parks. But one of the biggest highlights for kids is just steps from the parking lot at Mercer Slough Environmental Education Center. After you explore the complex of classrooms and stairs that allows visitors to see the forest from many levels, collect a key from the ranger to climb the ladder to the "tree house," essentially an elevated platform with handrails and a roof. Here, you are at eye level with the surrounding forest canopy. After taking in the view, take a hike on the 7 miles of shady trails.

GOOD TO KNOW: The center also hosts camps (through a partnership with Pacific Science Center), classes and nature movie nights, as well as free ranger-led walks.

FINE PRINT: Open daily. Mercer Slough Environmental Education Center, 1625 118th Ave. S.E., Bellevue. 425-452-2565. No parking pass needed. parks.bellevuewa.gov

Fort Worden State Park

Port Townsend

An active military base from 1902 to 1953, Fort Worden is now a stunning state park with more than 2 miles of saltwater shoreline, historic buildings and miles of trails, some of which lead to battery structures and underground bunkers. Young explorers can walk the dank, unlit tunnels of 12 former batteries on Artillery Hill. Also check out Memory's Vault, an area with pillars of poetry written by poet Sam Hamill that speaks to the fort's sights, sounds, history and weather. Trail maps are available at Fort Worden's Commons building, where you can also pick up coffee and snacks, and use the spiffy restrooms.

SAFETY TIPS: Use caution when climbing the stairs of the gun emplacements, since many lack handrails. Bring a flashlight to explore the fun but very dark and twisty tunnels and stay close to kids. There are open areas with no barriers in front of most of the gun emplacements, which lead to the bluff overlooking the Strait of Juan de Fuca and the Sound.

FINE PRINT: Fort Worden State Park, 200 Battery Way, Port Townsend. Call 888-226-7688 to book campsites or houses. Discover Pass needed. parks.state.wa.us/511/Fort-Worden

Fort Casey Historical State Park
Coupeville, Whidbey Island

Whidbey Island's Fort Casey was another important point, along with Fort Worden, in the former "Triangle of Fire" defense system constructed to protect Puget Sound. It's home to an even vaster network of gun emplacements, batteries and cannons. Children enjoy running the expansive grounds and climbing the stairs around the batteries, taking in the long view provided by these features. Tour the Admiralty Head Lighthouse before you leave.

GOOD TO KNOW: Turn your day trip into a getaway by staying in former officers' quarters at the Fort Casey Inn, booking a campsite at the state park or bringing a group to Camp Casey.

FINE PRINT: Fort Casey Historical State Park, 1280 Engle Rd., Coupeville. Call 888-226-7688 to book campsites. Discover Pass needed. parks.state.wa.us/505/Fort-Casey

Stump house at Guillemot Cove   FREE
Seabeck

At the end of the Guillemot Cove trail on the Kitsap Peninsula, families are rewarded with a stump house, which was created from an old western cedar tree stump after it was logged. While no one knows who built the stump house, urban legend suggests an outlaw used the stump as a hideout. A bonus to this hike is the beach: At low tide, look for oysters, sand dollars and sea stars.

GOOD TO KNOW: The hike down and then back up can be tiring for young children. After or during rainy periods, the meadow may be flooded; be sure to pack extra shoes or rain boots. No pets are allowed in the park.

FINE PRINT: 2.5 miles round-trip, 360 feet elevation. Guillemot Cove trailhead, 19484 N.W. Stavis Bay Rd., Seabeck. Find directions and trip reports at WTA.org. *No parking pass needed.* wta.org/go-hiking/hikes/guillemot-cove

IslandWood Canopy Tower   FREE
Bainbridge Island

Reasons abound to visit this 255-acre outdoor learning center on Bainbridge, from 6 miles of wooded trails to tree houses to an amazing garden. But the most exciting feature for kids is probably the 125-foot forest canopy tower, a rebuilt fire tower (formerly situated in the North Cascades) located on the edge of IslandWood's ravine. At the top, the view offers sightlines to Puget Sound and the mountains.

NEARBY BONUS: While exploring IslandWood's miles of trails, don't miss the 190-foot suspension bridge 60 feet above Mac's Dam Creek.

FINE PRINT: You can only visit IslandWood during public site tours or other public events; check the schedule online. Public events are usually free, but reserve your spot. Island-Wood, 4450 Blakely Ave. N.E., Bainbridge Island. 206-855-4300. No parking pass needed. islandwood.org

More like this:

> **Stairway Walks (Adventure 9)**
> **Dino-Mite Destinations (Adventure 35)**
> **Winning Winter Tours (Adventure 51)**

3.
Oh, Baby Animals!

By Allison Holm

Spring around the Sound means rain, mud, cherry blossoms, tulips — and baby animals. Take your kids to one of these farms, zoos and other critter-centric spots to ooh and ahh over furry and feathered friends, take a pony ride, and learn about fishing and farming. Some of these facilities are open year-round; others are open only in the spring and summer.

IMPORTANT: Before visiting, check a

farm's Facebook page or website (or call) to double-check hours and fees.

Forest Park Animal Farm   FREE

Everett

Everett's 197-acre Forest Park has everything from trails and picnic areas to a huge playground and a spray park. But for critter-loving kids, the highlight is the Animal Farm, just a short walk down from the playground. During open hours, kids can look at and interact with goats, chickens, ducks, sheep, pigs, beautiful bunnies and other farm animals. On select mornings, kids ages 2 and older can even get a free pony ride.

GOOD TO KNOW: Water-crazy kids? In hot weather, check out the Rotary Centennial sprayground, next to the playground. On a drizzly day, it's time for the indoor pool.

FINE PRINT: *The animal farm is open daily from late June through mid-August. Free, although donations are appreciated. Forest Park, 802 E. Mukilteo Blvd., Everett. 425-257-8700.* everettwa.gov/773/Animal-Farm

Maltby Produce Markets   FREE

Snohomish

Get your shopping covered while the kids get their animal fix at this hidden gem. Flower World's Maltby Produce Markets is just down the street from the huge nursery and features an on-site petting zoo where kids can get close to chickens and peacocks while watching sheep and goats roam the grassy area. Round out the experience by shopping for farm-fresh produce, herbs and eggs. Note: No dogs allowed.

NEARBY BONUS: Charming Snohomish, with its antique stores, river walk, eateries and Centennial biking trail, is just a mile away.

FINE PRINT: *Open year-round, daily. Free. Malty Produce Markets, 19523 Broadway Ave., Snohomish. 360-668-0174.* maltbyproducemarkets.com

Farrel-McWhirter Farm Park   FREE

Redmond

Tucked away in Redmond, Farrel-McWhirter is a 68-acre, city-owned park that offers an escape from urban life, with beautiful nature trails, large, grassy fields, picnic tables and barbecue pits. Kids can get up close and personal with pigs, goats, cows, ponies and turkeys.

GOOD TO KNOW: The park also hosts pony-riding classes, summer day camps and a preschool.

FINE PRINT: *Open year-round, daily, from 7 a.m. to dusk (barnyard hours are 9 a.m.–4*

p.m.). Free. Farrel-McWhirter Farm Park, 19545 N.E. Redmond Rd., Redmond. 425-556-2300. redmond.gov

Fox Hollow Farm
Issaquah

Set in the Squak Mountain area of Issaquah, Fox Hollow Farm — with its charming homestead and well-manicured surroundings — is a treat for kids of all ages (and parents, too). The open-farm days allow children to interact with sheep, goats, pigs, peacocks, chickens, miniature horses and kittens. Admission also includes the chance to drive mini John Deere tractors, bounce on giant inflatables and play house in the kid-size Cottage Area. Ramble down to the Issaquah Creek for a picnic or wading.

GOOD TO KNOW: Fox Hollow's Easter egg hunts are locally famous and usually held on several weekend days prior to Easter. Book ahead.

FINE PRINT: Open-farm sessions occur on weekends and select weekdays; reserve online. $10, kids younger than 12 months free. Fox Hollow Farm, 12123 Issaquah-Hobart Rd. S.E., Issaquah. 253-459-9095. foxhollowfamilyfarm.com

Kelsey Creek Farm   FREE
Bellevue

Not far from the trendy restaurants and shops of downtown Bellevue, this 1930s-style working farm, with white clapboard barns, open pastures and distant chatter of animals, sets a scene reminiscent of old-fashioned rural America. Kelsey Creek offers families a chance to view ponies, cows, sheep, bunnies, chickens and pigs in their pastures. There are also woodland paths, a playground and picnic tables.

GOOD TO KNOW: If you're just visiting, you can't pet the animals, but guided interaction is allowed at Kelsey Creek's farm classes, school

MORE CRITTER PICKS

Cougar Mountain Zoo: Emu chicks, wolf pups and reindeer calves, oh my! Issaquah's small zoo focuses on endangered species and education.

Northwest Trek: While riding the tram at this Eatonville wildlife park, you might spot baby bison, moose calves or fox kits.

Remlinger Farms: This farm/amusement park in Carnation includes a petting zoo with goats, peacocks and bunnies; pony rides are included in admission.

Outback Kangaroo Farm: This Arlington farm offers a Down Under experience, with tours featuring kangaroos, wallabies, wallaroos and other critters.

Woodland Park Zoo's Family Farm: Take a break from the wild animals and interact with the domestic set, including goats, pigs, bunnies, cows and chicks.

tours and birthday parties.

FINE PRINT: Open year-round, daily, from 9:30 a.m. to 3:30 p.m. Free, although donations are welcome. Kelsey Creek Farm, 410 130th Place S.E., Bellevue. 425-452-7688. farmer-jayne.com

Old McDebbie's Farm/Jim's U Fish
Spanaway

Jim and Debbie Pruitt love sharing their working farm in Spanaway with the community. Kids can ride a pony, walk the "Eye Spy" trail, create rhythms in the musical forest and go on a wildlife scavenger hunt. Families are invited to visit with the animals — everything from lambs, goats and bunnies to kangaroos and even a camel and a zebra. A favorite activity is fishing in the pond; bring your own rod or rent gear there.

GOOD TO KNOW: Want to catch fish but not clean it? The Pruitts will do it for you for a small fee. Also, it's fine to bring outside food in for a picnic.

FINE PRINT: Open March through November; the schedule varies by season. $8 admission, $5 pony rides, $6 for each fish caught. Old McDebbie's Farm/Jim's U Fish, 4924 268th St. E., Spanaway. 253-875-0356. oldmcdebbiesfarm.net

> ## More like this:
> ➤ **Berry-Pickin' Fun (Adventure 15)**
> ➤ **Easy Apple Picking (Adventure 30)**
> ➤ **Great Pumpkin Patches (Adventure 33)**

4.
Dig Into Clamming

By Nancy Schatz Alton

Digging for clams on a cold, wet spring day might not sound alluring. But there is something positively magical about this iconic Pacific Northwest hobby. Even if the rain is spitting out of the sky, you forget about getting wet within minutes of stepping onto the beach. For an hour or two, the drizzle doesn't matter, your family takes time to examine the wild world, and dinner that night is centered on delicious clams.

Clamming basics

TIDE CHARTS: Find out the time of the low tide for your clamming beach by looking online at tide charts. You have about a four-hour window around the low tide.

TYPE OF CLAMS: Clams available on Washington public beaches include littleneck, horse and butter clams, cockles, geoducks (the world's biggest burrowing clam) and razor clams.

LICENSE: The most important item is a shellfish/seaweed license, which is valid from April 1 to March 31 of the following year. Purchase one online at *fishhunt.dfw.wa.gov*, or buy a license at retailers such as Walmart, Fred Meyer and Big 5 Sporting Goods. Children younger than 15 do not need a license.

LIMIT: The daily personal limit for most marine clams (other than razor clams) is up to 40 clams but not to exceed 10 lbs. in the shell. Horse clams have a separate daily limit of seven, and you are allowed three geoducks daily. (Confirm limits on the Washington Department of Fish and Wildlife (WDFW) website.)

SHOVEL AND BUCKET: Depending on the type of clam you're digging, you might bring simple, small garden tools, such as a rake or trowel, or a shovel. You'll need a 5-gallon bucket with a tight-fitting lid in which to bring your clams home. Each person's limits must be kept separate until leaving the beach, so you'll need a net bag for each harvester; this also is helpful for rinsing clams of sand and grit.

GAUGES AND SCALES: You'll need plastic clam, shrimp and crab gauges, as well as a scale that hooks onto a bucket for larger clams (like butter clams).

BOOTS AND CLOTHES: Pack rubber boots and a complete change of clothes.

Top clamming tips

FOLLOW THE CLAMMERS: To find the area of the beach to start digging, look for people on the beach who are successfully harvesting clams. Each type of clam lives along a certain band of the beach and at a certain depth. The WDFW website has a page with information on every species.

LOOK FOR THE SHOW: Before you start digging, look for a hole or dimple in the sand or mud. This is called the "clam show" and it means the clam has withdrawn its neck after feeding and started to dig back down in the sand. Sometimes water or sand squirts out of a hole when you walk nearby it. Dig until you reach the clams.

MEASURE: Measure each clam with your gauge (most species need to be at least 1.5 inches wide) and count your limit.

INVOLVE THE KIDS: Kids can participate by digging, throwing clams in the bag, measuring or counting, or, of course, simply playing on the beach.

FILL EACH HOLE: After you are done digging, fill the hole. Some clam species need the holes filled up for survival, and the humans on the beach need the holes filled so they don't trip and possibly fall. WDFW officers can cite shellfishers for not filling holes.

PACK THE CLAMS TO TAKE HOME: On clamming days, you may meet a WDFW staff member counting limits in the parking lot. After you have had your limits counted, fill your bucket with seawater for the drive home. The clams need a minimum of four hours in this water to purge their bodies of grit and sand. Some experts recommend longer; look online for more instructions for purging and preparing.

RAZOR CLAMMING: Digging for the hardy razor clam is a different experience. Razor clam season opens in October every year and stays open until sometime in May (check the WDFW website for dig days). During the fall and winter, the low tides are in the evening, so people start as the light fades from the sky and they finish in the dark with lanterns lighting the digs. In the spring, the low tides are in the morning, making for easier razor clam digging in the daylight.

Razor clammers use a specialized digging tool such as a PVC tube or an aluminum tube, which brings up a core of sand. Sometimes the clam comes up on your first try, and other times the clam burrows back into the hole your tool made; if you're lucky you can dig the clam out with your hands. The daily limit for razor clams is the first 15 you dig up, regardless of size or condition, and each limit must be in a separate container. Learn how to shuck the clams and take out the digestive material on the WDFW website.

Kid-friendly clamming beaches around Puget Sound

There are many ways to find a great clamming beach, including the WDFW website, which has excellent beach-finding tools. Also check the WDFW and the Department of Health websites to make sure that the beaches are open and the shellfish is safe to eat. WDFW's hotline for consumption advisories is 800-562-5632.

Here are a few kid-friendly clamming beaches to try

Dosewallips State Park

Some people consider this beach the holy grail of clamming in the Pacific Northwest, with one of our state's largest, most productive tidelands. Make your outing an over-nighter by booking a campsite or cabin.

Quilcene Bay WDFW Tidelands

This beach on Hood Canal has pit toilets and an easy trail to the beach, with clamming just a few hundred feet from the parking lot. Although it isn't the most scenic beach, small clams are plentiful here.

Birch Bay State Park

This huge beach in Whatcom County, with a campground, has an abundant butter clam population, a decent Manila clam population and is a good place for crabbing.

West Penn Cove

This Whidbey Island beach has two access points (one of which has benefited from Penn Cove mussels from the nearby aquaculture operation), and there are good populations of native littlenecks and butter clams.

Twanoh State Park

Located on Hood Canal, this beautiful beach has camping and a swim area, and you can harvest oysters here year-round.

Razor clam beaches

Pacific Coast beaches with razor clam fisheries include some of the state's most spectacular stretches of sand, including Long Beach, Copalis Beach, Mocrocks Beach and Kalaloch Beach.

More like this:

➤ Berry-Pickin' Fun (Adventure 15)
➤ Bring on the Beach (Adventure 17)
➤ Family Birding Takes Flight (Adventure 43)

ELISA MURRAY

Kubota Garden

5.

Secret Gardens

By Jennifer Kakutani

Want a new spot for spring nature renewal with your family? These wonderful, lesser-known gardens have something special to offer, from a West Seattle garden designed to teach about honeybees to a pocket park that's also a cosmological adventure. Follow us on a dirt path to some of the Seattle area's secret gardens.

Kruckeberg Botanic Garden FREE

Shoreline

There might not be a more welcoming local garden for children than Kruckeberg, a 4-acre botanic garden that features a mix of native and exotic plants in a beautiful wooded setting. On an enchanting self-guided tour, my children thoroughly enjoyed finding treasures throughout, even as I was learning about the plants and trees. Hidden in the woods there is a stunning driftwood climbing structure, which kids are allowed to climb.

GOOD TO KNOW: Look for wonderful seasonal events for families, such as the "Garden Tots" program in the summer.

FINE PRINT: Open Friday–Sunday, 10 a.m.–5 p.m. Kruckeberg Botanic Garden, 20312 15th Ave. N.W., Shoreline. 206-546-1281. kruckeberg.org

Fremont Peak Park   FREE
North Seattle

Located on a west-facing bluff in Seattle's Fremont neighborhood, Fremont Peak Park invites visitors on a mythological and cosmological adventure. You can walk a labyrinth of blooming roses and tall trees and admire a view of the Olympic Mountains and Puget Sound. The center of the half-acre park is a sculpture that marks the solstices and equinoxes. Fun fact: Fremont Peak Park was once recognized as one of the 45 best public art projects in the U.S.

NEARBY BONUS: Just a few blocks north, stop by the Woodland Park Zoo Rose Garden and its new branch, the Seattle Sensory Garden, for more fragrant adventures.

FINE PRINT: Fremont Peak Park, 4357 Palatine Ave. N., Seattle. No restrooms. seattle.gov/parks/find/parks/fremont-peak-park

Danny Woo Community Garden   FREE
Chinatown–International District, Seattle

Climb up into Danny Woo Community Garden, with its steeply terraced gardens, and you will witness a culture of elderly folks that is sweet and inviting. Located in Seattle's Chinatown–International District, near the freeway, the garden is a social hub for immigrant gardeners to gather, grow food and pass on their practices. The children's garden is a multigenerational gardening effort that makes a powerful statement about the importance of homegrown food.

NEARBY BONUS: Across the street from the garden entrance is the historic Panama Hotel, which serves Macrina pastries and other snacks, and drinks. It's also a museum, complete with photographs, a phonograph, artifacts and a glass floor viewing area that shares the history of Seattle's Japanese community.

FINE PRINT: Danny Woo Community Garden, 620 S. Main St., Seattle. dannywoogarden.org

West Seattle Bee Garden   FREE
West Seattle

This busy garden, located in High Point Commons Park, is a must if your kids are curious about honeybees, especially if you want to observe them from a safe distance. The centerpiece of the park includes two hives nestled within an enclosure. The enclosure is covered in hexagonal panels that list fascinating bee facts. The honeycomb-style structure is located in a community garden (called a P-Patch) with a playground nearby and a large green space.

NEARBY BONUS: Take the short walk to Viewpoint Park for an amazing panorama of the Seattle skyline.

FINE PRINT: High Point Commons Park, 3201 S.W. Graham St., Seattle. westseattlebeegarden.com

Seattle Chinese Garden   FREE
West Seattle

Sometimes called the best-kept secret of West Seattle, the Seattle Chinese Garden, located at South Seattle College, employs water, stone, plants and architecture to create a spectacular landscape. Within this beautiful garden on a hilltop, families are surrounded by ancient symbolism. The bones of the earth are seen in stone bridges and rocky gorges. The blood of the earth is suggested by water, which infuses the garden with vital, rejuvenating chi.

NEARBY BONUS: The South Seattle College Arboretum is adjacent to the Chinese Garden and is free to the public.

FINE PRINT: Seattle Chinese Garden, 6000 16th Ave. S.W., Seattle. seattlechinesegarden.org

Kubota Garden   FREE
Rainier Beach, Seattle

This wild 20-acre Japanese garden in Rainier Beach — which was designated a historical landmark in 1981 — isn't quite the secret garden it once was. It's now counted as a favorite backdrop for family and couple photos. But there are still many days when you can have the lovely winding paths, ponds, waterfalls and hidden bridges all to yourself. Kids get almost magically pulled along by the paths that slope downhill from the entrance. It's delightful in all seasons.

GOOD TO KNOW: Kubota Garden Foundation offers free public tours one Saturday a month.

FINE PRINT: Kubota Garden, 9817 55th Ave. S., Seattle. kubotagarden.org

Bellevue Botanical Garden   FREE
Bellevue

Also not exactly a secret, Bellevue Botanical Garden has 20 acres of paths and innovative gardens that make it the ideal first hike for a preschooler. Take the "Lost Meadow" trail through wetlands and woodlands to a rock garden. Then continue on to the ultimate adventure for young kids — a 0.3-mile nature trail that crosses a ravine via a 150-foot suspension bridge (the Ravine Experience). Don't miss a meditative walk through the Yao Garden.

GOOD TO KNOW: Pick up a map of trails at the visitor center, and take a break at the Copper Kettle Coffee Bar in the Shorts House, right on garden grounds.

FINE PRINT: Bellevue Botanical Garden, 12001 Main St., Bellevue. bellevuebotanical.org

Highline SeaTac Botanical Garden   FREE

SeaTac

The heart of this unique 10-acre garden is Elda Behm's Paradise Garden. Elda Behm was an award-winning landscape designer, horticulturist and flower arranger. Her original garden was condemned to make way for the Port of Seattle's third runway expansion at Sea-Tac airport. It was saved and re-created by relocating thousands of Behm's plants that she had grown from seeds and cuttings. Stroll the garden and you will find ponds and four waterfalls that empty into a 100-foot stream.

GOOD TO KNOW: Visit the garden in May to see large bearded irises and rhododendrons in full bloom.

FINE PRINT: Highline SeaTac Botanical Garden, 13735 24th Ave. S., SeaTac. 206-391-4003. highlinegarden.org

More like this:
➤ **Oh, Baby Animals!**
  (Adventure 3)
➤ **Shady Summer Hikes**
  (Adventure 18)
➤ **Quirky Landmarks**
  (Adventure 45)

MORE BLOOMIN' FUN

Bloedel Reserve. Bainbridge Island's internationally recognized 150-acre landscape of woodlands and gardens is worth a visit any time of year.

Cherry blossoms. The University of Washington quad is the most famous local spot to view the show, but there are many other hot blossom spots. *parentmap.com/cherries*

Ethel L. Dupar's Fragrant Garden. You can only visit by appointment, but this South Seattle jewel is wheelchair accessible and designed for people who are blind. It is filled with more than 60 types of fragrant plants.

Picardo Farm P-Patch. Visit Seattle's original (and biggest) community garden and explore the sweetest children's garden around.

PowellsWood. This Federal Way garden serves as a source of inspiration for how to use natural land features to develop stunning landscapes.

Discovery Park

6.

Spring Hikes, Warm-Up Included

By Jennifer Johnson

In the spring, my kids and I go a little stir-crazy. We long to go hiking, but the weather is still drippy and our favorite trails in the mountains are laden with snow. It's time to get creative and explore treks closer to home. We especially like areas with indoor nature centers, where we can duck out of the rain and keep learning and exploring. An added bonus is that most of these hikes don't require a parking pass.

IMPORTANT: Be sure to pack your rain gear, mittens and a warm hat, plus a change of clothes for the car ride home. Hot chocolate is always a welcome addition, too.

Padilla Bay   FREE

Mount Vernon

An hour-and-a-half drive north of Seattle, near Anacortes, is a marvelous estuarine research reserve and interpretive center. You have several choices of trails: From the center's parking lot, take the wooded loop (a little less than a mile long). Add a few hundred yards by walking the paved path down to the beach and explore the mudflats. Or drive a mile south of the interpretive center to the South Shore Trail and walk along the tops of dikes, with water on one side and fields on the other. All trails are great for birding, too.

INDOOR TIP: The Breazeale Interpretive Center has a free museum chronicling life in the estuaries of the Salish Sea. We love the floor-to-ceiling aquarium full of sea life, and the hands-on room will keep the youngest children busy.

FINE PRINT: Padilla Bay South Shore Trail: 4.4 miles round-trip, 30 feet elevation gain. Find directions and trip reports on WTA.org. Breazeale Center open Tuesday–Saturday. Padilla Bay National Estuarine Research Reserve, Mount Vernon. 360-428-1558. No parking pass required. ecology.wa.gov

Discovery Park FREE
Magnolia, Seattle

This urban nature reserve, Seattle's largest park, is accessible in all seasons, has miles of trails, and will fill your need for green trees, birdsong and fresh air. Park at the Environmental Learning Center (east parking lot) and start on the 2.8-mile loop trail, which ambles through the woods, along bluffs with stunning views and through meadows; there's even a sandy area where kids can dig. Before or after your hike, check out the wonderful playground, just a short walk south of the center. From the north parking lot, you can walk the short Wolf Tree Nature Trail.

INDOOR TIP: Hop into the Environmental Learning Center to escape the cold and play with the hands-on exhibits.

FINE PRINT: Discovery Park Loop Trail: 2.8 miles, 140 feet elevation gain; many other trails available. Find directions and trip reports on WTA.org or look for an online trail map. Environmental Learning Center open Tuesday–Sunday. 3801 Discovery Park Blvd., Seattle. 206-386-4236. No parking pass required. seattle.gov/parks/find/parks/discovery-park

Brightwater Education Center FREE
Woodinville

You might think a wastewater treatment plant in Woodinville wouldn't be a pleasant place to hike, but King County designed the 70-acre site surrounding Brightwater for recreation, wildlife and education. Three miles of trails wander around ponds, along streams and through forest. You can choose from a couple of short loops on varied terrain and good surfaces. Be sure to stop and visit one of the ponds. Look for engaging art on the Brightwater campus, such as glass microbes and industrial pipes in the shapes of tree branches.

INDOOR TIP: At the Brightwater campus, kids and adults can learn about our water system through interactive exhibits, and visitors ages 9 and older can take a tour of the treatment plant. Bainbridge Island's IslandWood, which offers educational experiences at Brightwater, also offers popular family programs and summer camps.

FINE PRINT: Grounds and trails are open from dawn to dusk; the Education Center is open Monday–Friday, and occasional Saturdays. 22505 State Route 9 S.E., Woodinville. 206-296-0100. kingcounty.gov/services/environment/brightwater-center.aspx

Cedar River Watershed Education Center FREE
North Bend

My kids have fond memories of puddle stomping along a trail in this wonderful area, and watching ospreys dive for fish in the lake. You can park your car at Rattlesnake Lake and walk the gentle gravel path a half-mile up to the Cedar River Watershed Education Center. If the weather is nice, connect with trails up to Rattlesnake Ledge (for older kids and adults) or along the Iron Horse Trail.

INDOOR TIP: In the education center, kids can learn about the water cycle by popping pingpong balls into a fabulous system of pipes or touching fascinating items collected from nature. A variety of naturalist-led programs are offered.

FINE PRINT: A number of trails available, including Rattlesnake Ledge (4 miles round-trip, 1,160 feet elevation gain) and Iron Horse Trail (1.4 miles from the center to Iron Horse State Park). Find directions and trip reports on WTA.org. *Center open Tuesday–Sunday. Cedar River Watershed Education Center, 17905 Cedar Falls Rd. S.E., North Bend. Some parking spaces near the Iron Horse trailhead may require a Discover Pass. 206-733-9421.* seattle.gov

SAFETY FIRST

Always check conditions of trails and roads before your hike; a great resource is Washington Trails Association's trip reports (*WTA.org*). Bring the 10 Essentials, including snacks, water, extra layers, hats and sunscreen, and be sure kids know how to be safe on the trail. Find out more at *parentmap.com/outdoorsafety.*

Tacoma Nature Center FREE
Tacoma

Visit this urban wetland preserve in the South Sound area for a chance to view wildlife and birds in all seasons. Two and a half miles of gentle trails meander through the park, including a 1-mile loop circling Snake Lake. If you are up for more distance, take the Hillside Loop away from the lake. Kids will also enjoy Discovery Pond, an innovative nature-themed play area with a tree house and a pond with waterfalls.

INDOOR TIP: The nature center has activities and games for children. You can also take a class, go for a guided walk with a naturalist or buy plants from the on-site native plant nursery.

FINE PRINT: 2.5 miles of trails at the center. Center open Monday–Saturday. Download a trail map and trail guide from the website. Tacoma Nature Center, 1919 S. Tyler St., Tacoma. 253-404-3930. No parking pass needed. metroparkstacoma.org/tacomanaturecenter

Billy Frank Jr. Nisqually National Wildlife Refuge
Olympia

Located between Tacoma and Olympia, just off Interstate 5, this sprawling nature reserve encompasses a vast area around the Nisqually River Delta. Walk the boardwalk through the tangled wetlands, observing ducks and geese and listening for songbirds and frogs. Keep your eyes open for signs of beavers and other wildlife. You can also take longer walks farther out into the estuary.

INDOOR TIP: When you are ready to retreat indoors, children will enjoy the displays in the visitor center about the ecosystems in the refuge. Note: No dogs allowed.

FINE PRINT: Variety of hiking distances available, up to 5 miles round-trip. Find directions and trip reports on WTA.org. Visitor center open Wednesday–Sunday. Billy Frank Jr. Nisqually National Wildlife Refuge, 100 Brown Farm Rd. N.E., Olympia. 360-753-9467. $3 refuge pass to park. fws.gov/refuge/Billy_Frank_Jr_Nisqually

More like this:
➤ Secret Gardens (Adventure 5)
➤ Shady Summer Hikes (Adventure 18)
➤ Hidden-Gem Playgrounds With a View (Adventure 25)

7.
Kid-Friendly Indie Bookstores

By JiaYing Grygiel

Move over, Kindles and Nooks. Turning the pages of a printed book will always be in style, and it'll never run low on batteries. Independent Bookstore Day is a fun spring event (held on the last Saturday of April), but if you're raising bookworms, browsing (and buying) books is a welcome activity 365 days a year.

Third Place Books

Lake Forest Park; Ravenna, Seward Park, Seattle

Sociologist Ray Oldenburg wrote that everyone needs three places: the first place is the home, the second is school or work and the third place is community. A community hub based on books — that's the idea behind Third Place Books. The family of bookstores hosts everything from live music to language groups to knitting clubs. The original location, in Lake Forest Park Town Center, has a massive children's section. Third Place added a store in Ravenna in 2002, and in Seward Park in 2016.

GOOD TO KNOW: All three locations have food options on-site (and the Ravenna and Lake Forest Park locations have play areas), so once you're there, you can settle in.

FINE PRINT: Open daily. Multiple locations. thirdplacebooks.com

The Elliott Bay Book Company

Capitol Hill, Seattle

Just as Portland has Powell's Books, Seattle has The Elliott Bay Book Company. This granddaddy of Seattle bookstores moved to its Capitol Hill home in 2010, turning a former auto warehouse into a sanctuary for book lovers. There's story time every Saturday at 11 a.m. at the children's castle (inside the children's section).

NEARBY BONUS: Pair your literary outing with a cone at legendary ice creamery Salt & Straw, just two blocks away.

FINE PRINT: Open daily. The Elliott Bay Book Company, 1521 10th Ave., Seattle. 206-624-6600. elliottbaybook.com

Queen Anne Book Company

Queen Anne, Seattle

Small but mighty: Queen Anne Book Company's petite square footage means the selection is highly curated. Children's book buyer Tegan Tigani is one of the store's secret weapons

— she's famous for launching the careers of local children's authors. She'll help you find that perfect birthday present.

GOOD TO KNOW: Look for story times at 10:30 a.m. on the first and third Fridays of every month.

FINE PRINT: Open daily. Queen Anne Book Company, 1811 Queen Anne Ave. N., Seattle. 206-284-2427. qabookco.com

University Book Store
University District, Seattle; Mill Creek, Tacoma

At University Book Store's flagship location in Seattle's U District, it's easy to get trapped at the bargain tables near the entrance (there's great stuff there!). But don't miss its wonderful children's section upstairs, with comfy chairs, a Lego table and a welcoming staff. Need a last-minute gift that's not a book? The University Book Store is a one-stop shop, carrying lots of Seattle-themed goodies and Husky gear (obviously).

NEARBY BONUS: Combine a visit to the U District location with exploration of the University of Washington campus.

FINE PRINT: Open daily. Multiple locations. ubookstore.com

Brick & Mortar Books
Redmond

With bookstores closing every year, you'd think most people would be wary of the printed-word business. Not Dan Ullom. The former schoolteacher opened Brick & Mortar Books in 2017; its co-owners are his wife and his parents. The store is located at Redmond Town Center, in the former Eddie Bauer space. Look for an excellent selection of science fiction and middle-grade titles in the children's section.

GOOD TO KNOW: In-house kid lit experts include Ullom's mom, a former Lake Washington school librarian, and his two bookworm kids.

FINE PRINT: Open daily. Brick & Mortar Books, Redmond Town Center, 7430 164th Ave. N.E., Ste. B105, Redmond. 425-869-0606. brickandmortarbooks.com

Island Books
Mercer Island

Island Books is just the type of community hub you want your local bookstore to be. The shop features an expansive children's section, with a super-cool playhouse, and grown-ups are sure to find their next read, too. Just ask the helpful staff.

GOOD TO KNOW: Families flock to Island Books' Wednesday story time, Storybook Corner, at 10:30 a.m. Additional events keep this community spot buzzing. Grab a tasty lunch at Homegrown next door.

FINE PRINT: *Open daily. Island Books, 3014 78th Ave. S.E., Mercer Island. 206-232-6920.* mercerislandbooks.com

King's Books
Tacoma

Looking for the purrrrr-fect book? King's Books has two sociable resident felines, so you may get some cuddles along with your reading. King's sells used and new titles, more than 100,000 in total, including a good children's picture book section, a growing nonfiction section and lots of middle-grade titles.

GOOD TO KNOW: The store holds community events ranging from author readings to craft fairs.

FINE PRINT: *Open daily. King's Books, 218 St. Helens Ave., Tacoma. 253-272-8801.* kingsbookstore.com

More like this
> ➤ **Cheap Summer Cinema (Adventure 19)**
> ➤ **Live Like a Tourist (Adventure 21)**
> ➤ **Destination Libraries (Adventure 48)**

8.
Pinball, Putt-Putt and More Old-School Fun

By Maegen Blue

Remember when bowling was something you did without a controller and you went to the arcade to play video games? If your kids think free time has to mean screen time, it's time to drag everyone out for some old-school-style fun in the real world. Sure, the Seattle area is known for all things hip and high tech, but there are many places that are proudly retro, too.

ALAN TEO

Seattle Pinball Museum
Chinatown–International District, Seattle

Pay one admission fee and have your fill of machines set to free play. At this retro gem in the heart of the International District, you'll find more than 50 machines, including some going back to the 1950s. Most kids will find pinball tricky at first, so this is a great way for them to learn without blowing through all your change.

GOOD TO KNOW: Because the machines are delicate, children younger than 7 aren't allowed, and this policy is enforced.

FINE PRINT: Closed Tuesday–Wednesday. $12–$15, all-day pass $17–$20. Seattle Pinball Museum, 508 Maynard Ave. S., Seattle. 206-623-0759. facebook.com/pages/Seattle-Pinball-Museum

West Seattle Bowl
West Seattle

There is archaeological evidence suggesting bowling may date back to ancient times. West Seattle Bowl isn't that old, but it has been around since 1948. Bumpers are available on every lane here, so you won't have any gutter balls. A really nice feature is that you can choose which bowlers get bumpers, so they are raised or lowered automatically depending on who is bowling. Look on the website for specials such as its Sunday "Breakfast & Bowl," where you get two free games if you buy a breakfast entrée.

GOOD TO KNOW: West Seattle Bowl is one of many area lanes participating in the Kids Bowl Free program (*kidsbowlfree.com*), where kids get two free games a day all summer.

FINE PRINT: Open daily. $21–$30/hour per lane; Monday–Friday, 3–6 p.m., is happy hour

SPRING

CULTURE

($15/lane). Shoe rental $4. West Seattle Bowl, 4505 39th Ave. S.W., Seattle. 206-932-3731. westseattlebowl.com

Interbay Miniature Golf
Interbay, Seattle
A round of mini golf is always great fun (or frustration) for all ages. You won't find wind-mills at this 18-hole golf course right in the Interbay neighborhood of Seattle (between Ballard and Magnolia); instead, it showcases natural features such as waterfalls, creeks and rocks.

GOOD TO KNOW: The course is closed to families during the Pints and Putts league for adults in the summer. Call ahead to confirm openings.

FINE PRINT: *Open daily. $6.50–$9. Interbay Golf Center, 2501 15th Ave. W., Seattle. 206-285-2200.* premiergc.com/-mini-golf

Discovery Trail Golf Course at Willows Run
Redmond
There are also no windmills in sight on this 18-hole mini golf course (formerly called Rainbow Run, and part of the expansive Willows Run golf complex), located in the lush Sammamish River Valley. You will find tunnels, caves and surprise special effects such as a bear roar. Note: The course sometimes closes for private parties, so call before you head out.

NEARBY BONUS: Stop by downtown Redmond before or after your mini golf experi-ence for a gourmet cone at Molly Moon's.

FINE PRINT: *Schedule varies seasonally. $6–$11; you can save $1 by going before 11 a.m. Willows Run, 10402 Willows Rd., Redmond. 425-883-1200.* willowsrun.com

Triple XXX Rootbeer Drive-In
Issaquah
The decor and eats are straight out of "Happy Days" at Triple XXX Rootbeer Drive-In, where the walls are literally covered with memorabilia. Reviews on the food are mixed, but everyone agrees it's worth a trip for the ambiance, especially if you're a nostalgia lover. Burger and sandwich portions are enormous, so plan on paying a small fee to share unless you've burned off some serious calories on nearby Tiger Mountain first.

GOOD TO KNOW: Triple XXX hosts vintage car shows, "Cruz-Ins," on most Saturdays year-round. You can see the schedule on its website.

MORE OLD-SCHOOL FINDS

Don's Ruston Market and Deli: Sit at the counter and order a malted or another classic treat at this little spot in picture-perfect Ruston, just outside Tacoma.

Full Tilt: The combo of ice cream, video games and pinball makes this local chain of ice cream stores great fun.

Husky Deli: Stepping into this popular ice cream spot in West Seattle is like walking into an old-time general store.

Luna Park Cafe: At the West Seattle diner, you'll find jukeboxes, walls full of funky '50s memorabilia and plentiful portions.

Shug's Soda Fountain: This soda fountain in Pike Place Market mixes up sundaes, sodas and floats with house-made ice cream, syrups and toppings.

FINE PRINT: Open daily. Cash only, although there is an ATM. Triple XXX Rootbeer Drive-In, 98 N.E. Gilman Blvd. Issaquah. 425-392-1266. triplexrootbeer.com

Dorky's Video Arcade

Tacoma

If you remember Pac-Man and Frogger, you'll be right at home at Dorky's, located in the heart of downtown Tacoma, not far from Wright Park. It boasts several rooms of old-school video games and pinball machines. Beer is available, but there is an equal mix of young families, teenagers and twentysomethings on first dates.

GOOD TO KNOW: All ages are welcome only until 9 p.m., after which this spot is strictly 21 and older. Children must be with a grown-up at all times. There is no ATM on-site. You can add cash back on your card purchases for a fee, but we suggest you come with cash.

FINE PRINT: Open daily. Dorky's Video Arcade, 754 Pacific Ave., Tacoma. 253-627-4156. dorkysarcade.com

Skate Tiffany's

Puyallup

Lucky South Sound families have several great roller rinks to choose from, but Skate Tiffany's is especially beloved for its wood floors, friendly staff and family-friendly music selections. The snack bar and video game area have been updated, but it still has that old roller-rink smell you'll remember. Two other nearby rinks with a similar vibe are Pattison's West in Federal Way and the Auburn Skate in Auburn. Tip: Young skaters can have their wheels tightened to make them roll less — a great idea for beginners.

NEARBY BONUS: Skate Tiffany's operates a mini golf course next to the skating rink, so you can double your retro experience.

SPRING

CULTURE

FINE PRINT: Open daily. Prices vary; Tuesday is $2 skate (rental not included). Skate Tiffany's, 1113 N. Meridian, Puyallup. 253-848-1153. skatetiffanys.com

Shake, Shake, Shake
Tacoma

This hamburger and milkshake spot in Tacoma's Stadium District has a super-cool interior — imagine the Jetsons opening a diner — but it's the tasty burgers and real ice cream shakes that will keep you coming back. Try one of their inventive flavors — like the Tiger shake, made with the area's most famous confection: Almond Roca.

GOOD TO KNOW: The fries are big enough to share. So are the shakes, but you won't want to!

FINE PRINT: Open daily. Shake, Shake, Shake, 124 N. Tacoma Ave., Tacoma. 253-507-4060. shakeshakeshake.me

> **More like this:**
> ➤ **Live Like a Tourist (Adventure 21)**
> ➤ **Sweet Ice Cream Spots (Adventure 22)**
> ➤ **Geektastic Outings (Adventure 47)**

9.

Stairway Walks

By Annie Fanning

Because of the rugged topography of the Puget Sound area, hundreds of stairways were built up and down hillsides all over the region. In "Seattle Stairway Walks: An Up-and-Down Guide to City Neighborhoods," authors Jake and Cathy Jaramillo explain why: Many of the older neighborhood stairways around Seattle were first built "as a way for developers to expand and extend the links between trolley stops and residential tracks."

Many stairways are secret shortcuts through quiet neighborhoods. Some trail into hidden woods. Some lead to water. Some give rise to amazing views. Others are spectacular in themselves, feats of design and engineering. Their rising steps beckon to the imagination, daring us to see where they lead.

Wilcox Wall   FREE

Queen Anne, Seattle

The perfect exercise for aspiring sleuths: See if you can find all 785 steps in the Wilcox Wall on the west slope of Seattle's Queen Anne hill. Actually an ornate brick-and-concrete retaining wall, Wilcox Wall has three double staircases, Gothic arches and Art Deco streetlights. Walking up and down this Byzantine beauty may make you feel like you've walked into a M.C. Escher print. Designed by architect and namesake Walter Wilcox (who also designed the Washington Park Arboretum bridge) and built in 1913, the Wilcox Wall runs along Eighth Pl. W. for almost a half-mile. Approach its southern end from Marshall Park.

NEARBY BONUS: Bring a picnic and enjoy the fairy-tale splendor of nearby Parsons Gardens.

FINE PRINT: Access the stairs at Eighth Ave. W. at W. Lee St., Seattle. qastairs.com/wilcox.html

ANNIE FANNING

Kelsey Creek Farm stairs

Howe St. and Blaine St. Stairs   FREE

Capitol Hill–Eastlake, Seattle

Explore Seattle's longest continuous stairway as it cascades 388 steps (and 160 feet) down E. Howe St. on Capitol Hill through the I-5 Colonnade bike/trail park to Franklin Ave. E. in Eastlake. Make your return trip one block south via the charming 293-step Blaine St. stairs, which escorts climbers into the hidden Streissguth Gardens of North Capitol Hill, a family-maintained public garden built on the hill.

These parallel stairways date from trolley days and both start at 10th Ave. E., near Highland Cemetery. Be prepared to sweat.

NEARBY BONUS: Make a detour for excellent sandwiches and pastries (and restrooms) at Grand Central Bakery at Eastlake Ave. E. and E. Blaine St.

FINE PRINT: Access the Howe Street stairs at 810 E. Howe St., Seattle; and the Blaine Street stairs at 10th Ave. E. and E. Blaine St. I-5 Colonnade Park is at 1701 Lakeview Blvd. E., Seattle. seattle.gov/parks/find/parks/i-5-colonnade

Thornton Creek Water Channel Stairs FREE
Northgate, Seattle

Just south of Northgate Mall, the stairways below and around Thornton Place will take you into a Dr. Seuss landscape, where colorful art mixes with water, nature, science and educational elements. Look for one of two street-access stairways — the 64 steps down from N.E. 100th St. or the 32 steps that jog down from Fifth Ave. N.E. — that lead to the Thornton Creek Water Quality Channel, a series of paths, terraces, bioswales and artful buoys around the formerly covered Thornton Creek. Designed to filter pollutants from runoff and stormwater draining into the creek, the landscaped channel is fun to explore, with whimsical public art and interpretive signs.

NEARBY BONUS: After walking around the channel, take steps up to Thornton Place for lunch at the Jewel Box Café or Tengu Sushi (a conveyor-belt sushi spot), or a splash at the fountain.

FINE PRINT: Park on the streets around Thornton Place, or at Northgate Park-and-Ride. In addition to the two access points described above, you can find stairs leading to the channel at Third Ave. N.E., just by The Watershed Pub & Kitchen.

Mercerdale Hillside Stairway FREE
Mercer Island

Leafy and lovely, this 321-step stairway in downtown Mercer Island skirts the upland forest along the north edge of Mercerdale Park. If you can coax your kids away from the delights of Mercerdale Park (slides! A skate dot!), follow the curving sidewalk deeper into the park to the plaza of Bicentennial Park. Here you can find restrooms and the trail

ERRATIC ROCK EXPLORES

Are your kids more interested in pre-history than urban history? Go erratic rock hopping. When glaciers advanced into the Puget Sound region 2 million years ago, they picked up hunks of rock and carried them along. When the ice melted, these huge, irregularly shaped boulders were left miles away from their place of origin. You can find (and sometimes climb) these magnificent relics in city neighborhoods (Wedgwood), on beaches (Des Moines) and along mountain trails (Cougar Mountain). *parentmap.com/erratic* to the Mercerdale Hillside stairway. The north stairway will lead you to a wooded wonderland. For a longer hike, take one of the trails down the slope and into the forest.

NEARBY BONUS: Hungry? Fill up on fish and chips or fish tacos at Freshy's Seafood Shack, less than a mile away.

FINE PRINT: Mercerdale Park, 3009 77th Ave. S.E., Mercer Island. mercergov.org/page.asp?navid=406

Kelsey Creek Farm FREE
Bellevue

For a bucolic excursion, hike shady trails to the 163-step stairway that leads to a forested hillside near the historic white barns at Kelsey Creek Farm. To find the stairway, start at the north end of the parking lot, at the bridge crossing over Kelsey Creek's tributary. Following signs for the Lake to Lake trail, you'll head left, walk up and over a small hill, and take another footbridge over Kelsey Creek, enjoying the sights and sounds of the creek. Keep left until you get to the timber stairs. You can loop back to your starting point, less than a mile total, or continue exploring trails that connect nine Bellevue parks.

NEARBY BONUS: After your stair walk, bring the kids to see the pigs, cows and ponies at the farm (see p.18). If you visit in the fall, you may spy salmon in Kelsey Creek, as well as catch the forest's brilliant autumnal show.

FINE PRINT: Kelsey Creek Farm, 410 130th Pl. S.E., Bellevue. parks.bellevuewa.gov

More like this:
➤ **Spring Hikes, Warm-Up Included (Adventure 6)**
➤ **Family Birding Takes Flight (Adventure 43)**
➤ **Quirky Landmarks (Adventure 45)**

10.
Beginning Bike Paths

By Kate Missine

The Seattle area has no shortage of excellent biking trails. But while some of our best-known routes may be perfect for capable cyclists, those just getting the hang of the sport may need a quieter spot to work on skills. Whether your child is mastering the balance bike, getting ready to ditch the training wheels or cruising on a scooter, we've scouted the best beginner stretches around Seattle and the Eastside.

Paramount School Park   FREE
Shoreline

This Shoreline park caters to everyone. A flat, lightly trafficked path circles a large grassy area, a perfect spot for wobbly bikers to practice their skills. A cool skate park lets scooter and skateboard pros show off rad moves. Siblings not up to biking can have a blast at the large, updated playground. The open, partially fenced layout makes it easy for parents to keep an eye on playing kiddos while supervising a little one riding around the looping path. Bonus: There's adult exercise equipment right next to the play structure.

NEARBY BONUS: Kick back with a caffeine dose at nearby Café Aroma while the kiddos play in its well-stocked playroom; or catch a budget movie ($4 seats) at neighborhood favorite Crest Cinema Center.

FINE PRINT: Paramount School Park, 15300 Eighth Ave. N.E., Shoreline. shorelinewa.gov

Washington Park Arboretum   FREE
Montlake, Seattle

Covering 230 acres and with more than 20,000 varieties of trees and plants, this botanical gem on the shores of Lake Washington has long been a favorite for serene family walks. The loop trail adds to the park's appeal to families with youngsters on wheels.

The fully paved path stretches for 1.2 miles from E. Madison St. to the Graham Visitors Center (find restrooms there). A creek, restored wetlands and plenty of trees along the way make for cool exploratory stopovers, and lots of benches let kiddos and parents take a breather between bursts of pedaling.

NEARBY BONUS: The Montlake Tot Lot — a playground at the park's western edge — is a small but cute stop.

FINE PRINT: Washington Park Arboretum, 2300 Arboretum Dr. E., Seattle. Park at the Graham Visitors Center and access the trail nearby. botanicgardens.uw.edu

Maple Leaf Reservoir Park   FREE
Maple Leaf, Seattle

A smooth, flat path of about half a mile loops around this 16-acre park, which also includes a covered picnic shelter, sport courts and a huge grassy playfield. (On clear days, keep an eye out for Mount Rainier.) Walk down the steps (or pedal down the sidewalk) to the park's lower level, which features a terrific, all-accessible playground, a zipline, a sweet butterfly garden and a sand pit.

NEARBY BONUS: Just across Roosevelt Way N.E. from the park, you'll find neighborhood favorite Cloud City Coffee, which offers sandwiches, baked goods and a tot play area. Or check out the monthly Parents Night Out at the magical Moonpaper Tent for a future date night.

FINE PRINT: Maple Leaf Reservoir Park, 1020 N.E. 82nd St., Seattle. seattle.gov/parks/find/parks/maple-leaf-reservoir-park

Seward Park   FREE
South Seattle

Combine a family cycling ses-

MORE PEDAL PICKS

Alki Beach Trail: Calm it's not. But it is wide and paved and offers unparalleled people watching at Alki Beach. Tip: Rent a six-person surrey bike from Wheel Fun Rentals.

Cedar River Trail: A 17.4-mile rail-trail from Renton to Maple Valley. In the fall, stop at the Renton Library, built over the Cedar River, and look for salmon.

Centennial Trail: This 30-mile trail system that runs from Snohomish to the Skagit County line is surprisingly quiet.

Duthie Hill Mountain Bike Park: This Issaquah park is like no other, with trails, berms and jumps ranging from beginner to expert, and there's even a kiddie pump track.

Snoqualmie Trail tunnel: Bike the section of the 100-mile Palouse to Cascades trail (formerly the John Wayne Trail) that takes you through an exciting 2.3-mile-long tunnel.

sion with an educational adventure at this iconic southeast Seattle park on Lake Washington. Start at the Seward Park Audubon Center, where kids can learn all about local flora and fauna, and then follow the 2.4-mile paved path along the beach. Those who are more stable on two wheels can explore the more rugged trails through the forest. Finish up with a romp at the nature-themed play area. Note: From mid-May through September, Lake Washington Boulevard's Bicycle Sundays program closes the street to cars.

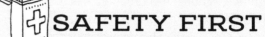

SAFETY FIRST
Make sure to get bikes tuned up and helmets checked every year, and invest in safety gear such as reflective clothes. Teach kids road skills and safety and consider enrolling them in a camp or class.

NEARBY BONUS: Follow with a browse through the amazing children's section at Third Place Books and dine at its on-site joint, Raconteur (or carbo-load on its popular brunch dishes before your ride!).

FINE PRINT: Seward Park, 5900 Lake Washington Blvd. S, Seattle. seattle.gov/parks/find/parks/seward-park

Lincoln Park   FREE
West Seattle

Almost 4 miles of bike paths is just the start of what West Seattle's signature waterfront park has to offer. A paved trail perfect for starter cyclists begins by the Fauntleroy ferry terminal and runs along the beach, where riders can dismount to collect shells and build sandcastles. The path then continues toward the recently renovated playground at the park's north end. Check out the new south playground, too.

NEARBY BONUS: During the summer months, cool off after your ride with a dip at Lincoln Park's Colman Pool, an outdoor saltwater pool with ocean views, waterslide and diving boards. (Get there at least 15 minutes before a session to ensure admittance.)

FINE PRINT: Lincoln Park, 8011 Fauntleroy Way S.W., Seattle. seattle.gov/parks/find/parks/lincoln-park

Redmond Central Connector   FREE
Redmond

Linking Redmond's Bear Creek Trail and the ever-popular Sammamish River Trail, the 2.3-mile-long Redmond Central Connector cuts right through vibrant downtown Redmond. Flanked by grassy fields for running around, cool lounging benches and nighttime lighting, this urban path is usually calm, even on nice-weather weekends. Once the ride is over, play and shop (and use the restroom) at Redmond Town Center, and look for the city's brand-new downtown park.

NEARBY BONUS: Refuel with burgers and shakes at Tipsy Cow Burger Bar in downtown Redmond, followed by a cone at Molly Moon's, one block away.

FINE PRINT: Redmond Central Connector: Park at Bear Creek Park, located behind Bear Creek Village shopping center, between Redmond Way and Avondale Way N.E., Redmond, or at Redmond Town Center, 7525 166th Ave. N.E., Redmond. redmond.gov, traillink.com

East Lake Sammamish Trail FREE
Redmond, Sammamish

This recently updated trail includes new paving, restrooms and seating along the eastern shore of Lake Sammamish from Redmond to Issaquah. The popular 11-mile trail has six entrance points; our favorite is Sammamish Landing Park, which turns into a buzzing beach destination in the summer months. Ride the wide, quiet stretch of paved trail with pretty lake views, then walk on the dock and have a picnic by the water. More seasoned cyclists can follow the route south toward Issaquah's Gilman Boulevard, or north to Redmond's Marymoor Park.

NEARBY BONUS: Explore Lake Sammamish State Park (Discover Pass required to park) and its phenomenal destination playground in Issaquah.

FINE PRINT: Access East Lake Sammamish Trail at Sammamish Landing Park, 4607 E. Lake Sammamish Pkwy. N.E., Sammamish (as well as other locations). kingcounty.gov

Rainier Trail FREE
Issaquah

Bring train lovers to downtown Issaquah to chug alongside a slice of railway history. Running parallel to the former Lake Shore and Eastern Railway, Issaquah's 2.5-mile Rainier Trail lets young riders practice their moves on the paved, minimal-traffic path. They'll also enjoy hopping off to play on the real (inactive) railroad tracks at its southern side. Head north past Confluence Park and toward the Darigold dairy plant; then come back for a tour of the Depot Museum, in downtown Issaquah, with its historic engines and railroad exhibits.

NEARBY BONUS: Play at the train-themed Depot Park, right next to the trail.

FINE PRINT: Park and access the Rainier Trail at the Issaquah Community Center, 301 Rainier Blvd. S., Issaquah, or in downtown Issaquah. traillink.com/trail/rainier-trail

More like this:
➤ Choo-Choo! Train Adventures (Adventure 11)
➤ Mountain Biking Thrills (Adventure 37)
➤ Summer Splurges (Adventure 24)

ALLENS PHOTOGRAPHIC

One of the trains at Mt. Rainier Railroad and Logging Museum

11.

Choo-Choo! Train Adventures

By Nancy Chaney

Train obsession is a stage many kids go through. Some never outgrow it. Given the Puget Sound region's rich railway history, there are multiple ways to learn about, observe and ride the rails, from seeing a real Thomas the Tank Engine to riding on miniature steam trains engineered by seasoned train buffs, who are only too happy to share their interest with the next generation.

SPRING

ADVENTURE

Great Northern & Cascade Railway FREE
Skykomish

During the summer, head to the mountains for a free ride on a miniature steam train (1/8 scale) in the historic railroad town of Skykomish on scenic U.S. Highway 2. The riverside town is working to restore its vintage train depot and revive its position as an important railroad waypoint. Volunteer train buffs run the mini trains, which wend their way on a mile of track (including two tunnels and a bridge) around the old train yard.

GOOD TO KNOW: You can also ride mini steam trains in Port Orchard, Washington, through the Kitsap Live Steamers program.

FINE PRINT: *Rides offered May–October, Saturday–Sunday, 10 a.m.–4 p.m. A museum, visitor center and gift shop is open Thursday–Monday. Free; donations appreciated. Great Northern & Cascade Railway, 101 Fifth St. N., Skykomish.* greatnortherncascaderailway.com

South Lake Union and First Hill Streetcars
Seattle

Explore one of Seattle's most rapidly changing neighborhoods by taking the South Lake Union Streetcar between the South Lake Union neighborhood and Westlake Center downtown. (Ride the monorail, too, for double the fun!) Streetcars sport bright colors and a nifty chime that kids can appreciate.

On the South Lake Union line, a good starting spot is Lake Union Park, where you can also visit the Museum of History and Industry, wave at the floatplanes and boats, and stroll over to the Center for Wooden Boats. The more recently opened First Hill Streetcar connects Capitol Hill, First Hill, Chinatown–International District and Pioneer Square for more in-city adventures. Extended streetcar lines are in the works.

GOOD TO KNOW: Street parking is free on Sundays; or consider walking or busing from surrounding neighborhoods.

FINE PRINT: *Streetcars run every 10–15 minutes. Buy tickets on the platform or on board, or use an ORCA card or valid Metro bus transfer. $1.50–$2.25, kids 5 and younger free.* seattlestreetcar.org; *real-time info at* seattlestreetcar.org/how-to-ride/streetcar-tracker

Link Light Rail
Seattle

Ride the urban rails! Now that Seattle has a 14-stop Link light rail line, opportunities to design your own light rail adventure abound. Traveling from points south, you could plan an outing to the International District, the Central Library or other downtown adventures. From the University of Washington Station, head south to Columbia City for window shopping and treats, or ride all the way to Seattle-Tacoma International Airport for airplane viewing. Tacoma is ripe for Link adventures as well. Park for free at the Tacoma Dome Station and take the Tacoma Link light rail for free to destinations downtown.

PARKING TIP: Parking near light rail stations in Seattle is limited; you will likely need to park in a pay lot, bus it to a station or find free street parking on Sundays.

FINE PRINT: Trains run every 10–15 minutes during peak times. $1.50–$3.25, ages 5 and younger free. Buy tickets prior to boarding the train, or use your ORCA card. soundtransit.org

Northwest Railway Museum
Snoqualmie

This restored train depot in the historic (and charming) town of Snoqualmie is a free museum that's open seven days a week. It's also the starting point for a 75-minute excursion in an antique coach car of a train that runs seasonally. Special events at the Railway Museum include the hugely popular Day Out With Thomas in July, when the "real" Thomas the Tank Engine drops in for a visit, and the annual Santa Train, featuring the big guy in red (book early for events).

GOOD TO KNOW: A fun time to visit Snoqualmie and ride the trains is during Railroad Days, the town's annual August festival.

FINE PRINT: Snoqualmie Depot is open daily, free to visit. Seventy-five-minute train excursions run on weekend days from April through October. $10–$20, kids younger than 2 free; special event tickets are pricier. Northwest Railway Museum, 38625 S.E. King St., Snoqualmie. 425-888-3030, ext. 7202. trainmuseum.org

MORE TRAINSPOTTING SPOTS

Balmer rail yard: There's always something to see at Seattle's Balmer Yard, near 20th Ave. W. and Thorndyke Ave. W. on the Magnolia side of Interbay.

Carkeek Park: Hang out on the bridge between the playground and the beach at this epic Seattle park for some prime train gawking.

Edmonds waterfront: Trains, ferries, the beach, a playground and solid seafood restaurants add up to a perfect day.

Georgetown Playfield: Play at this terrific South Seattle playground while keeping an eye out for trains nearby.

Golden Gardens Park: Spot trains and turtles at this huge Seattle beach park, which also has a pirate-themed playground and wetland trails.

SPRING

ADVENTURE

Washington State History Museum
Tacoma

For a bird's-eye view of a whole train system, check out the expansive model railroad setup at Tacoma's Washington State History Museum. Members of a model train club have built and continue to work on this impressive 1,800-square-foot display, showcasing a 1950s-era Northwest railroad network.

NEARBY BONUS: Within walking distance of the history museum (or a short ride on Tacoma's Link — double trains!), you can stop at the Museum of Glass and the pay-what-you-will Children's Museum of Tacoma. Also check out impressive, historic Stadium High School, just north of the downtown area.

FINE PRINT: *Open Tuesday–Sunday. $11–$14, ages 5 and younger free. Washington State History Museum, 1911 Pacific Ave., Tacoma. 888-238-4373.* washingtonhistory.org

Mt. Rainier Railroad and Logging Museum
Elbe

For a train adventure that takes you a bit further back in history, head to scenic Elbe for a two-hour, 14-mile ride on Mt. Rainier Railroad's vintage, steam-powered logging locomotive. The railroad runs all kinds of weekend excursions throughout the year, including very popular themed rides such as the Polar Express (buy tickets early). Its museum is home to the most comprehensive collection of steam logging locomotives in the country.

NEARBY BONUS: Try ScaleBurgers if you need lunch while in Elbe (call ahead, 360-569-2247, to confirm it's open) — and admire the collection of cabooses across the street while you eat.

FINE PRINT: *Trains depart multiple times on Friday, Saturday and Sunday for the two-hour, 14-mile round-trip experience, which includes a short stop at Mineral to visit the logging museum. $21–$41, ages 2 and younger free. Parking $4. Mt. Rainier Railroad and Logging Museum, 54124 Mountain Hwy. E., Elbe. 360-492-6000.* mtrainierrailroad.com

More like this:
- ➤ Beginning Bike Paths (Adventure 10)
- ➤ Walk-On Ferry Tales (Adventure 23)
- ➤ Getting to the Places You'll Go (p. 6)

ELISA MURRAY

Artists at Play playground

12.

Epic Playgrounds

By Linnea Westerlind

If you believe that playgrounds have become too safe, here's some good news: An increasing number of Seattle-area playgrounds — some old-school and some brand new — are designed for thrills, with steep slides, long ziplines and tall swings that encourage kids to safely test their limits. These epic parks around the Sound are worth the trek. (Find even more at *parentmap.com/adventureplayground*.)

IMPORTANT: Remember to always read signage at parks for safe play guidelines, and make sure your child knows his or her limits.

Shoreview Park FREE

Shoreline

Part of a huge greenspace that is actually two adjacent parks making up 88 acres, this playground sits near playfields and within easy wheelchair- and stroller-accessible reach of the parking lot. Two colorful climbing structures are bursting with slides — eight, by my count. Gutsy kids can climb to the top of the larger play tower, which has two tube slides that drop two stories. The smaller structure is just as fun for little tykes.

GOOD TO KNOW: The park also has kid-friendly hiking trails that connect to Boeing Creek Park, an off-leash dog park, tennis courts and a second playground (more slides!) near the baseball field.

FINE PRINT: Shoreview Park, 700 N.W. Innis Arden Way, Shoreline. shorelinewa.gov

Artists at Play FREE
Seattle Center

Opened in 2015, this artist-designed playground at Seattle Center is one of the most adventure-oriented playgrounds in Western Washington. Features include a jaw-dropping 35-foot climbing structure, one of the tallest such structures in North America. Kids (recommended ages 5–12) can scale the rope ladders that lead straight to the top or take the route up through the large climbing net and then traverse the narrow rope passageways to reach the top of two tall tube slides. Other highlights include the ADA-accessible swing set that prompts wind chimes to ring; an ingenious sound fence; a labyrinth; and a smaller play structure.

NEARBY BONUS: The Armory, right next door, often hosts free cultural festivals and other events, and has a standout food court.

FINE PRINT: Next 50 Plaza, Seattle Center, 305 Harrison St., Seattle. seattlecenter.com

Montlake Playfield FREE
Montlake, Seattle

This super-adventurous park outside the Montlake Community Center has some of the best climbing equipment around the Sound. Start on the challenge course, where kids (and adults!) take rope bridges and climb nets to reach a pinnacle and then exit through a long tube slide. On the other structure, take a ladder up to the top of the spaceship for a view of the entire park.

GOOD TO KNOW: The park also includes adult exercise equipment, so you can get your heart rate up while the kids play, and a wildlife-viewing trail along the Lake Union waterfront.

FINE PRINT: Montlake Playfield, 1618 E. Calhoun St., Seattle. seattle.gov/parks/find/parks/montlake-playfield

Bayview-Kinnear Park   FREE

Queen Anne, Seattle

Tucked underneath one of Seattle's most famous viewpoints, Kerry Park, is Bayview-Kinnear Park (also known as Lower Kerry Park). Rock-climbing holds cover a long cement wall along one side of the play area. Kids can practice "bouldering" back and forth and even get a little bit of height off the wood chips. The other big draw at this park is the set of fast slides that are built into the hillside.

NEARBY BONUS: Kerry Park, with its photogenic (and affordable) view of the city, is just up the tall staircase.

ROCK ON: CAMP LONG

No epic park list is complete without mention of Camp Long, the West Seattle park that is home to Schurman Rock, the country's first human-constructed rock climbing structure, built in the 1930s. Also take time to explore the hiking trails and an environmental learning center that offers nature programs and camps.

FINE PRINT: Bayview-Kinnear Park, 270 W. Prospect St., Seattle. seattle.gov/parks/find/parks/bayview-kinnear-(lower-kerry-park)

Jefferson Park   FREE

Beacon Hill, Seattle

Located at the top of Seattle's Beacon Hill neighborhood, with stunning views on clear days, this grand park is the place to go for a full day of activities to challenge your kids. At the top of the park's "Beacon Mountain," two ziplines cross the hillside — they are among the longest ziplines in Seattle. Nearby you'll find two slides — one is so steep that parents should watch little kids near the top. All ages will enjoy the spray park, and flat, paved paths all around the park are perfect for biking or scootering.

NEARBY BONUS: On the west side of Jefferson Park, explore the Beacon Food Forest, a public foraging garden with a community berry patch, nut groves, fruit trees and more. Read signs so you know what's available for picking.

FINE PRINT: Jefferson Park, 3801 Beacon Ave. S., Seattle. seattle.gov/parks/find/parks/jefferson-park

Inspiration Playground at Bellevue Downtown Park   FREE

Bellevue

There's so much to do at this incredible Eastside playground, your kids won't know where to start. Point your thrill-seekers to the enormous nontraditional climbing wall designed to look like vines and roots creeping across a wall of boulders. They'll soon find the in-ground trampoline, hillside slides and seasonal spray features.

NEARBY BONUS: Find lunch everyone will love at Lincoln South Food Hall, composed of six kitchens that offer everything from street tacos to pork belly ramen to ice cream.

FINE PRINT: Bellevue Downtown Park, N.E. First St. and 100th Ave. N.E., Bellevue. parks.bellevuewa.gov

Wilburton Hill Park   FREE
Bellevue

Although it covers more than 100 acres, Wilburton Hill Park is less well-known than Bellevue Botanical Garden, located next door. You can combine these parks for an adventurous half-day, and Wilburton's thrilling zipline is a great place to start. Sit or stand on the disc and give a good push off the small hill to get the most speed. The rest of the play area includes a colorful train, a net spinner, swings and a two-story tree-house-style structure.

NEARBY BONUS: After ziplining at the playground, walk the flat trails to the suspension bridge at The Ravine Experience at Bellevue Botanical Garden (free admission).

FINE PRINT: Wilburton Hill Park, 12400 Main St., Bellevue. parks.bellevuewa.gov/ parks-and-trails/parks/wilburton-hill-park

Summit Park   FREE
Issaquah

This little-known neighborhood park in the Issaquah Highlands community has two exhilarating slides that start at the top of a hill. Parents can check out views from the top as kids zoom down these curving plastic slides. Older kids will enjoy the Kompan climbing structure. Don't miss the oversize checkers and chess boards.

GOOD TO KNOW: Summit Park is a private park owned by the Issaquah Highlands Community Association, but it's open to the public.

FINE PRINT: Summit Park, corner of 30th Ave. N.E. and N.E. Harrison St., Issaquah. issaquahhighlands.com/explore/parks

Fisher Creek Park   FREE
Snoqualmie

This park should be on the summer bucket list of every adventure seeker. The seven steep slides are pretty scary, the two ziplines pick up a lot of speed and the net dome climber has an unusual, challenging shape. Don't miss the huge climbing wall or the obstacle-course-style play structure.

GOOD TO KNOW: Finally getting bored? Head into the small forest to find the kid-friendly bike course.

FINE PRINT: Fisher Creek Park, 7805 Fisher Ave. S.E., Snoqualmie. ci.snoqualmie.wa.us

More like this:
- ➤ **Hidden-Gem Playgrounds With a View (Adventure 25)**
- ➤ **Super Spray Parks (Adventure 26)**
- ➤ **Rainy-Day Playgrounds (Adventure 50)**

KATE MISSINE

Lower Woodland Skate Park

13.

Rad Skate Parks

By Kate Missine

City streets and emptied-out pools were the original skater's playground. Today, a skatescape with bowls, ramps, rails and ledges is a hipper — not to mention safer — option. The Seattle area has such pro-approved spaces for every age and skill level.

Lake City Skate Spot at Virgil Flaim Park   FREE

Lake City, Seattle

Designed to provide an opportunity for youth recreation and community building in Lake City's Virgil Flaim Park, this 8,000-square-foot skate spot is a place for every kind of user. It features a mix of traditional and street elements, and lots of spectator room to learn from the pros. When you're done, shoot some hoops at Virgil Flaim's basketball court, while the littles tumble on the playground (with old-school metal slides!).

NEARBY BONUS: Refuel at the Lake City location of Dick's Drive-In, just around the corner.

FINE PRINT: Virgil Flaim Park, 2700 N.E. 123rd St., Seattle. seattle.gov/parks/find/parks/virgil-flaim-park

Lower Woodland Skate Park, Woodland Park   FREE

North Seattle

This spacious skate park, located next to the tennis courts in Seattle's Woodland Park, is just for skateboarders: Scooters and bikes aren't allowed, although there's a steady stream of kids and adults who disregard this rule. Kids of all levels are bound to find the perfect pipe in one of the nine skate areas, including a smaller, four-sided bowl just for the newbies.

NEARBY BONUS: Kidd Valley makes for an easy lunch stop, and Green Lake is just across the road. (Green Lake's playground, however, is on the far side of the lake.)

FINE PRINT: Lower Woodland Skate Park, 1000 N. 50th St., Seattle. seattle.gov/parks/find/parks/woodland-park

Seattle Center Skatepark

FREE

Seattle Center

No Seattle skateboard experience would be complete without some spins and airs at Seattle Center's skate park, or "SeaSk8," as it's known. With 10,000 square feet packed with edgy elements, glass surfaces, skateable sculptures and a street-style plaza with stairs and ledges, there's something for everyone. The nonprofit Skate Like a Girl hosts free drop-in sessions for kids ages 12 and younger, as well as girls-only skate times.

RAD RESOURCES

Skate Like a Girl: This nonprofit runs camps and programs for all ages, all abilities and all genders. Look for its free workshops in the summer.

All Together Skatepark: Fremont's indoor skate destination gives kids access to all the practice terrain they need, plus lessons, kids-only skate times and more.

NEARBY BONUS: Play at Seattle Center's epic Artists at Play playground; snack at the Armory; and hit a museum or two.

FINE PRINT: Seattle Center Skatepark, Second Ave. N. and Thomas St., Seattle. seattlecenter.com/skatepark

Roxhill Park Skate Park   FREE
West Seattle

Roxhill Park's neat skatescape shows off several challenging features for skilled tricksters, but also includes less challenging bowls and lower ramps for the starter set. Scooter riders and bikers are good to go, and when they're ready for a rest, watching the experienced crowd perform pro moves makes for exciting entertainment.

NEARBY BONUS: Roxhill Park is known as "Castle Park" for its fantastic wooden castle-like play structure, a climbing net and a sandbox for the tots.

FINE PRINT: Roxhill Park, 2850 S.W. Roxbury St., Seattle. seattle.gov/parks/find/parks/roxhill-park

Edge Skate Park   FREE
Redmond

Easily accessible in Redmond's downtown core, this edgy Eastside arena has pipes, bowls and ramps galore for skateboarders young and old. Scooters and balance bikes are welcome, and riders who are just starting out get lots of practice space on the easier elements. A funky addition is the groovy graffiti wall, where budding street artists can show off their talents.

NEARBY BONUS: After practicing ollies, refuel at SoulFood CoffeeHouse, a couple of blocks away (a play area and a flavored milk menu are draws), and browse Snapdoodle Toys, next door.

FINE PRINT: Edge Skate Park, N.E. 83rd St. and 161st Ave. N.E., Redmond. redmond.gov/cms/One.aspx?portalId=169&pageId=4097

Bellevue Indoor Skate Park and Highland Skate Plaza
Bellevue

Rainy day? Grab those boards and head to Bellevue's indoor skate park, remodeled with polished pipes, banks and a thrilling "vert" wall. Several levels of ramps, from a soaring 6-footer to a micro-mini ramp, cater to all ages, with lessons available for those learning the basics. Highland Skate Plaza, a 13,000-square-foot outdoor skate area, is right next door, with a newly refinished surface and elements that replicate favorite global street spots. (Scooters, bikes and inline skates allowed at the outdoor plaza only.)

NEARBY BONUS: Grill lunch or dinner right at your table at Blue Ginger Korean BBQ.

FINE PRINT: Check website for hours. $5–$10/session; $10–$12/annual pass. Bellevue Indoor Skate Park, 14224 Bel-Red Rd., Bellevue. parks.bellevuewa.gov/sports-and-athletics/skate-parks

More like this:
- ➤ **Beginning Bike Paths (Adventure 10)**
- ➤ **Hidden Seattle Center (Adventure 20)**
- ➤ **Walk-On Ferry Tales (Adventure 23)**

14.

One-of-a-Kind Getaways

By Lauren Braden

Looking for a family getaway that your kids will be talking about for years? How about booking a weekend in a tree house, a lighthouse or an Airstream trailer? The Northwest is a hot spot for unusual lodgings that will transform your family's overnight stay into a memorable adventure.

IMPORTANT: Many of these places are fully booked far in advance, so plan your visit well ahead of time — even the year before. Also, we included a few places that are a long drive from Seattle because they are so special.

Iron Horse Inn Bed and Breakfast
South Cle Elum
All aboard! For more than half a century, this historic inn was a rooming house for railroad workers. Today, the inn's seven rooms and four caboose suites (the best bet for families) comprise a kid-friendly bed-and-breakfast, loaded with artifacts and railroad memorabilia from a bygone era, and furnished in period antiques. Kids will love sleeping in the caboose loft and playing in the gazebo. The inn's sitting room is a great place to read a book beside the woodstove before feasting on a home-cooked breakfast of waffles or pancakes.

ADAM CROWLEY/ ADAMCROWLEY.COM

TreeHouse Point

NEARBY BONUS: Right across the tracks, find a restored depot and railyard interpretive trail.

FINE PRINT: From $145/night. Iron Horse Inn Bed and Breakfast, 526 Marie Ave., South Cle Elum. 509-674-5939. ironhorseinnbb.com

TreeHouse Point

Preston

Want a getaway without the kids? This romantic retreat just outside Seattle features six beautiful bungalows, designed by tree house master Pete Nelson, built in a tree canopy beside a raging river. Wake up in your hand-hewn log bed to the sounds of birdsong before climbing down your ladder to a continental breakfast in the lodge. And no one younger than 13 is allowed to stay.

GOOD TO KNOW: You can also take a guided tour of the property, but advance tickets are required for any visit to TreeHouse Point.

FINE PRINT: See the website for prices and tips on how to book (new reservation blocks are added weekly for 60 days out). TreeHouse Point, 6922 Preston–Fall City Rd. S.E., Issaquah. 425-441-8087. treehousepoint.com

Point No Point Lighthouse

Hansville

Bunk down in a cool relic of Washington's maritime history on the Kitsap Peninsula.

Built in 1879, Puget Sound's oldest lighthouse still stands on the sandy beach at Point No Point, guiding ships of all sizes safely into Admiralty Inlet. The former lighthouse keepers' quarters are now vacation rentals. The larger of the two, the Historic Keeper's Quarters, has a full kitchen, living room, dining room, two bedrooms and a bathroom, all decked out in Victorian antique furniture and lighthouse-themed artwork. From the porch, you can take in the panoramic view.

NEARBY BONUS: The rental is adjacent to a wildlife habitat preserve, so bring binoculars.

FINE PRINT: $215/night. Point No Point Lighthouse, 9009 N.E. Point No Point Rd., Hansville. 415-362-7255. uslhs.org/about/point-no-point-vacation-rental, jeff@uslhs.org

Sou'wester Historic Lodge and Vintage Travel Trailer Resort ····➔

Seaview

Step out of your car on the Long Beach Peninsula at the Sou'wester and you'll immediately feel the old-school beach vibe that flows through this place like an ocean breeze. Silvery vintage travel trailers are lined up in a cute row as if they're posing for Instagram. Some are small and rustic, while others are palatial. All 10 are fully restored throughout, clean as a whistle and thoughtfully decorated. The three-story main lodge welcomes you with a huge front porch and cozy wood-paneled parlor.

NEARBY BONUS: Rolling dunes and the Pacific Ocean are a five-minute walk away.

FINE PRINT: From $95/night. Sou'wester Historic Lodge & Vintage Travel Trailer Resort, 3728 J Pl., Seaview. 360-642-2542. Three-hour drive from Seattle. souwesterlodge.com

Rolling Huts ····➔

Winthrop

Designed by renowned Seattle architecture firm Olson Kundig, this cluster of six compact glass-and-steel shelters on a grassy slope in the Methow Valley will make you feel right at home on the range — albeit with a modern twist. Although the huts' furnishings are simple but functional (bring your own bedding), all the important amenities are there: a woodstove, kitchenette, Wi-Fi and spacious deck that faces rugged Cascade peaks. Each hut has an adjacent portable toilet. Full bathrooms and showers are housed in the centrally located barn a short distance away.

GOOD TO KNOW: The Methow is a cross-country skiing mecca in the winter and a hiking paradise in the summer. Plan accordingly.

FINE PRINT: From $135/night. Rolling Huts, 18381 State Route 20, Winthrop. 877-223-1137, 509-996-4442. Three-and-a-half-hour drive from Seattle. rollinghuts.com

Out 'n' About Treehouse Treesort ····➔

Cave Junction, Oregon

Got a budding Tarzan or Jane in your family? In the Oregon Siskiyous, find a hotel in the trees, the vision of a local builder who dreamed of making a living off Oregon's most abundant natural resource without cutting them down. More than a dozen unique tree houses are scattered among the branches here, some just off the ground and others high in the canopy, accessed by ladders or staircases and connected by catwalks. Some are spacious; others are quite cozy. Kids never get bored here — the Treesort also has a swimming pool, ziplines, giant swings, hiking trails and horseback riding.

NEARBY BONUS: Oregon Caves National Monument and Preserve is only about an hour's drive away, and Crater Lake National Park is about two and a half hours away.

FINE PRINT: From $200/night for a four-person tree house; multiple-night stays required in summer. Out 'n' About Treehouse, 300 Page Creek Rd., Cave Junction, Oregon. 541-592-2208. Seven-and-a-half-hour drive from Seattle. treehouses.com

More like this:

- ➤ Volcano Escapes (Adventure 29)
- ➤ Yurts 101 (Adventure 39)
- ➤ San Juans on a Shoestring (Adventure 40)

WANDER LIST:
Great Escapes

Unfold a map of the Puget Sound region and in every direction, you'll find tiny, tantalizing destinations that offer relaxed fun for families, with the occasional thrill thrown in. Here's your dictionary of great daycations.

Anacortes: This historic ferry town isn't just a stop on the way to the San Juan Islands. Soak in views at Washington Park; visit the W.T. Preston, a stern-wheeler snag boat that used to run on the Skagit River; and enjoy not getting on a ferry. Stop at the stunning Deception Pass bridge on the way there or back.

Bellingham: Explore cool STEM museums (Spark Museum of Electrical Invention, Mindport), walk the boardwalk over Bellingham Bay and ride mountain bikes at Larrabee State Park. Then get your reward: a cone at one of the best ice creameries in Washington state: Mallard. *parentmap.com/bellingham*

Camano Island: Another "island" you can drive to, Camano's star stop is the historic fishing resort Cama Beach State Park, which rents out rustic cabins all year (book early). While away more beach hours at Cavalero Beach Park or Camano Island State Park.

Camlann Medieval Village: The year is 1376. The town is Somersetshire, ancient realm of King Arthur. From May to September, during a festival weekend, you can enthrall your kids with a visit to this living-history project near Carnation. Listen to minstrels, watch knightly combat, learn archery, visit the forge and eat medieval delicacies.

Duvall: Just off the Snoqualmie Valley Trail, Duvall has attained a rural yet artsy vibe without feeling too upscale. Fuel up on wood-fired pizza, browse antique stores and have a rail-trail bike adventure. Don't miss the town's summer SandBlast Festival.

Gig Harbor: Stunning Sound scenery, awesome parks and free museums: Those are just a few of the attractions you'll find in this South Sound town, just over the Tacoma Narrows Bridge. *parentmap.com/gigharbor*

Harstine Island: Drive over the bridge to Harstine, located in south Puget Sound, and you'll step back to a simpler time. Hike and beachcomb at Harstine Island State Park and Jarrell Cove State Park. Make reservations ahead to visit the Wild Felid Advocacy Center, an unusual sanctuary for big cats.

Mima Mounds: Are your kids into geology and mystery? Take them to the Mima Mounds Natural Area Preserve, southwest of Olympia, to come up with their own theories of how these up to 6-foot-tall mounds came to exist in this grassland prairie.

Northwest Trek: Arrive early to make the most of your ticket to this unique wildlife park in Eatonville. Take the tram tour first — keep your eyes open for moose or elk — and let the kids climb and swing at Kids' Trek, one of the most adventurous playgrounds in the Puget Sound region.

Port Townsend: Grown-up pleasures in PT are many — the views and the Victorian homes, to name two. But the surefire hook for kids is that you can actually lock yourself in an old-time jail at the Jefferson Museum of Art and History, housed in the former City Hall. Follow by playing at gorgeous Fort Worden State Park.

Poulsbo: Celebrate our region's Scandinavian heritage with a trip to this Kitsap town that's often called "Little Norway." Touch sea stars at the free aquarium (the SEA Discovery Center), stroll the waterfront park and eat doughnuts or lefse at Sluys Bakery.

Roslyn: Just off Interstate 90, this mountain mining town is all about history and natural beauty. Grab coffee at the cafe made famous by the TV series "Northern Exposure," and walk along the Coal Mines Trail. Browse the old cemetery, which has a larger population than the town and is divided by ethnic background.

Snohomish: Want to pick pumpkins and apples at the same farm? Need a vintage typewriter or a 1950s-era school desk? This historic town is your answer. *parentmap.com/snohomish*

Tacoma: The City of Destiny, as Tacoma is sometimes called, is less gritty than it used to be and even more family-friendly. Race pinewood derby cars at LeMay-America's Car Museum. Bike along Ruston Way before heading to Point Defiance Zoo & Aquarium to gawk at red wolves, walruses and sharks.

Vashon and Maury Islands: Wander the beach, fly kites, jump off driftwood and climb the lighthouse at Point Robinson, followed by more of the same (minus the lighthouse) at Maury Island Marine Park. Snack at the Snapdragon Bakery and Café, and see one of Vashon's quirkiest sights, the Bike Tree. *parentmap.com/vashon*

Westport: Get a taste of Washington's coast (without driving forever) at Westport. Climb to the top of the viewing tower or Washington state's tallest lighthouse. Watch surfers chase waves, eat fish and chips, fly a kite and dig up a clam or two.

Whidbey Island: This long, skinny island is home to stunning beaches and parks (Deception Pass State Park is a must-visit), a lighthouse, military forts, charming towns and farm stands. There's also an actual drive-in movie theater, the Blue Fox.

SUMMER

While the rest of the world makes New Year's resolutions, Northwest families make summer resolutions — for camping, road tripping, picnicking and playground-hopping. Slow it down or ramp it up? This mix of mini adventures will help you do both.

SUMMER

NATURE

15.
Berry-Pickin' Fun

By Allison Holm

There's something about berry picking that captures the essence of summer. Gathering juicy, sun-ripened strawberries, raspberries and blueberries is a winning activity for any kid during summer break. And then there's the after-picking party: pie, jams, ice cream, smoothies. These Seattle-area farms grow everything from strawberries and blueberries to marionberries and tayberries.

TIPS: Strawberries are typically available starting in mid-June, with raspberries and blueberries following. Unless noted otherwise, a farm accepts credit cards. Double-check U-pick hours and availability, address and directions, and find out whether you need to bring containers. Berry fields typically have little shade so make sure you pack plenty of hats, sunscreen, water and snacks. Arrive early (or late) to avoid sun and crowds.

Broers Farms

Monroe

Located just south of Monroe, this 60-acre farm has been certified organic since 1989. It grows strawberries, raspberries, marionberries and thornless blackberries for the public to pick; you can also buy pre-picked berries. And they have a decent bathroom and a playground on the premises.

GOOD TO KNOW: Combine your berry picking with a trip to The Reptile Zoo, located right on U.S. Highway 2 about 4 miles from the farm.

FINE PRINT: Call 360-794-8125 or check the Facebook page for berry updates. 18228 Tualco Rd., Monroe. facebook.com/Broers-Farms-Inc-116161815124236

Biringer Farm

Arlington

Operating since 1948, grand-scale Biringer Farm is a favorite with many families for its strawberry and raspberry U-pick fields. You can also pick tayberries (a cross between a Scottish raspberry and an Oregon blackberry), blackcap raspberries and blackberries. Kids love riding the "Jolly Trolley" out to the fields and playing on the small playground. When you're finished, picnic near the historic barn. Note: Biringer minimizes use of pesticides and other chemicals.

GOOD TO KNOW: Shop the market for Slicers (15-lb. containers of fresh, sliced and sugared strawberries, which come ready to eat or freeze) and local honey. Biringer hosts an annual strawberry festival in mid-June with inflatables, rides, face painting and more.

FINE PRINT: Check online or call 425-259-0255 for U-pick hours and berry updates. 21412 59th Ave. N.E., Arlington. biringerfarm.com

Remlinger Farms

Carnation

If you'd like your berry-picking with a side of amusement park, Remlinger Farms is the place for you. After you pick your fill of strawberries or raspberries in the U-pick fields (no admission charge), head over to the Country Fair Family Fun Park, with more than 25 pint-size rides and attractions, including a mini roller coaster and small steam train, as well as a petting farm and pony rides. Note: The farm uses natural fertilizers.

GOOD TO KNOW: From mid-May until mid-June (and again in September), Remlinger offers an $8 "toddler weekday" discount ticket to the family fun park (not all rides are open). Pick up snacks at the Farm Market or eat at the on-site restaurant.

SUMMER

NATURE

FINE PRINT: The full family fun park is open on weekends starting in mid-May and daily from late June onward. $13.75–$15.75 admission to family fun park; no admission fee for U-pick fields (only cash is accepted to pay for berries). Check online or call 425-333-4135, ext. 250 for berry updates. Remlinger Farms, 32610 N.E. 32nd St., Carnation. remlingerfarms.com

Harvold Berry Farm
Carnation

This small and scenic family-owned farm in Carnation is a reader favorite. Harvold's U-pick strawberries and raspberries ring up at affordable prices, and containers are provided. Call before arriving to be sure the fields are open. No pets are allowed in the fields.

FORAGE AND FIND

You don't need to drive to a farm to find berries for the picking, of course. Just take a summer walk in the woods and — depending on the month — you're likely to find salmonberries, thimbleberries, huckleberries or our ever-present blackberries. Make sure you've identified the plant before eating. More tips at *parentmap.com/foraging.*

NEARBY BONUS: Lovely Tolt-MacDonald Park is just a mile away, with bike trails, camping and a cool suspension bridge.

FINE PRINT: Cash only. Check online or call 425-333-4185 for U-pick hours and berry updates. 32325 N.E. 55th St., Carnation. carnationwa.gov

Picha's Berry Farm
Puyallup

Third-generation farmers Dan and Russ Picha continue a family tradition of growing some of the sweetest berries around the South Sound. Strawberries and raspberries are available for U-pick; you can also purchase pre-picked blackberries.

GOOD TO KNOW: Picha's berries are available at stands in Puyallup and Tacoma; U-pick is only at the Puyallup location.

FINE PRINT: Cash and checks only at the Tacoma stand; the Puyallup location accepts credit cards, too. Check the Facebook page or call 253-841-4443 for U-pick hours and berry updates. 6502 52nd St. E., Puyallup. pichafarms.com

Bow Hill Blueberries
Bow

Just a mile from the foodie destination of Edison, Washington, this lovely blueberry farm uses certified organic growing practices. In addition to picking berries, you can shop for hand-crafted products such as blueberry juice, blueberry sauce, dried heirloom blueberries and (yum!) Lopez Island Creamery blueberry ice cream.

GOOD TO KNOW: Bow Hill requires that pickers each buy a $5 grazing pass (or $15 for as many as five family members), which lets you eat as much as you want while picking; it's refunded once you pick more than 10 pounds.

FINE PRINT: Check online or call 360-399-1006 for U-pick hours and berry updates. 15628 Bow Hill Rd., Bow. bowhillblueberries.com

Bryant Blueberry Farm
Arlington

Located conveniently just a few miles off Interstate 5, this farm's many kid-friendly perks include a playground, giant "jumping pillow," fields to play in, picnic tables, shady spots and farm animals for viewing. Bonus: It uses environmental and sustainable agricultural methods.

GOOD TO KNOW: Besides blueberries, Bryant grows currants, tayberries, blackberries, loganberries and boysenberries for U-pick, as well as some U-cut vegetables and flowers.

FINE PRINT: $5 fee to bounce on the "jumping pillow." Check online or call 360-474-8424 for U-pick hours and berry updates. 5628 Grandview Rd., Arlington. bryantblueberries.com

Larsen Lake Blueberry Farm
Bellevue

In the lovely Lake Hills Greenbelt area of Bellevue, find Larsen Lake Farm, operated by the Bellevue Parks and Community Services department to preserve Bellevue's agricultural heritage (as is its cousin, Mercer Slough Blueberry Farm). After picking, head up to the shaded produce stand to shop for reasonably priced produce. Note: Larsen Lake minimizes use

UNIQUE U-PICKS

Blue Dog Farm: This certified organic blueberry farm in the Snoqualmie Valley has a unique membership model for picking berries.

Charlotte's Blueberry Park: Pick blueberries for free at this 20-acre, volunteer-maintained park in Tacoma, which has been farmed since 1929.

Garden Treasures: Take your veggie lovers to this certified-organic farm in Arlington, where you can pick your own produce, including asparagus, beets, blackberries, tomatoes, melons and peas.

Lavender Hill Farm: Pick your own lavender at this quiet farm on Vashon Island, then explore the rest of the island.

Schuh Farms: Take a day trip to this historic 500-acre farm in Skagit Valley to pick strawberries, raspberries, tayberries and cherries.

SUMMER

NATURE

of pesticides and other chemicals.

NEARBY BONUS: After filling your pail, stroll the trail around Larsen Lake or do some fishing.

FINE PRINT: Bring checks or cash, and valid Washington state ID as a deposit for picking buckets. Check online or call 425-499-5322 for U-pick hours and berry updates. 700 148th Ave. S.E., Bellevue. ci.bellevue.wa.us/blueberry_farm.htm

Canter-Berry Farms
Auburn

Canter-Berry Farms grows eight different varieties of blueberries, boasting flavors from sweet to tart to (a little) spicy. You can also buy blueberry products such as jams, vinegars and chutneys. Though not certified organic, the farm does minimize its use of pesticides and other chemicals. Cool fact: Canter-Berry Farms also raises, trains and shows American Saddlebred horses.

NEARBY BONUS: Canter-Berry Farms is only a five-minute drive from Flaming Geyser State Park, along the Green River.

FINE PRINT: Check online or call 253-939-2706 or 800-548-8418 for U-pick hours and berry updates. 19102 S.E. Green Valley Rd., Auburn. canterberryfarms.com/upick.cfm

More like this:
- ➤ Roaring Waterfall Hikes (Adventure 1)
- ➤ Sweet Ice Cream Spots (Adventure 22)
- ➤ Easy Apple Picking (Adventure 30)

16.
Hikes With a Prize

By Jennifer Johnson

Sometimes kids are enthusiastic hikers, but many times they need an extra incentive to join parents on the trail. And parents need rewards, too. These treks include

JENNIFER JOHNSON

Panorama Point

fun features sure to entice a reluctant hiker of any age out into the wilderness, from rocks and snow to views and water play.

Pyramid Lake   FREE   ┈→

Rockport, North Cascades

This steep hike in North Cascades National Park is not for small children, but hardy hikers will enjoy the huckleberries, giant cedars, forest flowers and streams. The trail climbs straight up from Highway 20 through lodgepole pine forest, past a mossy stream and into the Pyramid Lake basin, which boasts a rare population of carnivorous sundew plants living on logs out in the water. My kids were also enchanted by the newts in the lake.

GOOD TO KNOW: Restrooms are available in Newhalem at the picnic area near the campground, and also in the parking area for the Gorge Waterfall overlook.

FINE PRINT: 4.6 miles round-trip, 1,500 feet elevation gain. Find directions and trip reports on WTA.org. Highway 20, Rockport. No parking pass needed. Two-hour, 30-minute drive from Seattle. nps.gov/noca/planyourvisit/pyramid-lake-trail.htm

Big Four Ice Caves

Granite Falls

Located in the Mountain Loop Highway area of the North Cascades, the trail to Big Four Ice Caves wanders through a bird-filled wetland, over a rushing river and within deep green forest. This beloved route has seen substantial development to make the trail wide, gentle and accessible to all ages and many ability levels.

SAFETY TIPS: Follow the directions of the warning signs and stay well back from the caves and the cliff face. Enjoy the view, but do not go inside the caves. Tragic deaths have resulted from caves collapsing and rocks and ice falling.

FINE PRINT: 2.2 miles round-trip, 220 feet elevation gain. Find directions and trip reports on WTA.org. Mountain Loop Highway, Granite Falls. Northwest Forest Pass needed. fs.usda.gov

Old Sauk River   FREE

Darrington

Meander among gargantuan old-growth trees next to a wild and scenic river on the Old Sauk River Trail. Also off the Mountain Loop Highway and close to the town of Darrington, the hike has two trailheads. The northern trailhead allows hikers to travel the entire mossy 3 miles to the southern end and back. The central trailhead offers restrooms and entry to an ADA-accessible section of trail with interpretive signs, and allows for a shorter hike to the southern end. The trail ends abruptly at Murphy Creek; look for striking rocks, and frogs!

GOOD TO KNOW: In mid- to late summer there are safe places to play on the river-banks.

FINE PRINT: 1–6 miles round-trip, less than 100 feet elevation gain. Find directions and trip reports on WTA.org. Mountain Loop Highway, Darrington. fs.usda.gov

Heybrook Lookout   FREE

Gold Bar

A view without (too) much work is what this U.S. Highway 2 hike offers families. To reach Heybrook Lookout, you'll climb steeply through shady green forest, to a sturdy tower that lets hikers see far over trees to surrounding peaks and valleys. A picnic table at the summit provides a spot for lunch.

GOOD TO KNOW: For a real adventure, book a night in Heybrook's newly refurbished lookout tower cabin for just $75/night, 360-degree views included. Find out details at *recreation.gov.*

SAFETY FIRST

Always check conditions of trails and roads before your hike; a great resource is Washington Trails Association's trip reports (*WTA. org*). Always bring the 10 Essentials, including snacks, water, extra layers, sun hats and sunscreen, and be sure kids know how to be safe on the trail. Find out more at *parentmap.com/outdoorsafety.*

FINE PRINT: 2.6 miles round-trip, 850 feet elevation gain. Find directions and trip reports on WTA.org. *Stevens Pass Highway, Gold Bar. No parking pass needed. No restrooms at the parking area.* fs.usda.gov

Meadowdale Beach Park FREE
Lynnwood

This stunner of a short hike, located a mere 30-minute drive from Seattle, is popular for good reason. Starting as a wide dirt trail, it descends sharply into Lunds Gulch, leveling out along a creek and within a half-mile of the beach. Parents will appreciate the deep shade of the mature forest, and kids will enjoy climbing trees along the way.

GOOD TO KNOW: Bring waders or old tennis shoes to walk through the tunnel — in the water — that carries the creek under the railroad tracks and to the beach. Check the water level and your comfort level first, of course.

FINE PRINT: 2.5 miles round-trip, 425 feet elevation gain. Find directions and trip reports on WTA.org. *6026 156th St. S.W., Edmonds. No parking permit needed, but the lot is small and often full; you may have to park on residential streets.* snohomishcountywa.gov

Ginkgo Petrified Forest State Park ⋯→
Vantage

This road trip east has several rewards, including an almost-guaranteed dose of summer sun, and a fascinating geological find. I recommend visiting the interpretive center at Ginkgo Petrified Forest State Park first. Look over the dramatic landscape — it sits on the banks of the Columbia River — before heading inside to see more than 30 varieties of petrified wood, and learn about how it was formed. Afterwards, take a 3-mile hike on nearby trails, spotting petrified logs in the ground and experiencing the desert landscape.

NEARBY BONUS: A fun side trip is to head back west along the Old Vantage Highway to the Wild Horse Wind and Solar Facility & Renewable Energy Center (open April 1–Nov. 15), where you'll get to see giant wind turbines up close and learn about how they work.

FINE PRINT: Gingko Petrified Forest Interpretive Trails: 3 miles round-trip, 200 feet elevation gain. Find directions and trip reports at WTA.org. *The interpretive center is open seasonally; check the schedule online. Ginkgo Petrified Forest State Park, Vantage.* 509-856-2700. *Discover Pass needed. Two-hour, 45-minute drive from Seattle.* parks.state.wa.us/288/Ginkgo-Petrified-Forest

Panorama Point ⋯→
Mount Rainier National Park

The deservedly popular trail from Paradise to Panorama Point isn't an easy hike, but delivers something for everyone, including glorious views and flowers. If you can encour-

SUMMER

NATURE

age or bribe youngsters to climb the steep paved paths in the first mile, the grade gets easier after that. You'll find blossoms of every color in July and August, jaw-dropping views and snow patches that can persist through the summer. Panorama Point makes a good snack stop and turnaround point. Look for the stone privy, with its rounded door, composting toilet, toilet paper and skylight.

GOOD TO KNOW: Get snacks and use the restrooms at the Jackson Visitor Center at Paradise.

FINE PRINT: 5 miles round-trip, 1,300 feet elevation gain. Find directions and trip reports on WTA.org. Mount Rainier National Park. National Park pass required. At least a three-hour drive from Seattle. visitrainier.com

More like this:
➤ **Roaring Waterfall Hikes (Adventure 1)**
➤ **Last-Minute Campgrounds (Adventure 28)**
➤ **Colorful Fall Hikes (Adventure 32)**

17.
Bring on the Beach

By Allison Holm

It's tough to beat a summer's day at a favorite beach: From sand castle building and shell seeking to wading and tide pool exploring, beach activities always win. These Seattle-area Sound and lake spots are all-day destinations, from rocky shores teeming with crawly critters to sandy paradises that call for flip-flops and picnic baskets. And beaches, of course, are an excellent destination in any season and almost any weather. Important: Keep an eye on kids; know whether there are lifeguards on duty. Cover up, apply sunscreen and follow other summer safety tips.

Jetty Island   FREE
Everett

Located just five minutes by boat from the Everett waterfront, Jetty Island is one of the region's best beaches for families, with more than 2 miles of sand, mudflats and warm, shallow water that's perfect for safe wading. The island is accessible from July 5

Jetty Island

through Labor Day, when Everett runs a free walk-on ferry between Marine Park and the island. Time your trip for one of the many fun activities scheduled at the island, from nature walks to puppet shows to bonfires.

GOOD TO KNOW: There are no services (just a portable toilet) on the island, and the all-sand paths are not suitable for strollers. Bring food, water, sun protection and anything else you'll need. Pick up boarding passes for the ferry at the boat launch kiosk. It's first come, first served unless you make a reservation (which you can do for free for groups of eight or more).

FINE PRINT: *Free, but suggested donation of $2 per adult and $1 per child for the ferry. Parking is $3 per car. Catch the ferry at the 10th Street boat launch and Marine Park, 607 10th St., Everett. Reservation line: 425-257-8304.* portofeverett.com/marina/facilities/jetty-island

Brackett's Landing/Marina Beach Park FREE

Edmonds

Just a short walk from charming downtown Edmonds you'll find a wonderful waterfront area. Brackett's Landing, with north and south sections divided by the ferry dock, features a paved walkway that leads to a jetty. In addition to playing on the beach and cruising the path, kids can peer through a large telescope, watch ferries come and go and observe scuba divers at one of the busiest underwater dive parks on the West Coast. Walk (or scooter) down the pedestrian path to Marina Beach Park, where you'll find picnic tables, a playground and a dog park. Hungry? Stop in at Anthony's Beach Cafe, where the kids can play in a sandbox while you enjoy fish tacos and the sunset.

GOOD TO KNOW: Parking fills up quickly in the summer, so you may end up parking around the downtown shopping area and walking a few blocks. There are restrooms and an outdoor shower for rinsing off sand.

FINE PRINT: Brackett's Landing, Main Street and Railroad Avenue, Edmonds. Marina Beach Park, 650 Admiral Way S., Edmonds. edmondswa.gov

Carkeek Park FREE
North Seattle

Venture down the curving, tree-canopied Carkeek Park Road in North Seattle and you'll end up at one of the most magnificent beaches (and parks) in the city, with 220 acres of nature trails, creek, wetlands and beach. Play at the salmon-themed playground before heading to the beach: You'll cross an overpass above the railroad tracks, a fun experience for train-loving kids. The beach is wide and sandy in parts, and when the tide goes out, the beachcombing is excellent. Kids can play on the driftwood while you enjoy the views.

GOOD TO KNOW: Carkeek has several parking lots, but only one lot is directly across from the beach, and it can fill up quickly. Continue to the lower meadow for additional parking.

FINE PRINT: Carkeek Park, 950 N.W. Carkeek Park Rd., Seattle. seattle.gov/parks/find/parks/carkeek-park

Me-Kwa-Mooks Park FREE
West Seattle

One mile south of the popular (and often crowded) Alki Beach lies this smaller and lesser-known beach. Me-Kwa-Mooks (meaning "shaped like a bear's head" in the Nisqually dialect) is a rocky haven for crabs, sea stars, sea slugs, sea cucumbers and anyone who takes an interest in these marine creatures. The erosion of clay and sand has created a series of tide pools; a seawall running the length of the beach protects the upper beach from further erosion.

GOOD TO KNOW: Be sure to wear shoes or sandals for walking on the rocks. There is no lot; park on the street. Time your visit for a low-tide day when Seattle Aquarium beach naturalists are out.

FINE PRINT: *Me-Kwa-Mooks Park, 4503 Beach Dr. S.W., Seattle.* seattle.gov/parks/find/parks/me-kwa-mooks-park

Juanita Beach Park FREE
Kirkland

Lake Washington's Juanita Beach Park is a true gem. A healthy strip of soft, white sand welcomes shovel-toting tots and sun-seeking parents alike. The water is very shallow, and the large wrap-around dock shelters the swimming area from the rest of the bay; it's a lifeguarded beach, too. Take a stroll (or scooter ride) on the footpath through the small marsh section, or rent a stand-up paddleboard. Another plus is the big playground.

NEARBY BONUS: Pick up dinner at the Friday-evening farmers market (3–7 p.m.) or at Spud Fish & Chips, across the street.

FINE PRINT: *Juanita Beach Park, 9703 N.E. Juanita Dr., Kirkland.* kirklandwa.gov

Idylwood Beach Park
FREE
Redmond

A flat, sandy beach and crystal-clear water make this Lake Sammamish location a winning spot for swimming and sand play. The roped-off swimming area is shallow, with a gradual slope. A wide lawn and a large playground beckon kids for after-beach play. Picnic shelters provide shade, and a full bathhouse includes restrooms and showers.

GOOD TO KNOW: Come early on sunny days; the fairly small parking lot fills up quickly (there is also an overflow lot about a half block away). Lifeguards are on duty throughout the summer.

FINE PRINT: *Idylwood Beach Park, 3650 W. Lake Sammamish Pkwy. N.E., Redmond.* ci.redmond.wa.us

MORE BEACH PICKS

Golden Gardens Park: This classic beach in Ballard has acres of sand, a huge pirate-themed playground and wetlands for turtle spotting. It's a serious scene in the summer.

Lake Sammamish State Park: Rent a kayak, swim at the lifeguard-posted beach, play at the awesome and accessible playground near the beach. (And bring your Discover Pass.)

Owen Beach: Soak up views, explore tide pools and rent a kayak at Tacoma's huge and wonderful beach park.

Saltwater State Park: A sandy swimming beach, forested hiking trails, beach playground and a snack shack are the highlights of this Des Moines beach.

Seward Park: Swim at the lifeguard-posted beach, hike through old-growth forest and play at the nature-themed playground at this 300-acre park in South Seattle.

SUMMER

NATURE

Seahurst Park FREE
Burien

From starfish to sea cucumbers, this tide-pool–rich marine reserve offers little scientists an opportunity to explore more than a mile of shoreline. When kids tire of searching for crabs and shells, you can wander the wooded trails above. Picnic shelters and tables are available, as well as barbecue grills and a playground.

GOOD TO KNOW: Come early to find parking or you'll end up in the upper lot, which involves a long walk downhill to the beach.

FINE PRINT: Seahurst Park, 1600 S.W. Seahurst Park Rd., Burien. burienwa.gov

Gene Coulon Memorial Beach Park FREE
Renton

At Lake Washington's southern tip, you'll find a huge, sandy beach with fun written all over it. The designated swimming area is bordered by a walkway; the large, grassy lawn is great for spreading picnic blankets; and there's a large playground. Need more? Check out the beach volleyball courts, horseshoe pits and the little fishing dock. Bring your binoculars for a walk to Bird Island. The beach also hosts festivals and a summer concert series.

GOOD TO KNOW: Lifeguards are on duty at scheduled times. Kidd Valley and Ivar's have outlets at the park for grab-and-go meals.

FINE PRINT: Gene Coulon Memorial Beach Park, 1201 Lake Washington Blvd. N., Renton. rentonwa.gov

Dash Point State Park
Federal Way

When the tide goes out at Dash Point State Park, the beach seems to go on forever. With the park's 3,301 feet of shoreline, kids can run, splash, swim and dig for hours. There are also 11 miles of hiking trails and a popular campground, so you might make a getaway out of it.

GOOD TO KNOW: Restrooms are close to the beach. On weekend days, arrive early. And book campsites early, too, especially for a weekend.

THE TIDE IS LOW

Every spring and summer, Puget Sound beaches have a number of "minus tide" (super low tide) days. Grab boots and a field guide and take the kids on a beach walk to observe sea stars, moon snails, crabs and other critters in their natural environment. If you're lucky, a beach naturalist will be on hand to help you identify creatures. *parentmap.com/tide*

FINE PRINT: Dash Point State Park, 5700 S.W. Dash Point Rd., Federal Way. Discover Pass required. parks.state.wa.us/496/Dash-Point

Scenic Beach State Park
Seabeck
Just a 90-minute drive from Seattle, this state park on Hood Canal more than delivers the views promised by its name — on clear days, you can see the entire Olympic Mountain Range. The large, rocky beach is perfect for tide-pool exploration; the volleyball courts offer sand for digging; and there are trails to hike. The campground at the park has large shady sites and a playground.

NEARBY BONUS: Make a snack stop in Seabeck, a cute town with a general store and espresso stand. And just 10 minutes away at Guillemot Cove, you can hike to a stump house (see Adventure 2).

FINE PRINT: 9565 Scenic Beach Rd. N.W., Seabeck. Book campsites at 888-226-7688. Discover Pass required. parks.state.wa.us/579/Scenic-Beach

More like this:
- ➤ **Super Spray Parks (Adventure 26)**
- ➤ **Diveworthy Outdoor Pools (Adventure 27)**
- ➤ **Thrilling Indoor Pools (Adventure 38)**

18.
Shady Summer Hikes

By Jennifer Johnson

The ideal outdoor activity for a steamy summer day involves both being active and staying cool. A hike on a shady green trail, with some kind of water-play opportunity, is your answer. These routes — a mix of Washington State Park and U.S. Forest Service trails — offer a variety of experiences to keep kids stimulated and active.

Bridle Trails State Park
Kirkland
When you only have a few hours to get out of the house, try Bridle Trails State Park in

Kirkland. With the park's 28 miles of trails, you'll have plenty of room to wander. Mature forest shades the paths, which hikers share with equestrians (a thrill for horse-loving kids!). Bird life is abundant; I once participated in a study of hawks there, as they use the park for nesting and hunting.

GOOD TO KNOW: You can find information about the plants and animals, get directions and print a map of the park at the Bridle Trails Park Foundation website.

FINE PRINT: Variety of loop trails offering hikes of up to 3.5 miles (the Coyote Trail), 450 feet elevation gain. Find directions and trip reports on WTA.org or call 425-649-4275. Bridle Trails State Park, 5300 116th Ave. N.E., Kirkland. Discover Pass needed. parks.state.wa.us/481/Bridle-Trails

Saint Edward State Park

Kenmore

Another park that's close to Seattle, Saint Edward State Park offers 7 miles of trails that wander through the upper forest and down the bluff to the shores of Lake Washington, where adventurous children can dip their toes. Birdsong filters down through tall firs and native shrubs. You can extend your visit by playing on the inventive wooden playground, built by members of the community. Note that some trails are shared with mountain bikers.

GOOD TO KNOW: Saint Edward Environmental Learning Center runs free Wild Wednesdays in the Park programs in the summer.

FINE PRINT: Variety of distances; a good loop is to take the Perimeter Trail down to the Beach Trail; then ascend back (steeply) on the Grotto Trail. You'll find directions and a printable trail map at the State Parks website; find directions and trip reports on WTA.org. Saint Edward State Park, 14445 Juanita Dr. N.E., Kenmore. Discover Pass needed. parks.state.wa.us/577/Saint-Edward

SAFETY FIRST

Always check conditions of trails and roads before your hike; a great resource is Washington Trails Association's trip reports (*WTA.org*). If anyone's swimming, use caution and common sense. Bring plastic bags to pack swimsuits and sandals, and extra layers for bundling up. Always bring the 10 Essentials, including snacks, water, sun hats and sunscreen. Find more tips at *parentmap.com/outdoorsafety*.

Deception Pass State Park

Whidbey Island

At the northern end of Whidbey Island, Deception Pass is a stunning state park that will help your kids get some exercise and cool off. Its 38 miles of trails range from the level West Beach Trail to a climb to the top of Goose Rock (the highest point on Whidbey Island) for a spectacular view. You'll also find trails on the Rosario Beach/Bowman Bay side of the park, along with tide pools to explore on low-tide days. Or head to freshwater Cranberry Lake for swimming or boating.

GOOD TO KNOW: Pop into the Civilian Conservation Corps (CCC) Interpretive Center to get a taste of the history of the park, and read about native history at the story pole at Rosario Beach. There are also three campgrounds at the park.

FINE PRINT: Variety of trail distances and elevation, including the 4.3-mile round-trip hike to Goose Rock. Find directions, trail ideas and trip reports on WTA.org. Deception Pass State Park, 41020 State Route 20, Oak Harbor. 360-675-3767. Discover Pass needed. parks.state.wa.us/497/Deception-Pass

Rockport State Park

State Route 20, North Cascades

Huge old-growth trees cast deep shade, and creeks run melodically next to some of the trails at this state park. The West Loop Interpretive Trail (approximately 1.5 miles long) is laid with hard-packed gravel and is suitable for wheelchairs or strollers. Kids will marvel at the moss and lichen, and interpretive signs will help them learn about this unique ecosystem.

GOOD TO KNOW: If you're up for more adventure, follow the 3-mile round-trip Evergreen Trail counterclockwise from the parking lot, around to the "Broken Fir" and up into the wildest section of the park.

SUMMER

NATURE

FINE PRINT: Variety of trail distances, from 1.5 to 3 miles round-trip. Find trip reports, directions and trail ideas on WTA.org. Rockport State Park, 51905 State Route 20, Rockport. 360-853-8461. Discover Pass needed. parks.state.wa.us

Boardman Lake
Granite Falls

One of my kids' favorite wading lakes is nestled in a shady basin above the Mountain Loop Highway, east of Granite Falls. Boardman Lake is an easy 2-mile walk with 300 feet of elevation gain through deep, quiet, mysterious forest. Some giant trees have fantastical branches — my children refer to them as "the claw trees." Where the trail meets the outlet of the lake, there is a flat, shallow area perfect for wading.

PRO TIP: Want an easy backpacking trip? Find campsites and a pit toilet across the outlet stream.

FINE PRINT: 2 miles round-trip, 300 feet elevation gain. Find directions and trip reports on WTA.org. Boardman Lake, NF-4020, Granite Falls. Northwest Forest Pass needed. fs.usda.gov

More like this:
➤ **Roaring Waterfall Hikes (Adventure 1)**
➤ **Diveworthy Outdoor Pools (Adventure 27)**
➤ **Secret Urban Hikes (Adventure 42)**

19.
Cheap Summer Cinema

By Gemma Alexander

Despite the rise of video games and YouTube, the dark, air-conditioned cave of the movie theater has never gone out of style in our film-loving metropolis. This is especially true on those rare summer days when it really is too hot to be outside. With a little bit of planning, your family can share the big-screen tradition for some very retro prices.

Regal Summer Movie Express
Multiple locations

Regal Entertainment Group runs a weekday family matinee series all summer long.

Each ticket costs $1 for movies beginning at 10 a.m. on Tuesdays and Wednesdays. The same movies will play at all participating Regal Cinemas. In the Puget Sound area, find participating locations in Seattle (Regal Thornton Place Stadium 14), Lynnwood (Alderwood Mall), Redmond and Renton.

GOOD TO KNOW: Check the Regal website for exact dates and locations; several theaters in the region do not participate in Summer Movie Express.

FINE PRINT: $1/ticket. Multiple locations. regmovies.com/movies/summer-movie-express

The Edmonds Theater
Edmonds

It's pricier than other bargain cinemas, but the independent Edmonds Theater, housed in a restored vintage building, plays first-run movies on its single screen for less than you'll pay at a cineplex. Matinees are $8. For evening showings, general admission is $9; children 12 and younger, $7.

NEARBY BONUS: Edmonds Theater is in the heart of this charming ferry town, where you can also eat world-class gelato (Canarino Gelato), plan your next big trip (Rick Steves' Travel Store) or watch ferries dock and sail.

FINE PRINT: $7–$9/ticket. Edmonds Theater, 415 Main St., Edmonds. 425-778-4554 (showtimes); 425-672-9366 (office). theedmondstheater.com

Crest Cinema Center
Shoreline

Once a little down at the heels, Shoreline's beloved second-run theater is a last chance to catch the movies you meant to see before they leave the big screen. Matinees show on weekdays, a new addition to the schedule (they used to show only on weekends), but whenever you go, all tickets are $4 (3-D flicks are $5.50 and special showings may be more).

SUMMER

CULTURE

GOOD TO KNOW: You can also order wine and beer at the Crest.

FINE PRINT: $4–$5.50/ticket. 16505 Fifth Ave. N.E., Shoreline. 206-363-6339. landmarktheatres.com/seattle/crest-cinema-center

Cinemark Summer Movie Clubhouse

Bellevue

Not as well-known as the Regal series, the Cinemark Summer Movie Clubhouse also offers $1 tickets to a different G- or PG-rated movie each week for 10 weeks. Buy a $1 ticket at the door, or the whole bundle in advance for $5. The participating theater is Cinemark Lincoln Square Cinemas in Bellevue (Wednesdays, 10 a.m.).

NEARBY BONUS: Walk to nearby Downtown Park for epic playground fun after the movie; or to KidsQuest Children's Museum for hands-on fun.

FINE PRINT: $1/ticket. Cinemark Lincoln Square, 700 Bellevue Way N.E., Ste. 310, Bellevue. 425-450-9100. cinemark.com

Blue Mouse Theatre

Tacoma

A 100-year-old independent movie theater, the Blue Mouse screens films for relatively low prices every day of the week, with adult tickets regularly priced at $6. But the deal gets even sweeter on Mondays and Tuesdays, when all tickets are only $4; Saturday and Sunday matinee tickets are also $4. Blue Mouse plays a mix of family, art house, independent and mainstream movies, so be sure to check out the listings online before you go.

NEARBY BONUS: Blue Mouse, located in Tacoma's vibrant Proctor District, is not far from Ruston Way's network of bike/pedestrian paths, fountains and eateries.

FINE PRINT: $4–$6. Blue Mouse Theatre, 2611 N. Proctor St., Tacoma. 253-752-9500. bluemousetheatre.com

MORE MOVIE MADNESS

Summer in the Puget Sound region brings a plethora of outdoor movies. Top choices for families include Marymoor Park's Outdoor Movies series, Bellevue's Summer Outdoor Movies in the Park or Kandle Park's Sunset Cinema in Tacoma. Find what's playing close to you on the ParentMap calendar at *parentmap.com/calendar*.

More like this:

➤ **Stairway Walks (Adventure 9)**
➤ **Crafty Museum Spaces (Adventure 34)**
➤ **Quirky Landmarks (Adventure 45)**

WILL AUSTIN

SUMMER

CULTURE

Dupen Fountain

20.
Hidden Seattle Center

By Gemma Alexander

Seattle Center is 74 acres of paths, public art, plantings, epic playground, fountains, museums, historical displays, street performers, skate park, arts organizations, eateries and food trucks. In other words, it's a one-stop shop for family fun. Because we know you already know a lot about Seattle Center's main attractions, we've highlighted lesser-known spots that are excellent for kids and families.

Dupen Fountain/'Fountain of Creation'   FREE

The International Fountain, with its super jets, is rightly the centerpiece of Seattle Center. But its steep slopes and screaming crowds can be too much for smaller children. Head west to find the courtyard that hides Dupen Fountain. Formally titled "Fountain of Creation," the large, unofficial wading pool hosts happily splashing children among its bronze statues and small fountain jets, while parents relax nearby on the bench wall in the shady breezeway.

GOOD TO KNOW: Engineers test the water quality of this pool, and all other water features at the center, daily.

FINE PRINT: Dupen Fountain is located between KeyArena and The Vera Project. seattlecenter.com/locations/detail.aspx?id=85

KEXP Gathering Space/La Marzocco   FREE

KEXP, a beloved listener-supported radio station and nonprofit arts organization, opened its spacious, light-filled home at Seattle Center, just north of KeyArena, in 2016. The space is also home to a La Marzocco coffee shop, where visitors can get their caffeine and pastry fix, check out music-themed art, shop at the in-house Light in the Attic record shop and peek into the glassed-in DJ booth. On sunny days, doors are open to the courtyard.

GOOD TO KNOW: Bring your music-loving older kids to one of KEXP's free all-ages in-studio performances. Sign up in person on the day of the show up to 90 minutes in advance. Free studio tours are also offered daily at 2 p.m.

FINE PRINT: Open daily. KEXP, 472 First Ave. N., Seattle. kexp.org

UpGarden   FREE

The roof of Seattle Center's four-story Mercer parking garage is the unlikely home of a charming oasis called the UpGarden, the largest rooftop community garden in America. Like all of Seattle's P-Patches, the UpGarden is open to the public, although the food and flowers belong to the individual gardeners who grow them.

GOOD TO KNOW: Look for quirky touches, such as flowers sprouting from a vintage car and an old Airstream serving as a toolshed, and don't hesitate to take a few selfies with the Space Needle in the background.

FINE PRINT: UpGarden, 300 Mercer St., Seattle. upgarden.org

Seattle Center Armory   FREE

Seattle Center's 2012 reboot of the Center House into the Armory is no best-kept secret, but it's easy to overlook just how much goes on in the "Center of the Center," as it's called. More than 3,000 free public performances are staged at the Armory every year, including the Festál cultural festivals, which take place most weekends. At the outstanding food court, you'll find outposts of top local restaurants, such as Skillet Counter and Plum Pantry (the latter is vegan), MOD Pizza and Blue Water Taco Grill. And on the lower level, Seattle Children's Museum welcomes kids with hands-on exhibits.

GOOD TO KNOW: Admission to Seattle Children's Museum is only $5 the last hour of the day (4–5 p.m.).

FINE PRINT: Open daily. Free to visit. Seattle Center Armory, 305 Harrison St., Seattle. 206-684-7200. seattlecenter.com/locations/detail.aspx?id=41

Chihuly Garden and Glass

Glass and kids might not seem like a good combo, but the surreal artwork at Chihuly Garden and Glass, next door to the Space Needle, is a surprise hit. Don't miss the Glasshouse, a 40-foot-tall, glass-and-steel structure housing a 100-foot-long suspended sculpture in a wild color palette; or the garden, where you can admire Chihuly works installed alongside dogwoods, fuchsias and handkerchief trees.

GOOD TO KNOW: Chihuly Garden and Glass offers stroller-friendly tours periodically. Check the website's events page.

FINE PRINT: Open daily. $17–$26, kids 4 and younger free; King County residents get $5 off adult admission price, paying $21 instead of $26 (but you have to buy tickets on-site). Chihuly Garden and Glass, 305 Harrison St., Seattle. 206-753-4940. chihulygardenandglass.com

Bill & Melinda Gates Foundation Discovery Center   FREE

Move from style to substance when you cross Fifth Avenue from MoPop to tour this free museum about global health and development. The center's many interactive exhibits explore everyday hurdles facing the world's poorest people and what we can all do to help, including an opportunity to take action right away. Kids will love sharing their selfie and message on the giant wall.

GOOD TO KNOW: The Discovery Center offers free public tours several times a week; you can also book your own.

FINE PRINT: Open Tuesday–Saturday. Free. Gates Foundation Discovery Center, 440 Fifth Ave. N., Seattle. 206-709-3100. discovergates.org

---

SEATTLE CENTER TRIP TIPS

Cheap thrills: Seattle Center abounds with free and affordable summer events, including Festál events; the free Movies at the Mural series; and the Concerts at the Mural series.

Early bird: Arrive early to find parking and avoid crowds. Street parking is free on Sunday.

Map it: The map at *seattlecenter.com/tours* can help you plan your day.

Seattle Children's Theatre: Time your visit to catch a show at this nationally recognized theater.

Anne Frank's Tree FREE

Nestled between the Space Needle's valet parking circle and the IMAX theater is a hidden treasure: the Peace Garden. Look for a small horse chestnut tree planted at the southwest entrance to the garden. A gift from the Anne Frank House to the Holocaust Center for Humanity, the tree is a seedling from the very same chestnut tree outside of Anne Frank's hiding place, which she wrote so poignantly about in her diary.

NEARBY BONUS: Another quiet pocket of vegetation worth finding is the Poetry Garden, located outside the Armory's west exit. The polished granite boulders are inscribed with short poems by artists as different as Shel Silverstein and Bashō.

FINE PRINT: The Peace Garden is located near the base of the Space Needle. seattlecenter.com/locations/detail.aspx?id=69

> ## More like this:
> ➤ **Walk-On Ferry Tales (Adventure 23)**
> ➤ **Dino-Mite Destinations (Adventure 35)**
> ➤ **Geektastic Outings (Adventure 47)**

21.
Live Like a Tourist

By Elisa Murray

Ferries and Ferris wheels, spraypads and Spheres: Playing tourist around Seattle is a blast, if you know where to go and how to avoid (the biggest) crowds. Here are some of our favorite well-known sites, with tips for making the most of your tourist dollars.

AND DON'T FORGET: A growing number of transit options, from water taxis to streetcars, help connect the dots on this frontier city and make the journey as fun as the destination (see p. 6).

Future of Flight Aviation Center & Boeing Tour
Mukilteo

An excellent cloudy-day option available seven days a week, the 90-minute tour of Boeing's production line in Everett — the only public tour of its kind in North America —

JEREMY DWYER-LINDGREN/WOODLAND PARK ZOO

Woodland Park Zoo's Assam Rhino Reserve

SUMMER

CULTURE

gives a bird's-eye view of commercial jets in various stages of assembly and testing. The building is the largest in the world, by volume. The Future of Flight Aviation Center, at press time, was in transition. Check the website for updates.

GOOD TO KNOW: Book tour tickets online as early as you can. Children must be at least 4 feet tall to go on the tour.

FINE PRINT: Open daily. Peak-season tickets $15–$25. 8415 Paine Field Blvd., Mukilteo. 800-464-1476. futureofflight.org.

Woodland Park Zoo

Phinney Ridge, Seattle

With award-winning exhibits designed to mimic natural animal habitats, Woodland Park Zoo is home to more than 1,000 animals and 300 species. Charismatic megafauna such as lions, gorillas, grizzlies and rhinos draw the crowds; but fascinating lesser-known species such as Komodo dragons, warthogs, and sloth bears are worth seeking out, too.

GOOD TO KNOW: Check the daily schedule of events for special add-on experiences such as getting close to a giraffe or feeding an Australian parrot in the Willawong Station area. On rainy days, the indoor Zoomazium is a fun, wear-'em-out option.

FINE PRINT: Peak-season tickets $12.95–$20.95, ages 2 and younger free; $2 discount for transit riders. Woodland Park Zoo, 750 N. 50th St., Seattle. 206-548-2500. zoo.org

Hiram M. Chittenden Locks FREE

Ballard, Seattle

See salmon run! The Ballard Locks, as it's called, is the link between saltwater Puget Sound and freshwater Lake Union. Watch the boats move up and down through the locks as you make your way across the swinging walkways (leave the stroller behind) to eventually reach the fish ladder at the other end. There, from June to October, you can marvel at salmon fighting their way home.

NEARBY BONUS: Look for free concerts on summer Sundays on the expansive lawns of the park.

FINE PRINT: Ballard Locks, 3015 N.W. 54th St., Seattle. 206-783-7059. nws.usace.army.mil

Pike Place Market FREE

Downtown Seattle

"It's the soul of the city," historian Alice Shorett has said of Seattle's venerable Pike Place Market. From the fish throwers, buskers and Hmong flower sellers in the open-air market to the kitschy magic and comic shops that burrow beneath, the market is all color and chaos. Enjoy the traditional highlights — the Gum Wall, Beecher's Cheese, Rachel's Ginger Beer — and visit Pike Place's stunning new MarketFront area. But find your own new favorite corners, too.

GOOD TO KNOW: Plan your visit for a Wednesday, when no cruise ships stop at the waterfront and there's an evening farmers market.

FINE PRINT: Pike Place Market, 1501 Pike Pl., Seattle. pikeplacemarket.org

Amazon Spheres FREE

South Lake Union, Seattle

It takes some wrangling to visit Seattle's wild new attraction, Amazon's three greenhouse domes featuring a 65-foot green wall and 40,000 plants. At press time, you could book a 90-minute tour of Amazon HQ, which includes some time in the Spheres (only for 6 and older) or go during a public visiting day (no age restrictions).

GOOD TO KNOW: You have to register online, and new reservations open up 30 days in advance (and when people cancel), so keep checking back.

FINE PRINT: Tours available on select days and times. Amazon Spheres, 2111 Seventh Ave., Seattle. seattlespheres.com

SUMMER
CULTURE

Volunteer Park FREE

Capitol Hill, Seattle

A 107-step water tower with one of the best free views in the city; a terrific playground and large wading pool that's open every hot day in the summer; a conservatory that's a tropical refuge on cold, wet days: You've struck it rich with a visit to this Olmsted-designed oasis in Seattle's Capitol Hill neighborhood. And let's not forget the park's grand trees (and stumps), which offer some of the best climbing in the city. In 2019, a renovated Seattle Asian Art Museum will reopen, with an update of its gorgeous Art Deco architecture.

NEARBY BONUS: Pick up gourmet picnic food at nearby Cone & Steiner (happy hour is 4–7 p.m. every day).

FINE PRINT: *Volunteer Park, 1247 15th Ave. E., Seattle.* seattle.gov/parks/find/parks/volunteer-park

Seattle Great Wheel

Downtown Seattle waterfront

As a special outing, it's hard to beat a few rotations in a glass-bottom gondola of Seattle's 175-foot waterfront Ferris wheel. Follow the wheel's

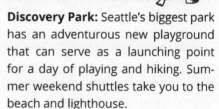

NEW AND NOTABLE

Discovery Park: Seattle's biggest park has an adventurous new playground that can serve as a launching point for a day of playing and hiking. Summer weekend shuttles take you to the beach and lighthouse.

High Trek Adventures: This thrilling aerial adventure park in Everett lets visitors challenge themselves by climbing, balancing and swinging through 60 aerial elements.

Nordic Museum: Modeled after a fjord, the museum's spacious new building in Ballard features kid-friendly elements such as interactive video displays on Nordic history and culture.

Redmond Downtown Park: Redmond's new downtown park features a raised "great lawn" with a wooden boardwalk, plaza, bermed gardens, and a spray park.

Space Needle 2.0: It's time to revisit that iconic Seattle landmark to see the new view offered by its $100 million renovation project.

SUMMER

CULTURE

Facebook page for updates on summer light shows, which you can check out for free as you wander the kitschy-fun waterfront. Note: Downtown Seattle's waterfront is in the middle of a multiyear redevelopment project that affects businesses and traffic. Keep updated at *waterfrontseattle.org*.

NEARBY BONUS: Pair with a trip to the world-class Seattle Aquarium (Pier 59), featuring a touchable tide pool exhibit, excellent octopuses, a unique underwater dome and a harbor seal exhibit area.

FINE PRINT: Open daily. $9–$14, ages 2 and younger free. Seattle Great Wheel, Pier 57, Seattle. 206-623-8607. seattlegreatwheel.com

Olympic Sculpture Park   FREE
Downtown Seattle

Get a big dose of art, nature and views at Seattle Art Museum's spectacular waterfront park. Pose your kids against the backdrop of sculptures, such as Alexander Calder's "Eagle," as you wander down the pedestrian paths that connect the upper park to the waterfront. Don't miss the greenhouse/nurse log installation titled "Neukom Vivarium."

NEARBY BONUS: Stroll on the scenic Elliott Bay bike and pedestrian trail at the bottom of the park.

FINE PRINT: Olympic Sculpture Park, 2901 Western Ave., Seattle. 206-654-3100. seattleartmuseum.org

Point Defiance
Tacoma

The forest. The beach. The zoo. The aquarium. The fort. The views. What doesn't this 760-acre urban park have? An easy starting point is Point Defiance Zoo & Aquarium, which just added the Pacific Seas Aquarium, featuring a 250,000-gallon habitat where visitors can view marine life through a curved glass underwater tunnel. The zoo's tigers, wolves and camel rides (!) are also big draws. Come back a second day to hike through forests, check out tide pools at Owen Beach and travel back in time at Fort Nisqually Living History Museum.

NEARBY BONUS: Bike or walk along Ruston Way's 2-mile pedestrian path on view-rich Commencement Bay.

FINE PRINT: Zoo open daily in the summer. $10–$18, kids 2 and younger free, $3 discount if you bike or bus. 5400 N. Pearl St., Tacoma. pdza.org

More like this:
➤ **For Love of Legos (Adventure 36)**
➤ **Destination Libraries (Adventure 48)**
➤ **Fall Wander List: Jumpin' Play Spaces (p. 168)**

22.
Sweet Ice Cream Spots

By JiaYing Grygiel

Seattle's artisanal ice cream scene has been booming for more than a decade, with new scoop shops, ice pop stands and gelaterías opening every year to help satiate our seemingly endless appetite for sweet, frozen treats. Whether you have a thing for unusual flavors, small-batch ice cream or ice cream paired with pinball, you'll find your nirvana at one of these sweet spots.

Salt & Straw
Capitol Hill and Ballard, Seattle
When Portland's legendary Salt & Straw ice creamery opened its two Seattle locations in 2017, owners (and cousins) Kim and Tyler Malek partnered with Seattle foodie icons to create several new flavors. In addition to Beecher's cheese with peppercorn toffee,

you'll find flavors such as Ellenos yogurt and matcha, Rachel's raspberry ginger beer, and Elm coffee and Westland whiskey. Try them all: The scoopers will literally let you sample every single flavor. My kids' favorite, hands down, is the chocolate gooey brownie.

GOOD TO KNOW: The tasting flight (four golf-ball-size scoops) is the most economical if you're going to share.

FINE PRINT: Open daily. Salt & Straw, 714 E. Pike St., Ste. A, Seattle. 206-258-4574. 5420 Ballard Ave. N.W., Seattle. 206-294-5581. saltandstraw.com

Central District Ice Cream Company
Central District, Seattle

At Central District Ice Cream Company, owners Darren and Kristine McGill draw inspiration for their ice cream from their backgrounds: He's Native American, and she's Filipina. You can try acorn and honey ice cream, inspired by the acorn mush Darren's grandmother would make for breakfast, and Filipino-inspired flavors such as champorado (rice porridge with sweet chocolate ice cream) and ube macapuno (coconut ice cream with purple yam and macapuno).

NEARBY BONUS: Time your ice cream trip for a Thursday afternoon, and you can head next door to Central Cinema for Cartoon Happy Hour, free showings of classic cartoons every Thursday, 5–7 p.m.

FINE PRINT: Open Tuesday–Sunday. Central District Ice Cream Company, 2016 E. Union St., Seattle. 206-519-1529. cdicecream.com

Full Tilt
Multiple locations

Bring a fistful of quarters for the kids and maybe some aspirin for yourself. If sugar alone isn't enough, the pinball, race-car-driving and video games at Full Tilt can get your kids really amped. The local family of ice creameries (with five locations) pairs locally sourced, handcrafted ice cream with soda, beer and arcade games. The ice cream menu changes regularly, from mint chip to birthday cake to Seattle-themed flavors such as Sub Pop, but you'll always find vegan options. Note: The original Full Tilt location, in White Center, is near another Seattle classic: Southgate Roller Rink.

GOOD TO KNOW: Book a birthday party at Full Tilt, and the birthday kid gets to design his or her own flavor and take two pints home.

FINE PRINT: Multiple locations; check website for addresses and hours. fulltilticecream.com

Parfait Ice Cream
Ballard, Seattle

Call it farm to cone. Parfait owner Adria Shimada grows berries and herbs in raised beds outside her shop, pasteurizes her own ice cream base and makes everything from scratch — even the sprinkles. This beautiful little ice cream shop isn't about wild flavor combinations; it's about fantastic versions of traditional ice cream. Try the butter toffee crunch or mint stracciatella, made with spearmint from the garden and drizzled with Theo dark chocolate.

NEARBY BONUS: Cool off at the fountains just a block away at Ballard Commons Park.

FINE PRINT: *Open daily. Parfait Ice Cream, 2034 N.W. 56th St., Seattle. 206-258-3066.* parfait-icecream.com

Husky Deli
West Seattle

Husky Deli doesn't have anything to do with the University of Washington. Through the Depression, Jack Miller's grandfather made ice cream cones called "huskies" because they were big, not because of the college mascot. The family-run West Seattle icon opened in 1932, and third-generation owner Jack Miller took it over from his dad 42 years ago. Husky Deli is known for its deli sandwiches and old-fashioned ice cream, made on the premises. Try salted caramel and coffee Oreo, or go with a classic like rocky road or maple walnut.

GOOD TO KNOW: There is also an old-fashioned candy counter where kids can buy their favorite goodies by the pound.

FINE PRINT: *Open daily. Husky Deli, 4721 California Ave. S.W., Seattle. 206-937-2810.* huskydeli.com

Bluebird Ice Cream
Greenwood and Fremont, Seattle; Capitol Hill store is relocating

Stepping into Bluebird Ice Cream is like entering a time warp — both locations feature restored vintage soda fountains. Sitting on the rotating stools at the marble counters, you get to experience how a Pioneer Square pharmacy felt like 100 years ago. The chocolate pudding and snickerdoodle flavors are sure hits for both kids and adults. For grown-ups, there's stout ice cream.

GOOD TO KNOW: Bluebird also serves beer that's brewed in-house; look for ice cream and beer pairings.

FINE PRINT: *Open daily. Bluebird Ice Cream, 7400 Greenwood Ave. N., Seattle, 3515 Fremont Ave. N., Seattle. 206-659-8154.* facebook.com/bluebirdicecrm

SUMMER

CULTURE

Snoqualmie Ice Cream Scoop Shop
Maltby

At Snoqualmie Ice Cream's flagship store, you can peek into the barn attached to the scoop shop to see how the ice cream is made. Chocolate and vanilla are always popular flavors, and you won't want to miss out on the lavender. Fun fact: This USDA-certified organic ice cream maker also supplies the base for several Seattle chains, including Molly Moon's and Full Tilt.

GOOD TO KNOW: The scoop shop has lots of seating inside and out. Take a look around the sustainably designed property, which features bioswales, rain gardens and energy-efficient equipment.

FINE PRINT: Open from late May until Labor Day. Snoqualmie Ice Cream Scoop Shop, 21106 86th Ave. S.E., Snohomish. 360-668-2912. snoqualmieicecream.com

Molly Moon's
Multiple locations

Owner Molly Moon Neitzel, who at last count had opened eight outlets of her wildly successful ice creamery has crafted a business model that's blended with political activism. For example, she's adamant about giving her employees solid pay and great benefits. So, you can eat your scoop entirely free of guilt. Find your favorite "always flavor" such as "Scout" mint, salted caramel or original strawberry, or try new flavors that are released every season (such as black sesame or Cali lime pie).

GOOD TO KNOW: You can also donate directly to one of Neitzel's pet causes, the Anna Banana Milk Fund, which provides local, organic milk to families in need.

FINE PRINT: Open daily. Multiple locations; check website for addresses and hours. mollymoon.com

Cloud Nine Creamery
Westfield Southcenter, Tukwila

Located right next to legendary Din Tai Fung in Westfield Southcenter, Cloud Nine Creamery makes your ice cream to order right in front of you. Pick your base and your flavors and a Cloud Nine "scientist" swirls everything together with liquid nitrogen. The ingredients freeze into ice cream in seconds, as smoke pours out of the KitchenAid mixer. More scientific touches abound: Enter through a beaker-shaped doorway. Employees wear lab coats. The toppings bar is organized with lab beakers.

GOOD TO KNOW: Signature dishes run $8.50–$10, but the portions are generous enough that you'll want to share each bowl.

FINE PRINT: Open daily. Cloud Nine Creamery, Westfield Southcenter (191 Southcenter Mall, Tukwila). 206-466-4989. cloudninecreamery.com

More like this:
- ➤ **Pinball, Putt-Putt and More Old-School Fun (Adventure 8)**
- ➤ **Global Bakeries (Adventure 46)**
- ➤ **Swimming Pool Getaways (Adventure 52)**

TOBIAS EAGEN

23.
Walk-On Ferry Tales

By Elisa Murray

As any Puget Sounder knows, ferry travel around here can be either, well, a nightmare (hours-long line, restless kids, endless snacks) or a "ferry tale" (you drive right on and enjoy a scenic, leisurely trip punctuated by whale spotting and a gorgeous sunset).

The San Juan Islands ferry reservation system has helped alleviate some of the stress of taking your car on the ferry, but we still love the walk-on solution, especially for day trips. No need to show up super early; simply park and amble on, and pay way less.

TIP: If you have young ones, the family bathrooms on Washington state ferries are your best friend; they're typically located between the men's and women's bathrooms.

Seattle to Bremerton

Pier 52, Seattle

The secret is out about Bremerton's wonderful, compact waterfront, which is steps from the ferry landing and has stroller-friendly boardwalk paths. Kids who love weapons and control panels will especially enjoy touring the Navy destroyer USS Turner Joy ($9–$15, kids 4 and younger free), which was deployed during the Vietnam War. Even closer to the ferry terminal is the free Puget Sound Navy Museum, which has interesting exhibits about Bremerton's illustrious naval history and naval intelligence. But the true summer highlight might be Harborside Fountain Park, a series of volcano-like fountains that accommodate many splashing kids on hot days.

GOOD TO KNOW: If you go on Sunday a farmers market is right at the Bremerton ferry terminal.

FINE PRINT: *A Washington state ferry runs from Seattle's Pier 52 to the Bremerton ferry terminal. $4.15–$8.35, free for ages 5 and younger.* wsdot.com/ferries. *The half-hour passenger-only Fast Ferry also runs from Pier 52 to the Bremerton ferry terminal. $12 round-trip.* kitsaptransit.com.

Seattle to Bainbridge Island

Pier 52, Seattle

The 35-minute ferry ride is a pleasant trip in itself, and once you're off the ferry, it's only a few blocks to the lovely town of Winslow, packed with natural and cultural (and edible!) activities. On a sunny day, wander the waterfront trail from the terminal to Waterfront Park to play on the beach or the playground. Play at the Kids Discovery Museum, with highlights that include a pirate tree house. Next door, browse the small, friendly Bainbridge Island Museum of Art (suggested donation) or hang out at the outdoor plaza. Two blocks away, explore the island's backstory at the Bainbridge Island Historical Museum.

NEARBY BONUS: Bainbridge is foodie heaven. Satisfy carb cravings at Blackbird Bakery. Eat a "wafflewich" for lunch at the retro-fun Madison Diner. Mora Iced Creamery is a must-visit for its fresh, gourmet flavors.

FINE PRINT: *As with the ferry to Bremerton, board at the Pier 52 ferry terminal in downtown Seattle. Ferry fare $4.15–$8.35, free for ages 5 and younger. Pier 52, Seattle.* wsdot.com/ferries

Edmonds to Kingston

Edmonds Ferry Terminal

Kingston — the gateway to the Olympic Peninsula — is at its best on a sunny summer day. Go on a Saturday in July or August, when you can explore the town before settling down at Mike Wallace Park on the waterfront for the farmers market (9 a.m.–2 p.m.) or a Saturday-evening concert in the park (6 p.m.). Don't forget the ice cream! Decent scoops are served at J'aime Les Crêpes and Mora Iced Creamery.

GOOD TO KNOW: Because there is so much to do on the Edmonds waterfront, from a boardwalk trail to sandy beach fun, you might leave extra time for exploring on the Edmonds side before or after taking the ferry.

FINE PRINT: Board at the terminal in downtown Edmonds for the 30-minute ride. You can often find free three-hour street parking near the ferry (harder on sunny days). Or to secure more time, park in a lot. Ferry fare $4.15–$8.35, free for ages 5 and younger. Edmonds Ferry Terminal, 199 Sunset Ave. S., Edmonds. wsdot.com/ferries

Anacortes to Friday Harbor

Anacortes Ferry Terminal

Because of the less-regular San Juan Islands ferry schedule, this trip works better as a weekend jaunt (though it can be done in a day). Picturesque Friday Harbor is home to world-class marine science laboratories, a fantastic whale museum and loads of outdoor activities. At the Whale Museum, the first museum in the country devoted to orcas, hear orca tales and see orca tails. On a sunny day, rent bikes at Island Bicycles for a pedal-powered tour; or skim the water in a kayak.

MORE WALK-ON FERRY FUN

Guemes Island: Catch a small car ferry from Anacortes to this gorgeous, oft-overlooked San Juan island. Five minutes later, on the Guemes side, grab lunch or ice cream.

King County Water Taxi: Bike down the wide Alki trail to the King County Water Taxi, catch a ride to Seattle, cycle to Olympic Sculpture Park and explore before looping back.

Lopez Island: Bring bikes on the Washington State ferry for a day trip to this flat, lovely San Juan island.

Victoria, British Columbia: Board the Victoria Clipper in downtown Seattle (look for Groupon deals) to the royal city for whale watching, parks and world-class museums.

Whidbey Island: This stunning island, reached via the state ferry from Mukilteo, is an excellent day destination: Don't forget to explore Mukilteo Lighthouse Park before boarding.

SUMMER

ADVENTURE

NEARBY BONUS: Boost the thrill quotient by booking a lofty excursion with San Juan Zip Tour. Find more activities at *visitsanjuans.com*.

FINE PRINT: At Anacortes (1.5–2 hours northwest of Seattle), park in one of three pay lots

above the ferry landing. Ferry fare $6.70–$13.50, free for ages 5 and younger. Anacortes Ferry Terminal, Ferry Terminal Road, Anacortes. wsdot.com/ferries

More like this:
- ➤ Choo-Choo! Train Adventures (Adventure 11)
- ➤ Bring on the Beach (Adventure 17)
- ➤ San Juans on a Shoestring (Adventure 40)

Diablo Lake

24.
Summer Splurges

By Fiona Cohen

From floatplanes to ziplines, these premium outings may cost a little more than an afternoon at the spray park, but the rewards are big. Your kid might gain a new perspective on our corner of the world from the back of the horse or a wildlife keeper's truck.

NOTE: These experiences also make great birthday presents.

Canopy Tours Northwest Zip Tour
Camano Island

Hook up to a zipline and whir from tree to tree on a Canopy Tours Northwest tour deep in the woods on peaceful Camano Island. During the two-and-a-half-hour experience, you'll ride six different ziplines (the longest one measures 660 feet), traverse a long bridge, explore trails and take a ride in a 1963 Unimog truck, originally built as a troop carrier for the Swiss Army.

GOOD TO KNOW: It's easy to build in a weekend getaway by staying in a historic cabin at Cama Beach State Park (book early) or renting a house.

FINE PRINT: *$65–$103. Minimum weight 65 lbs., maximum 300 lbs. Canopy Tours Northwest, 332 N.E. Camano Dr., Camano Island.* canopytoursnw.com

Tillicum Excursion
Blake Island

Argosy's Tillicum Excursion to Blake Island is a classic Seattle splurge. Forty-five minutes after you set off from downtown, you disembark into a quiet, wooded state park on an island in the middle of Puget Sound. You enter a Native American longhouse, where Native storytellers tell tales, followed by a meal of salmon cooked in the traditional Salish way: on stakes over an alderwood fire. No theme park goofiness here: It's a serious and respectful way to learn about the culture and art of the nonimmigrant people of this region.

GOOD TO KNOW: On select summer sailings, you can get an extra hour of island time to explore the beaches and trails. You can also book transportation on an Argosy boat to camp on the island (reserve on the Blake Island state park website).

FINE PRINT: *Seasonal sailings, Wednesday–Sunday. Advance tickets cost $35.50–$91.50, free for 3 and younger. Departs from Pier 54, downtown Seattle. 888-623-1445.* argosycruises.com/argosy-cruises/tillicum-excursion

Outdoor Odysseys paddling tours ····→
Friday Harbor, San Juan Island

Set where the surging waters of the Strait of Juan de Fuca mix with the quieter inland stretches of the Salish Sea, San Juan Island is surrounded by fertile waters that are home to a glorious assortment of wildlife, including Southern Resident orca whales. Paddlers on an Outdoor Odysseys tour see orcas often enough that guides instruct people on what to do when the animals venture too close: Stop paddling and band together until the whales pass by.

GOOD TO KNOW: Outdoor Odysseys offers a number of other tours (including a yoga kayaking package) and will also design a custom tour just for you.

SUMMER

ADVENTURE

FINE PRINT: Daily tours offered May–September, leaving from Friday Harbor. $109/person for the full-day tour, including a vegetarian lunch. Minimum age is 12, although custom family tours can be created. 360-378-3533. At least a 3.5-hour drive/ferry ride from Seattle. outdoorodysseys.com

Alpine Adventures rafting
Gold Bar and other locations

In spring and early summer, snowmelt comes surging into mountain rivers, creating a bumpy and thrilling playground for those with the expertise to raft it safely. Guides from Alpine Adventures, based in nearby Gold Bar, run rafting trips on a variety of rivers. Kids 6 and older can join beginner trips on the Upper Skagit River, which feature a mix of flat water and white water against a gorgeous backdrop of the North Cascades. On more difficult rivers the age limit is higher.

GOOD TO KNOW: If you reserve early, you can receive 15 percent off the regular price.

FINE PRINT: Prices start at $69–$79 for a half-day adventure and vary depending on the location and size of the group. 800-RAFT-FUN (723-8386). alpineadventures.com

North Cascades Institute Family Getaway ⋯➜
Diablo Lake, North Cascades National Park

Retreat to the North Cascades Institute for a Family Getaway weekend, a family camp experience that combines outdoor learning with glorious scenery and creature comforts. No tent is needed; you're housed in the institute's state-of-the-art ecolodge at Diablo Lake. Trek the trails, learn about nature or paddle a Salish-style 18-person canoe over the brilliant turquoise waters of the lake. Refuel with delicious, organic meals at the institute.

GOOD TO KNOW: For a cheaper (and shorter) alternative, you can book a quad room for a single Base Camp night ($75–$80/person, which includes one nature experience and three meals).

FINE PRINT: Family Getaway weekends are offered six or seven times a year, Friday–Sunday. $180–$280/weekend, free for ages 2 and younger. North Cascades Environmental Learning Center, 1940 Diablo Dam Rd., Rockport. 360-854-2599. At least a 2.5-hour drive from Seattle. ncascades.org

Icicle Outfitters horseback tour
Leavenworth

When you saddle up for a horseback tour of the Leavenworth area, you'll get a chance to explore the east slope of the Cascades from a unique perspective, going from one calendar-worthy view to another in the company of intelligent, sure-footed animals. Kids must be at least 6 to ride their own horse. Children younger than 6 can share a horse with an adult on the 2-mile ride (at half price).

GOOD TO KNOW: Make a weekend of it by camping near Icicle River or staying at Sleeping Lady Mountain Resort.

FINE PRINT: Two-mile rides are $30 per person, 4-mile rides are $60. 7505 Icicle Rd., Leavenworth. 509-669-1518. icicleoutfitters.com/generalinfo.html

Seattle Seaplanes Float Tour

Lake Union, Seattle

From its base on Lake Union, Seattle Seaplanes offers floatplane rides that present a thrilling perspective of the city and its setting. The cheapest option is the standard 20-minute loop around Seattle, or you could fly on one of the company's other routes, such as over the peaks of the Olympic Range, the glaciers of Mount Rainier or Mount St. Helens.

NEARBY BONUS: With the Seattle Seaplanes dock located less than a mile from the Museum of History and Industry and Lake Union Park, a floatplane excursion is easily combined with other Lake Union fun.

FINE PRINT: Flights start at $97.50 per passenger and leave from the southeast corner of Lake Union. 1325 Fairview Ave. E., Seattle. 800-637-5553. seattleseaplanes.com

Lake Union Charters schooner tour/ The Electric Boat Company

Special birthday for a young sailor? Sign up for a family sail with Lake Union Charters and Adventures and spend an hour and a half exploring the lake on a 63-foot gaff-rigged schooner built in 1926. You can take sailing lessons from the crew or just relax.

FAMILY-FRIENDLY TOURS

Alki Kayak Tours: Step into a sturdy double kayak and paddle behind your tour guide on an expedition from downtown and West Seattle.

Ride the Ducks: You're in for 90 minutes of stories, songs, silly jokes and quacking noises while riding a World War II–era amphibious vehicle.

Savor Seattle: A sweet treat for a young foodie is the Savor Seattle's Chocolate Indulgence Tour or the Pike Place Market Tour.

Seattle by Foot: Seattle Kid's Tour: The downtown destinations on this two-hour tour are picked with kids in mind.

The Fremont Tour: Billed as street theater, this family-friendly tour includes half a mile of walking, insights and improvised silliness.

SUMMER ADVENTURE

GOOD TO KNOW: Another Lake Union idea for a family party is a 10-seat electric boat, rented from The Electric Boat Company, which is furnished for comfort and is easy to operate (no experience necessary).

FINE PRINT: Go on a public charter sailboat rental for $65 per person or rent a private charter starting at $260 for as many as six people. Various locations. 360-399-6490. lakeunioncharters.com/charter/family-sail. For electric-boat rental, drivers must be 25 or older; a two-hour boat rental costs $218. The Electric Boat Company, 2046 Westlake Ave. N., Seattle. 206-223-7476. theelectricboatco.com

More like this:
- ➤ **Hidden Seattle Center (Adventure 20)**
- ➤ **Live Like a Tourist (Adventure 21)**
- ➤ **Winning Winter Tours (Adventure 51)**

25.
Hidden-Gem Playgrounds With a View

By Linnea Westerlind

Parents and other caregivers spend a lot of time at playgrounds, especially in nice weather. Wouldn't it be nice to have a gorgeous view to enjoy? After all, with all the water, hills and mountains that surround us, there's always another sweeping vista around the corner. These fantastic, lesser-known playgrounds feature some of the best lake, Sound and mountain views around. Bonus: Some of these parks have lifeguarded beaches, too.

Ella Bailey Park   FREE
Magnolia, Seattle

This excellent, and accessible, park offers heart-stopping views of Mount Rainier on a clear day. The playground has separate structures for older and younger kids, with dozens of climbing challenges and attractions. A flat, paved path circles the park, perfect for kids to bike on while parents stroll and enjoy the view.

NEARBY BONUS: Just 0.3 mile to the west, Magnolia Playfield has an outdoor swimming pool (Mounger Pool), playground and ballfields.

Ella Bailey Park

FINE PRINT: Ella Bailey Park, 2601 W. Smith St., Seattle. seattle.gov/parks/find/parks/ella-bailey-park

Ward Springs Park   FREE
Queen Anne, Seattle

Less well-known than famous Kerry Park, Ward Springs Park has great city views and is a blast for kids. A large wooden play structure resembling a fort offers lots of spots for climbing and sliding. Kids also get a kick out of the tire swing and sandbox, while parents or grandparents sit on benches and gaze at the Space Needle and city skyline. A gently sloped lawn is perfect for a picnic lunch.

NEARBY BONUS: Bhy Kracke Park, three blocks north, has equally amazing views from its upper section and a small playground in the lower area.

FINE PRINT: Ward Springs Park, Fourth Ave. N. and Ward St., Seattle. seattle.gov/parks/find/parks/ward-springs-park

Jack Block Park   FREE
West Seattle

This unusually shaped, little-known West Seattle park supplies one of the best views around of the downtown Seattle skyline. Although there's no real playground here, plenty of interesting features make it a fantastic spot for kids. Dig in the gigantic gravelly sandpit, play on the quiet beach, cross over pedestrian bridges and spy on activity at the port. Adults will be amazed at the sights from two viewpoints. The entire park is stroller- and wheelchair-friendly.

NEARBY BONUS: Ride or walk one-third of a mile down the Alki Trail to Seacrest Park, where you'll find a fishing pier, an awesome Hawaiian-Korean restaurant (Marination Ma Kai), boat and bike rentals, and beach access. It's also where the pedestrian-only King County Water Taxi docks on its route to downtown Seattle.

FINE PRINT: Jack Block Park, 2130 Harbor Ave. S.W. (at S.W. Florida St.), Seattle. Free parking available in two lots. portseattle.org/places/jack-block-park

Westcrest Park FREE
West Seattle

This popular West Seattle park was recently expanded and now has even more kid-friendly features. Bring bikes for kids to ride loops on the paved path that circles the upper section of the park. Parents can walk and look across at Beacon Hill and the Cascade Mountains or to a snowcapped Mount Baker in the far distance. The playground has a wooden play structure, two ziplines, a climbing net and a spinning net. Miles of easy hiking trails crisscross the forest at the south end of the park.

NEARBY BONUS: Highland Park Playground, just 0.2 mile to the west, has a popular spray park.

FINE PRINT: Westcrest Park, 9000 Eighth Ave. S.W., Seattle. Free parking is available in three lots. For the playground, enter at Eighth Ave. S.W. and S.W. Cloverdale St. seattle.gov/parks/find/parks/westcrest-park

Beer Sheva Park FREE
Rainier Beach, Seattle

Take in views of Lake Washington, Mercer Island and the Cascade Mountains from this waterfront park, which is perfect for picnicking, with tables and barbecue grills that are within sight of the large playground. Kids can play on the two climbing structures, which have blue curving slides, ladders and tunnels. Cross the bridge that goes over Mapes Creek to reach the waterfront, where you can look for ducks and watch boats being launched.

NEARBY BONUS: There is no lifeguard on duty here, but there is at Pritchard Island Beach, just 0.2 mile north.

FINE PRINT: Beer Sheva Park, 8650 55th Ave. S., Seattle. Free parking is available in the Atlantic City Boat Ramp parking lot next door. seattle.gov/parks/find/parks/beer-sheva-park

Groveland Beach FREE
Mercer Island

It's worth the steep descent from the parking lot to find this hidden park's treasures. First, you'll come to the playground, with slides, a climbing wall and musical instruments. Continue down the path to the beach, where a wide lawn with a small strip of sand waits for digging. Bonus on a hot day: This beachfront is almost entirely shaded in the morning. With its western position on the island, Groveland Beach has excellent views of forested Seward Park across Lake Washington. Note: Groveland does not have a lifeguard on duty.

NEARBY BONUS: Island Crest Park and its excellent Deane's Children's Park playground (and Adventure Playground program in the summer) are 2 miles away in the center of Mercer Island.

FINE PRINT: Groveland Beach, S.E. 58th St. and 80th Ave. S.E., Mercer Island. mercergov.org/Page.asp?NavID=497

Enatai Beach Park   FREE
Bellevue

Don't let its location almost underneath Interstate 90 deter you. Enatai Beach Park has some of the best views of Lake Washington around and is a very kid-friendly park. Stop first on the park's upper level, with its huge lawn of perfectly mowed grass and two brightly colored play structures. Then take the steps down to the sandy beach and dock. Kids can swim, dig in the sand and watch kayakers launch, while adults take in views of the lake and Mercer Island across the water. Lifeguards are on duty throughout the summer.

GOOD TO KNOW: You can rent kayaks or stand-up paddleboards right at Enatai Beach through Cascade Paddlesports. The city of Bellevue also offers three-hour canoe tours of Mercer Slough from Enatai Beach on weekends (kids have to be at least 5; $16–$18/person).

FINE PRINT: Enatai Beach Park, 3519 108th Ave. S.E., Bellevue. bellevuewa.gov

Redondo Beach and Pier
Des Moines

A long, curving beach offers hours of toe dipping, digging and exploring for kids, while adults take in views of Puget Sound, Vashon Island and the Olympic Mountains. Walk out on the wooden pier to see what the anglers are catching and take in even more sweeping views. On the pier, the Marine Science and Technology (MaST) Center includes a fine small aquarium that is free and open to the public on Saturdays, 10 a.m.–2 p.m. and Thursdays (summer only), 4–7 p.m.

NEARBY BONUS: Hungry? Salty's has a Redondo location with a sit-down restaurant and a fish bar.

SUMMER
ADVENTURE

FINE PRINT: Redondo Beach and Pier, Redondo Beach Dr. S. and Redondo Way S., Des Moines. Free parking is available on nearby streets, or in a paid parking lot off Redondo Way S. desmoineswa.gov

More like this:
➤ **Epic Playgrounds (Adventure 12)**
➤ **Rad Skate Parks (Adventure 13)**
➤ **Rainy-Day Playgrounds (Adventure 50)**

26.
Super Spray Parks

By Elisa Murray

How can kids swim without going swimming? The answer to this summer Zen koan is a spray park. On a hot — or just lukewarm — summer day, free spray parks are an easy opportunity for a screaming-fun time, what with all the water cannons, dumping buckets and jets. Spray parks are also open more often than their cousins: wading pools. Find a full list at *parentmap.com/spray.*

TIP: Always check hours; many spray parks don't open until 11 a.m. or even later. Remind kids to not drink the water. And keep an eye on kids.

Hazel Miller Spray Park   FREE
Edmonds
A North Sound favorite, this spray park is located in a woodsy park in the heart of downtown Edmonds next to a state-of-the-art play structure — in other words, it's perfect for a hot day. Kids will love the 55-gallon bucket, water cannons, arches that spray water and a toddler-friendly area. Look for the fun area where kids can build small dams to affect water flow. Conveniently, picnic tables are located nearby. The park also boasts a ballfield, trails and more.

NEARBY BONUS: Follow up with excellent gelato at Canarino in downtown Edmonds.

FINE PRINT: Open seasonally, 10 a.m.–7 p.m. daily. Hazel Miller Spray Park, 600 Third Ave. S., Edmonds. edmondswa.gov

SUMMER ADVENTURE

Seattle Center International Fountain FREE
Seattle Center

The big kahuna of spray parks is Seattle Center's famous International Fountain. It's open year-round, but it's at peak capacity only on hot days and during festivals, when it crawls with kids who stand and run (usually screaming) from the fountain's powerful water jets. You can sit on the sidelines and enjoy the show, which often includes music to which the jets are choreographed. Don't miss the thrilling Artists at Play playground, which will finish off the job of thoroughly exhausting your kids.

GOOD TO KNOW: Younger kids might prefer Seattle Center's other fountain, Dupen (aka "Fountain of Creation"), with its bronze sculptures and wading-pool feel.

FINE PRINT: Open year-round 11 a.m.–8 p.m. daily but it occasionally closes for cleaning; check online for updates. International Fountain, 305 Harrison St., Seattle. seattlecenter.com

Georgetown Playfield spray park FREE
Georgetown, Seattle

Yet another reason to visit this artsy-industrial neighborhood that sits south of downtown is this multi-activity park. Kids can divide their time between the spray park and the newly updated playground, which features an airplane-themed rope climbing structure and musical play elements. Grown-ups can hang in the shade or get a work-out on the adult fitness equipment.

NEARBY BONUS: Stellar Pizza is just north of the park.

FINE PRINT: Open seasonally, 11 a.m.–8 p.m. daily. Georgetown Playfield, 750 S. Homer St., Seattle. seattle.gov/parks/find/parks/georgetown-playfield

Crossroads Water Spray Playground FREE
Bellevue

Located in one of the Eastside's most culturally diverse neighborhoods, this North-west-themed spray park features a climbable orca, spitting frogs and clams. You'll also find a playground, walking trails, covered picnic shelters and even a nine-hole golf course.

NEARBY BONUS: Crossroads Bellevue shopping center, with ethnic eateries, quarter rides for kids and free entertainment on the Market Stage, is a short walk away.

FINE PRINT: Open seasonally, 10 a.m.–8 p.m. daily. Crossroads Water Spray Playground, 999 164th Ave. N.E., Bellevue. parks.bellevuewa.gov

Redmond Town Center fountains FREE
Redmond

Get your shopping and your kid's water play taken care of at the super family-friendly Redmond Town Center. Its outdoor areas are both play-friendly and safe, with a pe-destrian zone that encompasses the splash pad, as well as pavement games and picnic benches. The fountains are gentle and perfect for toddlers. Redmond Town Center also has an excellent family restroom and a nursing room.

NEARBY BONUS: Play at Uncle's Games (also located at Redmond Town Center), or head to nearby Marymoor Park for biking and playtime.

FINE PRINT: Fountains open daily during summer business hours; weather dependent. Red-mond Town Center, 7525 166th Ave. N.E., Redmond. redmondtowncenter.com

Les Gove Park Rotary Spray Playground FREE
Auburn

The colorful water-spray features make this park one of the most popular spray parks in the area. In addition, Les Gove includes the terrific, fully accessible Discovery Playground.

GOOD TO KNOW: The park also has bocce courts, a climbing wall and adult fitness equipment. The White River Valley Museum is right there, too.

FINE PRINT: Open seasonally, daily. Les Gove Park, 910 Ninth St. S.E., Auburn. auburnwa.gov

Point Ruston FREE

Tacoma

Tacoma's revitalized Ruston Way waterfront is packed with attractions for families. Play at the ferryboat-themed playground and sprayground at Point Ruston, and then bike down the 2-mile pedestrian path, enjoying stunning views of Commencement Bay along the way. Finish off with a cone at Ice Cream Social in Point Ruston.

GOOD TO KNOW: From June through September, you can take the Downtown to Defiance trolley bus from downtown Tacoma to Point Ruston, and then on to Point Defiance Zoo & Aquarium (just $1/ride).

FINE PRINT: Sprayground open seasonally, noon–10 p.m. daily. Point Ruston sprayground, 5005 Ruston Way, Tacoma. pointruston.com

Titlow Park FREE

Tacoma

Spray park and nature trails and a beach in one place? This 75-acre park on Tacoma's westside also boasts a lagoon, a recently updated playground, and basketball courts and playfields.

MORE WOW WATER SPOTS

Ballard Commons Park: This toddler-friendly series of small fountains is near the skate park and Sweet Mickey's candy and ice cream shop.

Northacres Park spray park: This shady park in North Seattle also boasts a wonderful playground, trails and picnic areas.

Green Lake wading pool: The large, shaded wading pool is open daily and located right next to the bike/pedestrian path.

Jefferson Park: Splash and play at the top of Seattle's Beacon Hill.

Volunteer Park wading pool: The large wading pool is open daily, and is next to the awesome playground and near Volunteer Park Conservatory.

Yesler Terrace: Seattle's new multi-level park offers super views, fort-like climbers, a slide built into a hill and a plaza with a spray park.

GOOD TO KNOW: Come on a low-tide day and get schooled in life as a sea star or moon snail by the Tiptoe Through the Tidepools program, held at Titlow Beach about once a month in the summer.

FINE PRINT: Open seasonally, 10 a.m.–8 p.m. daily. Titlow Park, 8425 Sixth Ave., Tacoma. metroparkstacoma.org

SUMMER

ADVENTURE

East Bay Public Plaza
Olympia

Heading to Olympia? Spend some quality splash time in the unique reclaimed-water stream on the East Bay Public Plaza in front of Hands On Children's Museum. The stream mimics a natural creek, with steppingstones that kids love to sit and balance on, and engineered seeps and springs that feed it. Take time to explore the demonstration wetland and water-themed art that teaches while beautifying: "All the water that will ever be is now."

GOOD TO KNOW: Next door, the WET (Water Education and Technology) Science Center is free and educational.

FINE PRINT: Open seasonally, 10 a.m.–8 p.m. daily. East Bay Public Plaza, 325 Marine Dr. N.E., Olympia. facebook.com/eastbaypublicplaza

More like this:
> ➤ **Shady Summer Hikes (Adventure 18)**
> ➤ **Diveworthy Outdoor Pools (Adventure 27)**
> ➤ **Yurts 101 (Adventure 39)**

27.
Diveworthy Outdoor Pools

By Kali Sakai

Wave pools, lazy rivers, zero-depth pool entries, aquatic play structures, and slides, slides and more slides. You'll find all these thrills and more at outdoor pools and water parks in Seattle and beyond.

Any of these pools makes a fine day trip to soak up sun and water. But don't just go on sunny days. Heated outdoor pools are a great destination on cool, cloudy days, too, and you'll have fewer crowds.

TIPS: Many facilities require admission for anyone entering the facility, even if you're not swimming. Most require a deep-water swim test if kids want to jump off a diving board or

SEATTLE PARKS/FLICKR CC

Colman Pool

swim in the deep area. Check rules online before going. Save by buying multi-visit passes or season passes, which are available for most facilities.

McCollum Park Pool

Everett

At this large, 87-degree pool, a short drive off Interstate 5 in Everett, kids will love the Water Walk, long slide, inner tubes, water basketball hoops and diving board. Other amenities include a barbecue on deck for picnics, and a sound system. The shallow end of the pool (depth of 2.5 feet) is for kids 48 inches and under with adult supervision.

GOOD TO KNOW: Arrive early on hot days to be ensured admission to the pool. Stay after swimming to explore McCollum Pioneer Park's playground, nature trails and BMX track. You can hike farther on the North Creek Trail, which connects to the park.

FINE PRINT: *Typically opens late June for the season. $5 for 75-minute session, ages 2 and younger free. McCollum Park Pool, 600 128th St. S.E., Everett. 425-357-6036.* snohomishcountywa.gov

Mounger Pool

Magnolia, Seattle

Magnolia's beloved outdoor pool is actually two pools in one: a larger, deeper pool (85 degrees), with a 50-foot corkscrew tube slide, and a separate warmer-water, shallow pool for young kids (94 degrees, ahhhh). It also recently installed a fixed shade structure. Check out Pool Playland, a "gentle" public swim in the warm-water pool for children 5 years and younger; Family Fun Fridays, with games and activities; and Free Slide Day.

NEARBY BONUS: Family-friendly Serendipity Café is just around the corner.

FINE PRINT: Typically opens mid-May for the season, daily from late June. $3.75–$5.50, $1 slide fee, babes younger than 1 are free. Check the Facebook page to find pool updates. Mounger Pool, 2535 32nd Ave. W., Seattle. 206-684-4708. seattle.gov/parks/find/pools/mounger-pool

Colman Pool
West Seattle
Overlooking the beach in Lincoln Park, this Olympic-size saltwater pool, recently renovated, features a diving board, corkscrew tube slide and a stunning view. Pool toys like water noodles and mats are available, too. The only two downsides for families: There is not a wading area for tots, nor shade at the pool (though you might be able to grab a small table with an umbrella). Water temps hover at about 85 degrees.

GOOD TO KNOW: It's a longish walk to the pool from one of the two parking lots (you can walk along the Sound or through the woods) and Colman sells out on hot days, so plan to show up early. A pool trip is easily combined with other fun at Lincoln Park, such as biking on the paths, exploring tide pools and playground time.

FINE PRINT: Typically opens around Memorial Day on weekends, daily from late June. $3.75–$5.50, $1 slide fee, babes younger than 1 are free. Colman Pool, 8603 Fauntleroy Way S.W., Seattle. 206-684-7494. seattle.gov/Parks/aquatics/colman.htm

Peter Kirk Pool
Kirkland
Located in the heart of downtown Kirkland, next to awesome Peter Kirk Park and Kirkland's public library, this large, L-shaped pool features a deep area with a low diving board and a separate wading pool for young kids. Look for special "wading pool only" sessions for kids younger than 7 and their caregivers. Both pools are 86 degrees.

GOOD TO KNOW: Buy a 10-visit pass and you can "fast pass" ahead of the line. After swimming, explore downtown Kirkland.

FINE PRINT: Opens for the season in early June. $5 per 90-minute session. Peter Kirk Pool, 340 Kirkland Ave., Kirkland. 425-587-3300. kirklandwa.gov

Henry Moses Aquatic Center
Renton
This water-park-like outdoor pool complex has 26-foot-high water slides, a lazy river, a

wave machine and an island lagoon. For tots, there is a zero-depth entry to a water play structure, and numerous spray features. Another plus: Long sessions (three hours) will seriously wear out kids. Water at the lap pool and activity pool is 85 degrees. Snacks are available at the Shark Bites Cafe on-site.

GOOD TO KNOW: Pre-sale admission begins three hours before a session. Combine pool time with a bike ride or walk along the lovely, stroller-friendly Cedar River Trail.

FINE PRINT: Opens mid-June for the season. $4.50–$8.50/residents, $8.50–$15/nonresidents, babes younger than 1 free. Henry Moses Aquatic Center, 1719 S.E. Maple Valley Hwy., Renton. 425-430-6780. rentonwa.gov

Kandle Pool
Tacoma

Tacoma has some of the most thrilling pools around the Sound, especially Kandle, Pierce County's first wave pool. At this 85-degree pool, you'll find a gradual zero-depth entry, a 100-gallon tumble bucket and, of course, the wave machine, which simulates an ocean wave experience. A separate shallow pool and "sprayground" sit adjacent to the main pool.

GOOD TO KNOW: Arrive early if you'd like a lounge chair, or bring your own. Concessions are available, but visitors can also bring their own (no glass). Kandle Park is also home to a state-of-the-art playground, skate park and (free) sprayground, open daily from late May through August.

FINE PRINT: Opens mid-June for the season. Five-hour session $8–$10; 2.5-hour half/evening session $6–$8, ages newborn–4 free. A season pass is good for Kandle and Tacoma's Stewart Heights Pool. Kandle Pool, 5302 N. 26th St., Tacoma. 253-404-3920. metroparkstacoma.org/kandle

Tenino rock quarry swimming pool
Tenino

Against the stunning backdrop of an old sandstone quarry, this 82-foot-deep freshwater pool promises the ultimate deep-water experience — if you can take the chill. (The water is usually about 45 degrees.) Kids who pass the deep-water test can jump off two diving boards and swim to a waterfall that flows into the quarry. There is also a slightly warmer wading pool for young kids.

NEARBY BONUS: Train-crazy kids will enjoy visiting the old train depot next door (made of sandstone, of course), which is open on weekends.

FINE PRINT: The pool is typically open from late June through August, Wednesday–Sunday. $3 residents, $5 nonresidents. Tenino City Park, Park Ave. E., Tenino. 360-264-2368. ci.tenino.wa.us

SUMMER ADVENTURE

Birch Bay Waterslides

Blaine

Just south of the Canadian border, this family-friendly water park has nine slides, a 40-person hot tub (for ages 7 and older), kiddie pool, volleyball, basketball and activity pool. The black slides include the Black Hole and a slide with a 60-foot drop (kids must be at least 12 years old and 100 lbs. to go on the drop). The kiddie pool, for ages 8 and younger, also has three slides.

GOOD TO KNOW: You can reserve a covered spot online. Outside food is allowed, but no competing fare (e.g., fast food and pizza). No coolers, alcohol or glass allowed. Make it a weekend by camping at Birch Bay State Park or lodging at luxe Semiahmoo.

FINE PRINT: *Typically opens for weekends after Memorial Day, open daily from late June. $13–$22.50 for full day. $11–$17.50 for "late day" (after 3 p.m.). Ages 2 and younger free. Birch Bay Waterslides, 4874 Birch Bay Lynden Rd., Blaine. 360-371-7500.* birchbaywaterslides.net

MEMBERS ONLY

Heard of those elusive, membership-only swim clubs that require years on a waiting list and a fat deposit? There's another way in: Many member pools allow nonmembers to take swim lessons, often for reasonable prices. Check clubs such as Samena Swim & Recreation Club, Wedgwood Swim Club and others for lesson sign-up dates.

Wild Waves Theme & Water Park

Federal Way

Located just off I-5 in Federal Way, the region's biggest water park stars attractions for every level of ability and comfort. Highlights include the super-thrilling Mountain Dew Slide Complex, Raging River Ride, 500,000-gallon wave pool and the Konga Lazy River. Little ones love Hook's Lagoon, a large pirate-themed water play area. Combined with the amusement park rides, there are more than 60 rides, slides and attractions.

GOOD TO KNOW: Weekdays in June are less crowded and admission is discounted. Bring your own stroller, as rentals aren't provided and the park is 70 acres. You can rent your own cabana 24 hours in advance. Buy tickets from a Seattle community center at a discount.

FINE PRINT: *Typically open from Memorial Day through Labor Day. Go before June 15 for discount admission and buy online to save. Peak-season admission is $22.99–$42.99 (kids 3 and younger free); parking is $10–$20. Wild Waves Theme & Water Park, 36201 Enchanted Pkwy. S., Federal Way. 253-661-8000.* wildwaves.com

More like this:
- ➤ **Super Spray Parks (Adventure 26)**
- ➤ **See Salmon Run (Adventure 31)**
- ➤ **Thrilling Indoor Pools (Adventure 38)**

28.
Last-Minute Campgrounds

By Nancy Schatz Alton

No camping reservations? That's okay. We're here to tell you — no promises, of course — that you can still find a tent spot for a last-minute jaunt. These excellent campgrounds are within a 90-minute drive of Seattle and might still have summer openings, especially if you're looking for midweek excursions. (Find even more ideas at *parentmap.com/procrasticamp*.)

CAVEAT: You should still book as early as you can for weekend camping. Also, keep checking back in, as some early campsite bookers will cancel a few weeks out.

Rasar State Park

Concrete

Just off the North Cascades Highway, this wonderful camping park on the Skagit River offers more than 40 campsites, including hike-in/bike-in sites, RV sites, tent sites and group campsites, as well as cabins. Kids will love circling the campground (which includes a playground) on their bikes, exploring the trails, digging in the sand by the river and completing the junior ranger program. Parents will love the shady sites and the chance to spot eagles feeding at the river.

GOOD TO KNOW: Book one of the cabins in January for the best chance of eagle spotting.

FINE PRINT: Campsites from $25 during peak season ($12 for primitive sites). Book online, or call 888-226-7688. Rasar State Park, 38730 Cape Horn Rd., Concrete. parks.state.wa.us/571/rasar

SUMMER

ESCAPES

ELISA MURRAY

Tolt MacDonald Park

Flowing Lake County Park

Snohomish

East of Everett and north of U.S. Highway 2, Flowing Lake is a busy campground, yet even when it's full, you'll find plenty of elbow room and a well-shaded forest setting. Don't forget your fishing pole: Flowing Lake is stocked with rainbow trout. The lake is great for swimming, but on warm summer days, there is a fair amount of boat traffic here, too. For a serene winter getaway, reserve one of the park's cabins. Note: Alcoholic beverages are not allowed in county parks.

NEARBY BONUS: Check for events at The Evergreen State Fairgrounds in Monroe, where you can also visit the free Western Heritage Museum (open Friday–Sunday).

FINE PRINT: Sites start at $28/night during peak season. Book online at the Snohomish County website or call 425-388-6600. Flowing Lake County Park, 17900 48th St. S.E., Snohomish. snohomishcountywa.gov

Tolt MacDonald Park & Campground

Carnation

Part of the excitement of camping in this King County park is walking over the 500-foot suspension bridge above the rushing Snoqualmie River. The park is at the confluence of the Snoqualmie and Tolt rivers; you will feel like you are in the country even though the campground is inside Carnation's city limits. Other highlights include miles of mountain bike trails, a playground and a nice riverfront area for play.

GOOD TO KNOW: Options include drive-in and hike-in campsites, yurts and a shipping container (!) that's been redesigned as a cabin, with heat and electricity.

FINE PRINT: You can't be too last-minute at Tolt MacDonald; the county requires that you book at least 10 days ahead (though any non-reserved sites are available as first come, first served). Campsites start at $20/night. Book online or at 206-477-6149. Tolt MacDonald Park, N.E. 40th St. and State Route 203, Carnation. kingcounty.gov

Millersylvania State Park
Olympia

This 120-site lakeside campground is a mere 5 miles off Interstate 5, but the surrounding forest will make you forget this fact. There are tent sites in the shade and in the sun, and they are all near Deep Lake. Take a dip at both of the swimming beaches and hike or bike along 8.5 miles of flat trails.

GOOD TO KNOW: Millersylvania also has luxury camping cabins, called Pampered Wilderness. Most are geared toward couples, but the Country Cabin has two full-size beds.

FINE PRINT: Sites start at $25/night. Book online, or call 888-226-7688. Millersylvania State Park, 12245 Tilley Rd. S., Olympia. parks.state.wa.us/546/millersylvania

Offut Lake Resort
Tenino

Book a campsite or a cabin at this historic south Thurston County resort. The small and beautiful Offut Lake has a 5-mph speed limit, so your children won't be bothered by boat wakes. At the resort, enjoy swimming, fishing and boating. Don't want to cook over the campfire? The resort's restaurant offers pub food as well as a few fancier entrée options.

PROCRASTI-CAMPER TIPS

There as many tricks for scoring last-minute campsites as there are campers. Keep checking online, as reservations are often canceled. Try campgrounds with non-reservable sites (best bet is to try midweek); see our guide at *parentmap.com/noreservations*. Or try Hipcamp, a new online platform that gives access to thousands of acres of private land for camping (*hipcamp.com*). Thrifty NW Mom has lists of free and low-cost campsites (*thriftynorthwestmom.com*).

SUMMER

ESCAPES

GOOD TO KNOW: Pets are allowed at the campground, but bikes are not. Nearby, visit Wolf Haven or Lattin's Country Cider Mill & Farm, a favorite South Sound farm that has a petting zoo, delicious doughnuts and no entrance fee.

FINE PRINT: Sites start at $30/night and include a dock pass for each guest. Offut Lake Resort, 4005 120th Ave. S.E., Tenino. 360-264-2438 (resort), 360-264-3474 (restaurant). offutlakeresort.com

Alder Lake Park

Eatonville

Water play is the name of the game at Alder Lake: Boat, swim, water-ski (bring your own boat), Jet Ski, play at the playgrounds, visit Alder Dam and watch the deer roam the park. There are also two no-wake areas and two small nonmotorized areas. During the peak summer season, there might be a dozen sites available on weekdays for one-night "walk-in" stays, but the only way to secure a site is with a reservation. There are 173 sites total.

NEARBY BONUS: Hike or bike at the University of Washington's Pack Forest, or visit Northwest Trek Wildlife Park, just north of Eatonville.

FINE PRINT: Sites start at $25/night. Book online or call 888-226-7688. Alder Lake Park, 50324 School Rd., Eatonville. mytpu.org

> ## More like this:
> ➤ One-of-a-Kind Getaways (Adventure 14)
> ➤ Spring Wander List: Great Escapes (p. 60)
> ➤ Yurts 101 (Adventure 39)

29.
Volcano Escapes

By E. Ashley Steel

Living on the famed "Ring of Fire" — the string of volcanoes and sites of seismic activity along the rim of the Pacific Ocean — has its perks. Your budding geologists can learn about stratovolcanoes, craters, lava domes and post-blast restoration firsthand. Each of these three vacations is a perfect starting point for exploring the Pacific Northwest's seismic wonders.

TINYPINES

SUMMER

ESCAPES

Mount Rainier National Park ····→

A beloved sight on the Seattle skyline, "the Mountain," as Rainier is often called, sits on a subduction zone atop colliding continental and oceanic plates. That means earthquakes galore (the mountain experiences more than 20 a year!).

WHAT TO DO: Mount Rainier is a wonderfully accessible national park, where you can learn about seismic activity and volcanic history. Past volcanic activity created the nearby mineral springs; find them on the short Trail of the Shadows near Longmire Museum (located on the road to Paradise, via the Nisqually entrance). The 49 springs are no longer open for soaking or drinking, but a visit to the historic Longmire Cabin — also along this trail — gives a glimpse into earlier times.

Another amazing artifact of volcanic activity to watch for: columnar lava — think hot lava meeting cold ice to create distinctive hexagonal columns. You'll spot it along the road to Sunrise, accessed from the northeast entrance to the park.

Unforgettable trail experiences include the Mount Fremont Lookout Trail at Sunrise, a 5.6-mile round-trip hike. It's suitable for teens or sure-footed younger kids and offers some stunning alpine and panoramic vistas. Or take the easier Grove of the Patriarchs Trail, a 1.5-mile round-trip hike through some of the most beautiful old-growth forests on Earth (including a magical suspension bridge). The Paradise region of the park offers stunning meadows of wildflowers and the Henry M. Jackson Memorial Visitor Center.

WHERE TO STAY: Consider a room at the historic Paradise Inn, built in 1916 and perched at an elevation of 5,420 feet. In summer, camping is also an option. Most of the 473 car-camping spots at the three campgrounds inside the park are fantastic. The charming Silver Springs campground is just outside the park boundary on State Route 410.

FINE PRINT: Double-occupancy rooms from $126/night at Paradise Inn, 52807 Paradise Rd. E., Ashford. 855-755-2275. mtrainierguestservices.com. $20/night for a campsite at one of the three campgrounds inside the park; reserve at nps.gov/mora/ planyourvisit. $20/night for a site at Silver Springs Campground; reserve at recreation.gov or 877-444-6777. Two-hour, 30-minute drive from Seattle. fs.usda.gov

Mount St. Helens ···→

Many of us can remember when Mount St. Helens erupted on May 18, 1980. The eruption removed more than 1,000 feet of mountain and left a horseshoe-shaped crater to commemorate the occasion. In the nearly 40 years since the blast, neighboring forests, lakes and rivers have, for the most part, recovered, but the altered landscape remains exciting to visit.

SEISMIC STUDY TIPS

Eruptive fiction: Fun titles about volcanoes include "Vacation Under the Volcano" by Mary Pope Osborne; "Ashfall" and "Ashen Winter" by Mike Mullin; and, of course, the Jules Verne classic "Journey to the Center of the Earth."

Explosive facts: Visit the volcano page on the Science Kids website or check your local library's juvenile nonfiction section. *sciencekids.co.nz/ sciencefacts/earth/volcano.html*

National parks know-how: The National Park Service also has great information about the geology and seismology of Mount Rainier and Mount St. Helens. *nps.gov/mora/ learn/nature/volcanoes.htm*

Volcano videos: Watch videos about volcanoes online at Bill Nye the Science Guy's YouTube channel or on the National Geographic website.

WHAT TO DO: Start your trip at the Forest Learning Center at mile marker 33 on State Route 504. It offers an impressive range of interpretive (and free!) exhibits and is a great starting point for short and long hikes. View geologic formations up close on the half-mile Eruption Trail, right behind the Forest Learning Center, or try the nearby 2.4-mile Hummocks Trail, a loop full of fascinating hummocks, debris left by the blast and small ponds.

At the far end of State Route 504 (about 52 miles east of Castle Rock, Washington), you'll find the Johnston Ridge Observatory. There you can enjoy views of the lava dome, crater, pumice plain and landslide deposit. The observatory regularly leads guided walks and talks as well as Junior Ranger programs, geared toward kids ages 6–12.

WHERE TO STAY: A particularly fun camping option is Seaquest State Park, which is connected by a pedestrian tunnel to the Mount St. Helens Visitor Center at Silver Lake. Even though the park is near Interstate 5, it has great views of the mountain, swimming nearby and lush hiking trails. Eco Park Resort, just down the road, offers somewhat more luxurious options, with cabins, yurts, campsites, a full-service restaurant and guided horseback rides. (Reservations are required.)

FINE PRINT: $30/night per campsite, Seaquest State Park, 3030 Spirit Lake Hwy., Castle Rock. 360-274-8633. parks.state.wa.us. $25–$150/night for campsites, yurts and cabins, Eco Park Resort, mile marker 24 on State Route 504, Toutle. 360-274-7007. ecoparkresort.com

Mount Bachelor ····➔

Located in central Oregon near Bend, Mount Bachelor is a dormant stratovolcano that formed more than 11,000 years ago, which now serves as a recreation center.

WHAT TO DO: Begin your visit at Lava Lands Visitor Center in Bend. Watch videos, check out the 3-D map and walk the Sun-Lava Path, a 5.5-mile paved trail along the edge of an actual lava field. In summer, you can hop a shuttle to the summit of Lava Butte, which erupted about 7,000 years ago. Also visit Newberry National Volcanic Monument, which has more than 50,000 acres of lakes, and lava, basalt, rhyolite and obsidian flows.

In summer, you can ride a Mount Bachelor chairlift or hike up to Pilot Butte State Scenic Viewpoint, an old cinder cone just east of Bend. Lava River Cave is a mile-long lava tube off U.S. Highway 97 at Exit 151/Cottonwood Road. It's a fairly steep descent into the cave, but it's cool inside all year long.

WHERE TO STAY: Camp at Little Crater Campground, or splurge and stay at Sunriver Resort, where kids can play all day at SHARC, a family-centered recreation area with an outdoor water park.

FINE PRINT: $18/night for a campsite at Little Crater Campground, La Pine, Oregon; reserve at recreation.gov or 877-444-6777. hoodoorecreation.com. Range of prices at Sunriver Resort. 855-420-8206. Six-hour drive from Seattle to Sunriver. destinationhotels.com/sunriver-resort

More like this:
- ➤ One-of-a-Kind Getaways (Adventure 14)
- ➤ San Juans on a Shoestring (Adventure 40)
- ➤ Swimming Pool Getaways (Adventure 52)

SUMMER

ESCAPES

WANDER LIST:
Free and Fun

The best things in the Puget Sound area are free — at least in the summer: beaches, spray parks, wading pools, wildflowers, natural waterslides, light-houses, skateboard lessons and bowling (if you're a kid). We especially love free programs that star in fun and community building.

Adventure Playground: The Adventure Playground program at Deane's Children's Park on Mercer Island lets kids build forts and other epic structures (tools and hard hats provided) several afternoons a week. It's free, but a donation is suggested.

Bat sense: Local nonprofit group Bats Northwest hosts bat walks on several evenings during the summer at Green Lake in Seattle, usually gathering about an hour before sunset.

Farmers market fun: Local farmers markets double as a source of fresh enter-tainment. The Wallingford farmers market is located next to the awesome Meridian playground (Wednesdays); Kirkland's Juanita Friday Market is across the street from the beach; and the Bellevue Farmers Market (Thursdays) rewards kids for trying new produce through its POP (Power of Produce) Club program. *parentmap.com/farmers*

Forage: Ditch the drive to a farm and head to a local park (or food forest) to pick not just blackberries, but thimbleberries, salmonberries and huckleberries, to name a few.

Free classes: Does your kid have a hankering to develop a new interest? Many kids' ac-tivities, such as karate studios, music classes and even STEM programs like Kids Science Labs, let first-timers sample a class for free. Just ask.

Free lunch: Some local cities offer free drop-in activities at playgrounds in the sum-mer, usually with lunch, such as Tacoma's summer playground program. Seattle also offers free lunches at many parks and other sites.

Hike and seek: There are so many ways to hunt for treasure, starting with geocaching. Less-er-known low-tech options include letterboxing, which involves following clues to a cached journal; and hiding and finding painted rocks (join a local Facebook group to get started).

Hike and slide: You want to hike, they want to water slide. Combine those two activi-ties with a ramble down the trail to Denny Creek's natural slides (exit 47 off Interstate 90, 1 mile hike in), where families can whoop it up on hot days. (Go early!)

Outdoor music and movies: Rock out at a free family concert, such as those presented as part of the Kirkland Summer Concert series at Juanita Beach Park (Tuesdays), or Kids SummerStage at Les Gove Park in Auburn (Wednesdays). For kids who can take a late night, outdoor movie series also abound.

Play streets: Want to connect with your neighbors and have more space for your kids to play outside? If you're in Seattle, it's a simple process to get a free permit to close down your street regularly to create a "play street." Tips at *parentmap.com/playstreet.*

Read, read, read: Summer reading programs at libraries are still the best summer deal in town, offering not only reading programs, but performances and workshops. Bookstores such as Barnes & Noble, Third Place Books and Half-Price Books also have fun programs.

Row, row: Take advantage of our water-logged wonderland. Boating spots such as the University of Washington's Waterfront Activities Center, Foss Harbor Marina in Tacoma and Issaquah Paddle Sports at Lake Sammamish offer affordable rentals. Every Sunday, Seattle's Center for Wooden Boats offers free boat rides (arrive early).

Shakespeare and the park: Swordfights, crazy costumes, free admission — Shakespeare in the park is kid-friendly right out of the gate. Try GreenStage's Backyard Bard program, featuring four actors in one-hour versions of the Bard's best. *greenstage.org/backyard-bard*

Skate and bowl for free: Beat the heat (or the rain) with free bowling time through Kids Bowl Free program (*kidsbowlfree.com*). Kids can roller skate for free on select evenings at Lynnwood Bowl and Skate through the Kids Skate Free (*kidsskatefree.com*) program.

Summer at the Sculpture Park: Starting in mid-July, Seattle Art Museum offers its free Summer at SAM program, with free live music and art activities at Olympic Sculpture Park on Thursday evenings and Saturdays, as well as food trucks at the ready.

SUMMER

WANDER LIST

Swimming lessons, free: Get free swimming lessons for your kids at nine Seattle beaches on weekdays. Sessions typically start in late June, with midday lessons and evening lessons.

Urban hikes: You don't have to escape to the forest to find great walks. Explore new corners of the city by following a designated trail, such as the Cheshiahud loop around Seattle's Lake Union (*parentmap.com/cheshiahud*), or creating your own route.

Wild learning: Saint Edward State Park's Environmental Learning Center hosts free "Wild Wednesdays" nature programs in the summer. Follow with play time at Saint Ed's amazing castle playground.

SUMMER

WANDER LIST

FALL

Where else but here can you see salmon fighting their way upstream in the middle of a metropolis? The season of dwindling light is a fine time to explore other kid obsessions, from Legos to dinos to apple pie.

FALL

NATURE

30.
Easy Apple Picking

By Lauren Braden

It's not autumn (or late summer) in the Northwest without a trip to pick your own apples. And you're in luck: Washington state produces about 60 percent of the nation's supply of apples, from super-sweet to pucker-producing tart varieties. Most of the region's apples are plucked from orchards in the Wenatchee Valley. But you can also find a few orchards closer to Puget Sound.

Important: Apples are usually ready for harvest from September through the end of October, but some farms start earlier.

Jones Creek Farms

Sedro-Woolley

Jones Creek Farms is a small, family-run operation in the fertile Skagit Valley, an area that was once dotted with apple orchards. It's your best bet in the Puget Sound region for heirloom varieties of apples, as this farm grows more than 100 unique varieties on its organically maintained orchard. Beyond apples, the farm offers U-pick Asian pears, squash and pumpkins.

GOOD TO KNOW: Pears and plums are also available for U-pick when ripe, and garlic is available for purchase.

FINE PRINT: *U-pick typically runs from late August through October. Check its harvest site (*jonescreekfarms.info*) for harvest updates. 32260 Burrese Rd., Sedro-Woolley.* skagitvalleyfruit.com

BelleWood Acres

Lynden

Just outside Bellingham, BelleWood Acres is a favorite for kids and adults alike. Little ones will enjoy a ride aboard the "Apple Bin Express," a small train that transports pickers to the U-pick area in the huge, 25,000-tree apple orchard. BelleWood offers apple varieties that include Sansa, Jonagold, Mountain Rose (pink inside!), Golden Supreme and Honeycrisp. Eat at BelleWood's Country Café and Bakery, and make a stop at the distillery's tasting bar. Check out the pumpkin patch (with corn maze, corn cannon and more) in October.

GOOD TO KNOW: BelleWood also hosts fun music and tasting events.

FINE PRINT: *U-pick typically opens around Sept. 1. Check the Facebook page or call 360-318-7720 for harvest updates. 6140 Guide Meridian Dr., Lynden.* bellewoodfarms.com

The Farm at Swan's Trail

Snohomish

For a quick trip from the Seattle area, The Farm at Swan's Trail, southeast of Everett, can't be beat. Set along the Snohomish River, it has a U-pick apple orchard as well as an enormous pumpkin patch. After your wagon is piled high with fruit, let the kids loose to find their way through an intricate corn maze in the shape of Washington state, then visit pigs and ducks at the petting zoo. There's also a mini train for kids, a playground and more.

GOOD TO KNOW: Hop on the wagon for a ride to the acre-wide orchard of Honeycrisp and Jonagold apples.

FALL

NATURE

FINE PRINT: Apple U-pick typically opens around mid-September. Check the Facebook page or call 425-334-4124 for harvest updates. 7301 Rivershore Rd., Snohomish. thefarm1.com

Skipley Farm
Snohomish

You won't find manicured areas for wedding receptions or pumpkin cannons at this working farm, but you will find more than 200 varieties of apples in the field, both the unusual types and the better-known Fuji and Honeycrisp. Try Bramley's Seedling apples for great pies and tart, crunchy eating. Also available for U-pick: William's Pride, Gravenstein, Redfree, Pristine, Zestar! and Sansa.

GOOD TO KNOW: Kids can visit the chickens, ducks and rabbits after picking. Earlier in the summer, stop by the farm to pick many kinds of berries.

FINE PRINT: Check the farm's Facebook page or call 206-679-6576 for harvest updates. 7228 Skipley Rd., Snohomish. skipleyfarm.com

Stutzman Ranch ····→
Wenatchee

Head east to Wenatchee's Stutzman Ranch if your kids love crunchy, juicy Fuji and Gala apples. If you get to the farm early in the day, you'll have your pick of farm-fresh eggs, too. Pay a visit to the farm animals, and then watch surplus pumpkins get hurled through the air from a real pumpkin cannon.

GOOD TO KNOW: You can also pick cherries, peaches, nectarines and pears earlier in the season.

FINE PRINT: U-pick for apples typically opens in late August. $5 U-pick minimum charged for all pickers older than 12. Check the Facebook page or call 509-667-1664 or 509-669-3276 for harvest updates. 2226 Easy St., Wenatchee. 2.5-hour drive from Seattle. thestutzmanranch.com

PICKIN' TIPS

Bring your own: Bring along your own bags, baskets or boxes; and pack rubber boots.

Dog gone: Many farms have a no-pet policy; check before going.

Organic or bust? While few U-pick apple orchards in the region are certified organic, many implement organic and natural growing practices in their orchards. Call ahead to ask.

Triple-check: Check an orchard's Facebook page or website, and/or call ahead to make sure it has U-pick options that day.

Wagon ho! Consider bringing a wagon to tote kids or apple baskets.

More like this:
➤ Berry-Pickin' Fun (Adventure 15)
➤ Hikes With a Prize (Adventure 16)
➤ Great Pumpkin Patches (Adventure 33)

FALL

NATURE

31.
See Salmon Run

By Fiona Cohen

What can your children learn from a fish? Plenty — about determination, perseverance, and the weird and fascinating drama of nature.

Every year, Pacific salmon travel hundreds of miles, relentlessly focused on arriving at the local streams where they were hatched. Their purpose: to mate and bury their eggs in the stream bottom before they die.

In September and October, sockeye and chinook (also known as "king") salmon arrive in the area. In November, chum and coho take their turn. By the time they fight their way into the creeks, the salmon's sleek bodies have been transformed, and they no longer eat. They die soon after spawning, and as they decompose, their bodies fertilize the streams.

When you take your kids to watch this action, don't feel silly if you find yourself cheering on a fish — people do it all the time.

Hiram M. Chittenden Locks FREE
Ballard, Seattle

From June through September, while the Hiram M. Chittenden Locks (more commonly called the Ballard Locks) ease boats in and out of Seattle's ship canal, returning salmon thrash their way up a 21-step fish ladder, which is more like a staircase of water. You can watch the salmon drama through underwater windows, a classic Seattle experience that every kid should witness.

GOOD TO KNOW: Sockeye, chinook and coho salmon all have runs through the Locks. Interpreter-led tours of the Locks and salmon ladder are offered seasonally.

FINE PRINT: Ballard Locks, 3015 N.W. 54th St., Seattle. 206-783-7059. ballardlocks.org/salmon-at-the-locks.html

Cedar River FREE
Renton

Sockeye and sometimes chinook and coho run this river from mid-September into early November. Join volunteer naturalists at four sites along the river on weekends in October, including the Renton Library (which is built over the river), Cedar River Park, Cavanaugh Pond and Landsburg Park and Dam.

NEARBY BONUS: Combine your salmon viewing with a fall hike or bike ride along Renton's Cedar River Trail.

FINE PRINT: Multiple locations. Call 206-792-5851 or visit Cedar River Salmon Journey online for maps and updates. govlink.org/watersheds/8/action/salmon-seeson

Issaquah Salmon Hatchery FREE
Issaquah

Conveniently located right in downtown Issaquah, the Issaquah Salmon Hatchery offers viewing along Issaquah Creek, glass windows into the fish ladders and interactive displays. The hatchery was created to restore the creek's historic salmon runs. Chinook and sockeye pass through from late August through mid-October, and coho follow from late September through November.

GOOD TO KNOW: Hatchery tours are offered on weekend days from September to early November. Tours are free, but donations are appreciated.

FINE PRINT: Check the Salmon Seeson Issaquah page at govlink.org for hours or call 425-392-1118 for updates. Issaquah Hatchery, 125 W. Sunset Way, Issaquah. issaquahfish.org

Piper's Creek, Carkeek Park
FREE
North Seattle

This stunning park along the Sound is Seattle's best spot to view a salmon run. Walk the trail along Piper's Creek from mid-October to December, a wonderful family hike any time of the year, and look for hundreds of chum returning to the creek. If you time it right, you can also pick apples at Piper's Orchard, the oldest known orchard in Seattle. Then go down the salmon slide at the playground and explore the beach.

GOOD TO KNOW: Volunteer salmon stewards usually staff the creek on weekends in November. Find tons more fun at Carkeek.

FINE PRINT: Check the Carkeek Park Salmon Stewards Facebook page for salmon updates. Carkeek Park, 950 N.W. Carkeek Park Rd., Seattle. govlink.org/watersheds/8/action/salmon-seeson

Duwamish River   FREE
Tukwila

Head to the Duwamish River valley to see habitat restoration in progress and salmon migrating to upstream spawning beds. Salmon Seeson recommends three viewing locations: North Wind's Weir, a 2.5-acre restored mudflat and marsh; the new Duwamish Gardens Park, designed to provide critical shallow water habitat for juvenile salmon; and Codiga Park. Look for pinks (July–September), chinook and coho (August–September) and chum (October–November).

MORE WILD FISH SPOTS

Adams River, B.C.: Put this on your bucket list. Every four years, millions of bright red sockeye jostle for position, an event that has been called one of the great migrations on earth.

Capilano River Regional Park, B.C.: Visit the Capilano Salmon Hatchery's viewing windows to see salmon returning to spawn, and then view the river surging through the Capilano Canyon.

Newhalem, North Cascades: Walk amid old-growth forest and watch salmon make their way through the glacier-fed Skagit River and Newhalem Creek.

Sol Duc River Salmon Cascades: Head to the western part of Olympic National Park in the fall to gawk at coho salmon leaping as far as 6 feet to reach their spawning grounds. (National Park pass required.)

FALL

NATURE

NEARBY BONUS: Combine a trip to North Wind's Weir with a bike ride on the 19-mile Green River Trail, which runs next to the park.

FINE PRINT: Multiple locations. Check the Salmon Seeson web pages and Duwamish Alive! website for details on where to go. govlink.org/watersheds/8/action/salmon-seeson

McLane Creek Nature Trail
Capitol State Forest, Olympia

This gentle, 1.5-mile nature loop offers dramatic streamside views of spawning chum salmon in November and early December, depending on rainfall. Salmon stewards are usually stationed at McLane Creek on November weekends, as well as on Thanksgiving Day and the day after.

GOOD TO KNOW: Kids will enjoy the boardwalk trail and the large observation deck over the creek.

FINE PRINT: Get directions and trip reports on WTA.org. McClane Creek Nature Trail, Capitol State Forest, Olympia. Discover Pass needed. streamteam.info

Kennedy Creek Salmon Trail FREE
Mason County

A fall hike along the 1.5-mile interpretive Kennedy Creek Salmon Trail, located on U.S. Highway 101 between Olympia and Shelton, is a fantastic day trip. About 40,000 chum cram into the lower 2 miles of this creek to spawn each fall (a heads-up: 5,000 people also cram onto the trail every November). The first half-mile of the trail is ADA accessible.

GOOD TO KNOW: Check for updates (and watch an awesome video about the trail) on the trail website. No dogs are allowed on the trail.

FINE PRINT: Open on weekends in November; schedule a midweek tour by emailing kennedycreek@spsseg.org. Find information and directions on the South Puget Sound Salmon Enhancement Group website. Kennedy Creek, Old Olympic Highway, Mason County. spsseg.org

SALMON SPOTTING 101

Bring binoculars for a better view of the salmon's physical changes, and wear boots and dress to stay warm. Stay out of the water and don't disturb the fish, dead or alive, in any way. And finally, keep pooches leashed or don't bring them. A dead salmon might look like an irresistible snack, but it can be deadly to dogs.

More like this:
- ➤ Colorful Fall Hikes (Adventure 32)
- ➤ Dino-Mite Destinations (Adventure 35)
- ➤ Winning Winter Tours (Adventure 51)

PETER STEVENS/FLICKR CC

Tonga Ridge

FALL

NATURE

32.
Colorful Fall Hikes

By Lauren Braden

Don't pack up the kids' hiking boots just yet. Autumn is a terrific season to hit the trail. Our wildlands burst with fall color — hues of flame red, bright orange and soft yellow. Summer crowds have dwindled, and pesky mosquitoes have disappeared, too. Critters such as marmots and songbirds are more visible as they hurry to find food. Just

SAFETY FIRST

Always check conditions of trails and roads before your hike; a great resource is Washington Trails Association's trip reports (*WTA.org*). Always bring the 10 Essentials, including snacks, water, extra layers, sun hats and sunscreen, and be sure kids know how to be safe on the trail. Find out more at *parentmap.com/outdoorsafety*.

make sure you bring extra layers for warmth and a thermos of hot cocoa.

Lake Ann ····➔
State Route 20,
North Cascades

This classic kid-friendly hike in the North Cascades is dazzling when saved for autumn. Late-season huckleberries cling to fiery-hued bushes along the trail, and wide-open vistas remind you of why you live in the Northwest (despite the winter that is just around the corner). The star attraction of this hike, however, is the flame yellow of the autumn alpine larches, which are usually at their peak in mid-October.

GOOD TO KNOW: A short distance from the trailhead is a junction; head to the right off the paved path and onto the trail. At 1.3 miles, there is a side trail to beautiful Lake Ann.

FINE PRINT: *3.4 miles round-trip, 700 feet elevation gain. Find directions and trip reports on* WTA.org. *Okanogan National Forest, North Cascades Highway. Northwest Forest Pass needed. Three-hour drive from Seattle.* fs.usda.gov

Tonga Ridge FREE ····➔
Skykomish, U.S. Highway 2

Known as the easiest ridge walk on the west slope of the Cascades, Tonga Ridge is also one of the most popular in late summer. Fall will afford you some solitude to enjoy the brilliant huckleberry and heather meadows in quiet peace. Hike to Sawyer Pass or as far as your kids wish, then turn around. Keep an eye out for deer, and don't miss the gorgeous views of the Cascades on a clear day.

NEARBY BONUS: Stop at a Snohomish farm on the way back for pumpkins or apples.

FINE PRINT: *8 miles round-trip, 400 feet elevation gain. Find directions and trip reports at* WTA.org. *Mount Baker–Snoqualmie National Forest, U.S. Highway 2. Two-hour, 15-minute drive from Seattle.* fs.usda.gov

Naches Peak Loop ····➔
Mount Rainier National Park

Fall color abounds on this easy loop hike that skirts the eastern boundary of Mount

Rainier National Park. The trail begins in the subalpine zone, where open meadows carpeted with huckleberry bushes look like they're on fire from all the red and orange hues. What could make such a scene even more beautiful? The constant backdrop of "the mountain." Hike the loop in a clockwise direction for the best views.

NEARBY BONUS: Refuel on the way home at the Historic Mint Restaurant and Alehouse in Enumclaw, just off State Route 410.

FINE PRINT: 3.2 miles round-trip, 600 feet elevation gain. 360-569-6650. Find directions and trip reports at WTA.org. Mount Rainier National Park at Chinook Pass. Northwest Forest Pass needed. At least a two-hour drive from Seattle. nps.gov

Lime Kiln Trail   FREE
Granite Falls

Step into this mossy canyon, where lush emerald ferns are layered against soft yellow and orange maple leaves, creating an autumn palette that is quintessentially Northwest. Kids will enjoy this easy hike along the South Fork of the Stillaguamish River for its rich history linked to limestone mining and the long-gone Everett–Monte Cristo railway, first built in the 1890s. Artifacts of this era are left all along the trail, from moss-cloaked saw blades to old bricks and rotting worker boots from centuries past. At 2.5 miles in, you'll reach the old 20-foot-tall lime kiln, the highlight of the hike.

GOOD TO KNOW: If you continue another mile to the trail's end, you'll find a riverbank vantage point where you can look for spawning salmon.

FINE PRINT: 7 miles round-trip, 625 feet elevation gain. Find directions and trip reports on WTA.org. Robe Canyon Historic Park, Granite Falls. No parking pass needed. snohomishcountywa.gov

Lord Hill Regional Park   FREE
Snohomish

The perfect autumn respite for urban hikers and equestrians, Lord Hill comprises 1,400 acres of upland nature preserve along the Snohomish River, just a 50-minute drive from Seattle. More than 5 miles of designated trails crisscross an old homestead. Varied river, forest and pond habitats support a lot of wildlife here, with animals being more active in autumn, including bears, bobcats, beavers, birds and garter snakes. Use the map to create a loop of your desired distance; the trails are well-signed.

GOOD TO KNOW: For a varied path with great fall color and possible wildlife sightings, hike the Beaver Lake Loop: the Beaver Lake trail to the Pipeline connector trail.

FALL

NATURE

FINE PRINT: 3–6 miles round-trip, scant elevation gain. Find directions and trip reports on WTA.org. 12921 150th St. S.E., Snohomish. No parking pass needed. snohomishcountywa.gov

More like this:
- ➤ **Roaring Waterfall Hikes (Adventure 1)**
- ➤ **Beginning Bike Paths (Adventure 10)**
- ➤ **Yurts 101 (Adventure 39)**

33.
Great Pumpkin Patches

By Elisa Murray

Need a new destination for your annual pumpkin pilgrimage? There's nothing wrong with visiting the same farm year after year, but be informed about what you're missing: From pumpkin cannonballs to intricate corn mazes to personalized pumpkins, Puget Sound–area farms truly do offer it all these days. And if you're a purist — nothing but an organic heirloom pumpkin and a steaming cup of cider, please — you can find that, too.

IMPORTANT: Check a farm's Facebook page (or website) before going, to double-check hours and offerings.

Craven Farm
Snohomish
Named one of the nation's best pumpkin patches by "Travel and Leisure" in 2016, this farm is hugely popular, especially with families who have younger kids. Find vehicles, tractors and pirate ships to climb on; a 15-acre corn maze (including a non-scary route that's open at night); hayrides; farm animals; and the Adventure Maze, complete with an obstacle course. A snack shack is open on weekends.

NEARBY BONUS: Another fantastic farm, The Farm at Swan's Trail, is just a couple of miles away, offering U-pick apples and pumpkins.

FINE PRINT: Open seasonally. Various fees. Check online or call 360-568-2601 for updates. Craven Farm, 13817 Short School Rd., Snohomish. cravenfarm.com

Bob's Corn and Pumpkin Farm

Snohomish

Want to plan a fun fall party? Reserve a fire pit in the 10-acre corn maze at this 30-acre pumpkin patch. Bob's staff will build and maintain the fire for you as well as transport any roasting sticks and supplies you bring. Other attractions at the farm include two smaller mazes for little ones, a corn pit, slides, farm animals, face painting and mazes. Special events include a Lumberjack Run and a Sweet Corn Festival in September.

GOOD TO KNOW: Are you a nursing mom? Bob's has a "nursing cabin" on the premises with two private rooms, as well as a wraparound porch outside with rocking chairs.

FINE PRINT: *Open seasonally. Various fees. Check the Facebook page or call 360-668-2506 for updates. Bob's Corn and Pumpkin Farm, 10917 Elliott Rd., Snohomish. bobscorn.com*

Fairbank Animal Farm

Edmonds

An experience geared to younger kids, this rustic farm offers rough paths and barnyard smells, and the kids can get their fill of animals to watch and feed (!), including chicks, ducklings, goats, ponies, rabbits and pigs. There is also a U-pick pumpkin patch, tiny tot "maize maze" and a hay tunnel.

NEARBY BONUS: After you've finished feeding critters, go for a short but spectacular

FALL

NATURE

hike at Meadowdale Beach Park, less than a mile away.

FINE PRINT: Open seasonally. Admission $3/person (younger than 10 months free), but only cash is accepted. Check online or call 425-743-3694 for updates. Fairbank Animal Farm, 15308 52nd Ave. W., Edmonds. fairbankfarm.com

Jubilee Farm FREE
Carnation

Jubilee grows vegetables and fruits and raises grassfed beef, using organic practices. The picturesque farm celebrates fall with many free harvest activities, including its famous trebuchet — a giant pumpkin catapult. Take a hayride out to the U-pick pumpkin fields in a wagon pulled by beautiful draft horses, buy hand-cranked cider, visit the farm animals and navigate a kids' hay maze.

GOOD TO KNOW: You can pick up a peck of organic produce at the farm stand while you're there.

FINE PRINT: Open on October weekends. Admission, parking and most activities are free. Check online or call 425-240-4929 for updates. Jubilee Farm, 229 W. Snoqualmie River Rd. N.E., Carnation. jubileefarm.org/harvestfestival

Remlinger Farms
Carnation

Remlinger has the pumpkin patch/amusement park combo cornered. After taking a wagon ride out to the U-pick pumpkin fields, head to the Country Fair Family Fun Park for kid-size thrills. Take note: There are lovely picnic spots at Remlinger, but you're supposed to buy food on the premises — there is a snack bar and full restaurant.

GOOD TO KNOW: If you have littles and a flexible schedule, don't miss the "toddler weekday" tickets to the family fun park in September, when families with young kids enjoy limited attractions at a discounted price.

FINE PRINT: Fall harvest festival runs late September through late October. Free admission to pumpkin patch and various fees for other activities. Check online or call 425-333-4135 for updates. Remlinger Farms, 32610 N.E. 32nd St., Carnation. remlingerfarms.com

Oxbow Farm & Conservation Center
Carnation

Oxbow isn't just a farm, it's an education and conservation center that is dedicated to stewarding 230 acres of forest and farmland and inspiring visitors to eat healthy, sustainably grown food. At its annual "Oxtober" festival, purchase pumpkins (including

FALL

NATURE

sugar pie and heirloom varieties), take a hayride, shoot a pumpkin slingshot, tumble in the House of Hay and explore the Kids' Farm.

GOOD TO KNOW: Oxbow runs wonderful summer camps and workshops for kids; you can also organize a field trip.

PUMPKIN PASS

If you like to patch-hop, then Snohomish County's Festival of Pumpkins, a collaboration between seven popular Snohomish farms, might be for you. You can buy one pass for all farms, saving big compared to buying tickets individually. *festivalofpumpkins.org*

FINE PRINT: Pumpkin patch and farm stand open Thursday–Sunday in October; festival events on weekends. Fees for some activities. Check online or call 425-788-1134 for updates. Oxbow Farm, 10819 Carnation-Duvall Rd. N.E., Carnation. oxbow.org

Carpinito Brothers
Kent

After you get lost in one of the two giant corn mazes, enjoy Carpinito's snack specialty: roasted corn. Visit the Farm Fun Yard across the street to see the farm animals, take a tractor-drawn hayride, race rubber ducks, feed the goats on the goat walk and "swim" in the corn pen.

NEARBY BONUS: Not far from Carpinito Brothers, catch another fall happening at Soos Creek Hatchery, where you can see salmon returning to spawn.

FINE PRINT: Open seasonally. Various fees. Check the Facebook page or call 253-854-5692 for updates. Pumpkin patch and corn maze: 27508 W. Valley Hwy. N., Kent. Farm Fun Yard: 6720 S. 277th St., Kent. carpinito.com

Thomasson Family Farm
Enumclaw

Another reader favorite in South King County, this working dairy farm runs a 216,000-square-foot corn maze during pumpkin season that is sponsored by Darigold. Other old-fashioned farm attractions include apple-lobbing slingshot competitions, tractor train rides, hayrides, a hay maze, duck races, a petting farm, a corn box (filled with 9 tons of corn) for the kids, and laser tag.

FUN FACT: Three generations of Thomassons help run the farm, including 14 grandkids.

FINE PRINT: Open seasonally. Various fees. Check online or call 360-802-0503 for updates. 38223 236th Ave. S.E., Enumclaw. thomassonfarm.com

FALL

NATURE

Creek House Farm
Port Orchard

Located in Kitsap County, Creek House raises organic, heirloom pumpkins. You'll find many typical activities, such as U-pick pumpkins, farm animals, a pumpkin slingshot and hayrides. But the real highlight of the farm is personalized pumpkins. Order by Aug. 31 to have names (or other text) scratched into young pumpkins and then search for your special pumpkin in the patch when it comes time to harvest!

NEARBY BONUS: Take a beach hike in Manchester State Park, just three miles away.

FINE PRINT: Open weekends in October. Adding personalization to a pumpkin costs $5 for as many as 10 letters. Pumpkins are sold by final weight. Check online or call 360-602-1273 for updates. Creek House Farm, 6060 E. Collins Rd., Port Orchard. creekhousefarm.com

> ## More like this:
> ➤ **Oh, Baby Animals! (Adventure 3)**
> ➤ **Dig into Clamming (Adventure 4)**
> ➤ **One-of-a-Kind Getaways (Adventure 14)**

FALL

NATURE

34.
Crafty Museum Spaces

By JiaYing Grygiel

Museums are notorious for being no-touch zones, and who wants to pony up for admission only to have a screaming toddler cut the visit short? But did you know that many Seattle-area museums offer art spaces — some free of charge — and other programs that encourage crafting, art exploration and sensory fun? These family- and wallet-friendly options will brighten up your fall and winter.

Seattle Art Museum lobby space
Downtown Seattle

The most amazing thing about Seattle Art Museum's lobby space is how huge it is. Come in through the entrance at First Avenue and University Street and pay admission only for the upper two floors of galleries; the entire lower level is free. Toddlers will love exploring the toy-filled terrace outside the museum's restaurant and climbing the grand staircase

JIAYING GRYGIEL

Bellevue Arts Museum

that's punctuated by Chinese marble statues. For school-age kids, there's an open studio stocked with art supplies halfway up the staircase. Look for the wheelchair ramp winding around the Think Tank space — there's a surprise mural inside.

GOOD TO KNOW: To visit the upstairs galleries with a group, you can request free community passes on the museum website; or reserve passes at the Seattle Public Library's website.

FINE PRINT: Open Wednesday–Sunday (open Monday in summer), late on Thursday. $14.95–$24.95, free for kids 12 and younger. Lobby art spaces are always free; museum free on first Thursday. Seattle Art Museum, 1300 First Ave., Seattle. 206-654-3100. seattleartmuseum.org

Wing Luke Museum of the Asian Pacific American Experience

Chinatown–International District, Seattle

Located in a beautifully restored historic building in Seattle's Chinatown–International District, this museum is dedicated to Asian-American history and art. On First Thursdays, the museum's free admission day, sit in for toddler story time at 11 a.m., followed by an art activity. Look for the colorful room just for small children, tucked among the galleries upstairs.

GOOD TO KNOW: Parents and school-age kids can sign up for a themed tour that ex-

FALL

CULTURE

plores the International District (most are an additional cost), such as "Bruce Lee's Chinatown" or a dumpling crawl.

FINE PRINT: Open daily except Monday. $10–$17, kids 5 and younger free. Free on first Thursday (and open late). Wing Luke Museum, 719 S. King St., Seattle. 206-623-5124. wingluke.org

Bellevue Arts Museum

Bellevue

Bellevue Arts Museum's ground floor is completely free. It won't cost you a penny to see the art in the atrium, the community education gallery or an art activity area tucked in back. But it's worth your museum dollars to visit the two upper levels of galleries, with their "Imagination Stations," where visitors can cut, draw and create.

GOOD TO KNOW: Many Saturday afternoons from 1 to 3 p.m., the museum hosts a drop-in "Get Crafty" activity in its lobby. You don't need to pay museum admission to participate, just a small fee for materials.

FINE PRINT: Open Wednesday–Sunday. $5–$15, $35 family, 5 and younger free. Free on first Friday. Bellevue Arts Museum, 510 Bellevue Way N.E., Bellevue. 425-519-0770. bellevuearts.org

Henry Art Gallery

University District, Seattle

Visit this small, friendly contemporary art museum on the University of Washington campus on a Sunday, when admission and parking (inside the UW Central Parking Garage next door) are free. A must-do activity at the museum is to cross the bridge to James Turrell's "Light Reign" skyspace, an outdoor, circular room with a wood-paneled interior and a retractable roof that reveals an ever-changing view of the sky.

GOOD TO KNOW: Sweeten the deal by visiting on select Sundays of the month to participate in a free drop-in ArtVenture program for families.

FALL

CULTURE

MIXING MUSEUMS AND KIDS

Gallery fun: Stop to sketch. Or use brochures as a scavenger hunt (they can find items listed). Small children can look for faces, shapes or colors.

Hands off: Talk to your kids about what to do in the no-touch zones at museums. They can hold hands, put their hands in their pockets or hold a favorite toy.

Play with art: Have kids move like an image in a painting or pose like a sculpture.

Rest plan: Be aware of where the bathrooms and family spaces are for when you need a break.

Stroller help: You can always bring along a stroller to corral little ones and keep 'em moving.

FINE PRINT: *Open Wednesday–Sunday, late on Thursday. $6–$10, children 10 and younger always free. Free every Sunday and on first Thursday. Henry Art Gallery, 15th Ave. N.E. and N.E. 41st St., Seattle. 206-543-2280.* henryart.org

Frye Art Museum   FREE
First Hill, Seattle

Your first stop in the museum should be the "Frye Salon," a gallery exhibit in which paintings are hung "salon style," resembling a giant jigsaw puzzle, with the walls filled from floor to ceiling. It's how art was displayed at the home of Charles and Emma Frye almost a century ago. (That exhibit runs until Sept. 22, 2019.) My two kids and I love to play "I spy," looking for ducks, horses, boats, flowers — all objects small children can identify in the paintings.

GOOD TO KNOW: One of the best kids' art activities in town is "Small Frye," held on the first Friday of each month, with a performance by storytellers from Seattle Children's Theatre, followed by an art-making project with the Frye's art educators. It's free.

FINE PRINT: *Open daily except Monday, late on Thursday. Always free. Frye Museum, 704 Terry Ave., Seattle. 206-622-9250.* fryemuseum.org.

Tacoma Art Museum
Tacoma

The art studio at Tacoma Art Museum (TAM) is free all the time, with easily accessible art supplies and inspiration. If you decide to pay the admission fee, browse the other exhibits dedicated to Northwest and Western art. When your kids are done creating, play at the nearby Children's Museum of Tacoma (CMT), where admission is pay what you will every day. CMT also has a program where families can do an art project inspired by a TAM work, and then receive free passes to TAM.

NEARBY BONUS: Take the Tacoma Link light rail to other Tacoma museum destinations, such as the Museum of Glass or the Washington State History Museum.

FINE PRINT: *Open daily except Monday. $13–$15, $40 family, kids 5 and younger free. Free on third Thursday (and open late). Tacoma Art Museum, 1701 Pacific Ave., Tacoma. 253-272-4258.* tacomaartmuseum.org

FALL

CULTURE

More like this:
- ➤ Holiday Magic on the Cheap (Adventure 44)
- ➤ Live Like a Tourist (Adventure 21)
- ➤ Summer Wander List: Free and Fun, p. 125

DANIEL STOCKMAN/FLICKR CC

A dino at Pacific Science Center

35.
Dino-Mite Destinations

By JiaYing Grygiel

October might be International Dinosaur Month, but budding paleontologists never take a month off. If you know all the Jane Yolen books by heart ("How Do Dinosaurs ... " do anything) and the T.rex costume is still in the daily rotation six months after Halloween, you'll want to have these dino-mite spots on your radar.

Burke Museum of Natural History & Culture
University District, Seattle
If you time your visit to the University of Washington's natural history museum right, you might be able to see real paleontologists at work on, say, a T.rex skull. This museum on the UW campus has the only real dinosaur fossils on display in the state. Stay tuned: Its epic new museum building opens in fall 2019 in a 113,000-square-foot LEED Gold building where exhibit spaces will be integrated with lab spaces and viewable collections, offering even more opportunities to see the scientific process at work. The new museum will also include a gallery devoted to paleontology and the

Ice Age and two different play spaces for kids.

GOOD TO KNOW: The Burke's old museum building will close on Dec. 31, 2018, and the new building is slated to open in the fall of 2019. Get updates at *newburke.org*.

FINE PRINT: *Open daily, late on first Thursday. $7.50–$10, ages 4 and younger free. Free on first Thursday. Burke Museum, 17th Ave. N.E. and N.E. 45th St. (on the UW campus), Seattle. 206-616-3962.* burkemuseum.org

Pacific Science Center

Seattle Center

There are so many reasons to visit Pacific Science Center (planetarium, Tinker Tank, Tropical Butterfly House, High-Rail Bicycle), but for prehistory buffs, it's all about the dinos. After you get your apatosaurus hand stamp at the ticket window, head to Building 1 to see the 11 large model dinosaurs — find two more in the outdoor courtyard. Some of these dinosaurs even move! Below the big dinosaurs are interactive panels at kid height, and miniature dioramas at toddler height. Don't miss the chunks of coprolite (fossilized dinosaur poop) you can touch.

GOOD TO KNOW: A Pacific Science Center membership pays for itself in as little as three visits (try the Cyber Monday deal), includes perks such as IMAX tickets, and gets you reciprocal admission to other science museums.

FINE PRINT: *Open daily. $13.95–$23.95, ages 2 and younger free. Pacific Science Center, 200 Second Ave. N., Seattle. 206-443-2001.* pacificsciencecenter.org

Fremont topiaries FREE

Fremont, Seattle

Fremont is famous for being quirky: naked bicyclists at the Solstice Parade, the Lenin statue, the Troll under the bridge ... and mama and baby apatosaurus topiaries next to the Burke-Gilman Trail. The 66-foot-long metal frames were built in the 1980s for the Pacific Science Center and later purchased for $1. The Fremont Rotary maintains these living sculptures; it took more than 12 years for the ivy to grow mama apatosaurus's head.

MORE DINO LOVE ♡♡♡♡

Birds are the only living dinosaur descendants, but other creatures living today are related to dinosaurs, including alligators and crocodiles, lizards, snakes and turtles. To see these creatures, head to The Reptile Zoo in Monroe (home to more than 85 species of reptiles); Woodland Park Zoo (where you can see Komodo dragons in an indoor exhibit); and Point Defiance Zoo & Aquarium, home to five species of sharks, which have been swimming since dinosaurs roamed the earth.

FALL

CULTURE

NEARBY BONUS: After your photo op, head across the street to eat samples of organic, fair-trade chocolate at Theo Chocolate's factory and retail store. Theo also offers a sweet factory tour for ages 6 and older, and a chocolate-themed story time for tykes.

FINE PRINT: Find the topiaries at N. Canal St. at Phinney Ave. N., Seattle.

Deane's Children's Park (aka Dragon Park) FREE

Mercer Island

Technically, it's a dragon, not a dinosaur. But the famous 45-foot-long dragon sculpture at Deane's Children's Park is big and scaly, and kids can slide down its tail, climb into its belly and walk into its mouth. Designed and built by artist Kenton Pies, it was installed in 2013, replacing the well-worn original dragon built by Pies in 1965. When your kids are done with the dragon, three more play structures in the shady, wooded park beckon, including a knights' castle.

GOOD TO KNOW: In the summer, the park hosts an Adventure Playground program on select afternoons: Kids can use hammers and nails to build their own tree forts.

FINE PRINT: Deane's Children's Park, 5500 Island Crest Way, Mercer Island. mercergov.org/Page.asp?NavID=3099

More like this:
➤ **Volcano Escapes (Adventure 29)**
➤ **Crafty Museum Spaces (Adventure 34)**
➤ **Quirky Landmarks (Adventure 45)**

FALL

CULTURE

36.
For Love of Legos

By April Chan

Legos are popular around the world, but the Seattle area seems to nurture a particularly potent brand of brick fanatic. And our region has brick fun to spare, including a standout October festival, BrickCon, which is reputed to be the longest-running fan-based Lego convention around. Here are other hot Lego spots.

Wunderkind

Northeast Seattle

This spacious café, just a brick toss from Seattle's University Village, provides an inviting environment where parents can let their children loose on Legos on two different floors. On the first floor, nurse an Americano while helping little ones figure out the intricacies of Duplo train sets. Or head upstairs and keep an eye on older builders as you catch the latest game on multiple overhead TVs. The small snack bar features an assortment of food and drink options, including (happy-hour alert!) craft beers and wines.

GOOD TO KNOW: Wunderkind also hosts frequent workshops, camps and guided Lego builds (check its Facebook page). Or book it for your Lego fan's next party.

FINE PRINT: Open daily. $6/child day pass, $15/monthly pass; other passes also available. Wunderkind, 3318 N.E. 55th St., Seattle. 206-854-7186. wunderkindseattle.com

Pacific Science Center Tinker Tank

Seattle Center

Located in Pacific Science Center near the entrance to the Boeing IMAX Theater, this hands-on building and crafting area includes two large tables of colorful Lego 2x4 blocks, along with impressive creations safely ensconced behind a display case. Don't be surprised to see a massive color-coordinated wall, an inverted pyramid and towers that stretch toward the ceiling.

FALL

CULTURE

GOOD TO KNOW: You can also sign up for a 90-minute Tinker Tank session on a specific topic, from soldering to animation. (Pick up a free workshop ticket at the admission window.)

FINE PRINT: Open daily. $13.95–$23.95, ages 2 and younger free. Pacific Science Center, 200 Second Ave. N., Seattle. 206-443-2001. pacificsciencecenter.org

Math 'n' Stuff

Maple Leaf, Seattle

Beloved by local Lego lovers, this toy and game store became a Lego Gold Standard store in 2013, and it is absolutely worth a field trip to this northeast Seattle neighborhood to browse and buy. It carries an assortment of Lego products, as well as lots of other cool toys, science kits, math games, board games and role-playing games.

MORE BRICK FUN

Bricks 4 Kidz: This international program brings STEM concepts via toys and blocks to children through classes, camps and workshops.

Dan Parker: Lego artist Parker, who has produced more than 4,000 structures, is the equivalent of our local brick Olympian. He often leads builds and displays at festivals and other events.

Fun Assembly Required: Based out of Seattle, this traveling local business brings the Legos to you, either in the form of themed birthday parties or classes at a predetermined venue.

Libraries: All library systems around the Sound host regular STEM-related events that often include or feature Lego builds.

The Brickhouse: Olympia's unofficial Lego store is family-owned. Play at the bulk block tables before picking up the scooper.

GOOD TO KNOW: Math 'n' Stuff has an annex location where it hosts build events, game nights, make-and-take events and more. Check its calendar. You can also book a birthday party there.

FINE PRINT: Closed Sunday and Monday, and even its store hours are quirky: 9:53 a.m.–6:07 p.m. Math 'n' Stuff, 8926 Roosevelt Way N.E., Seattle. 206-522-8891. mathnificent.com

Bricks & Wheels

Bellevue, Kent

With well-stocked Lego shops in Factoria and in Kent, Bricks & Wheels offers sets, minifigures and even full models to buy, sell, trade or simply admire. Don't miss the fill-a-bag bulk table and the build-your-own minifigures table to play around with before finding that perfect piece or set to take home.

NEARBY BONUS: At Factoria, combine your Lego excursion with wiggle time at Funtastic Playtorium.

FINE PRINT: Open daily. Bricks & Wheels, 12678 S.E. 38th St., Ste. B, Bellevue. 425-643-8028. 12135 S.E. Kent-Kangley Rd., Kent. 253-277-4085. bricksandwheels.com

Lego Stores

Head to one of three official Lego Stores in the Seattle area to play at interactive tables, make custom minifigures and buy bricks with the help of specialists. Check out your local store's calendar for updates on building events, parties and other fun events.

GOOD TO KNOW: A Lego Store best practice is to figure out how much you'll spend (if any) before you get there, to minimize in-store negotiations.

FINE PRINT: Open daily at three Puget Sound locations: 3000 184th S.W., #428, Lynnwood, 425-640-2281. Bellevue Square, 119 Bellevue Square, Bellevue, 425-451-2271. 633 Southcenter, Unit 1450, Seattle, 206-243-1554. lego.com/en-us/stores

More like this:
- ➤ **Pinball, Putt-Putt and More Old-School Fun (Adventure 8)**
- ➤ **Dino-Mite Destinations (Adventure 35)**
- ➤ **Geektastic Outings (Adventure 47)**

FALL

CULTURE

37.
Mountain Biking Thrills

By Elisa Murray

Mountain biking is a sport where everyone gets to be a kid again — even we middle-aged, risk-averse parents. That's something you'll find out as soon as you follow your kid down a single track at Duthie Hill Mountain Bike Park, hooting the whole way.

The good thing is that, contrary to the sport's gnarly reputation, the thrill scale in mountain biking is set by you. If you'd rather leave the bumps and jumps to your progeny, you can simply ride off-road and enjoy the scenery and the break from pollution. Because that's the other huge perk of mountain biking: It offers thrills in nature with no cars in sight.

COURTESY EVERGREEN MOUNTAIN BIKE ALLIANCE

Duthie Hill Mountain Bike Park

Duthie Hill, Issaquah's famed mountain bike park, is an excellent site for a first ride. A partnership between Evergreen Mountain Bike Alliance and King County Parks, the 120-acre park is set in gorgeous evergreen forest and was designed with every kind of rider in mind. Beginners will get easy thrills riding the up-and-down cross-country trails, some with exciting downhill portions as well as berms and bumps, while those wanting more challenges can try the more technical "freeride" trails, which include log sections, wooden jumps and other features.

Trails all loop back to a large central clearing, which has two pump tracks (one just right for kids) as well as seating, picnic tables, a shelter and pit toilets. A large trail map is posted, and each trail is clearly marked by skill level.

Duthie has also become a center for mountain bike education: Evergreen Mountain Bike Alliance leads regular camps and classes there. Kat Sweet, who owns a mountain bike business called Sweetlines, runs camps and clinics at Duthie, and coaches a girls' junior racing team. They share a mission: making mountain biking more accessible to people of all ages and all skill levels.

Gearing up for the first ride

According to Sweet, there are only a few essentials you need to try mountain biking.

➤ For adults, a mountain-specific bike with knobby tires and a front suspension fork is best, as it's more forgiving on bumps.

➤ Kids should ideally have a bike with knobby tires and a few gears. Their bikes should also have hand brakes, essential for braking evenly on the downhills.

➤ An essential for everyone is a properly fitting bike helmet.

➤ Optional gear includes knee pads and gloves to protect the hands. Flat shoes, such as Vans, are better than running shoes for kids.

Sweet also shared some tips for newbies.

➤ Practice going downhill and standing up on the pedals with evenly weighted feet and slightly dropped heels.

➤ Keep elbows out for stability.

➤ "Always look ahead, don't read the tread," as she tells her students. In other words, look ahead to where you want to go next.

➤ Have kids practice braking evenly, a critical skill.

➤ Remind kids that mountain biking often includes walking up hills (and sometimes down).

➤ Never underestimate the power of treats in encouraging a successful hill climb.

As your children gain more mountain biking skills, they might pick up some tips about life, too: Commit to the downhill so you can achieve the uphill, look ahead to see where you're going next and always keep your feet on the pedals. Also: There's no shame in getting off and walking.

FALL

ADVENTURE

PEDAL POWERED

Compass Outdoor Adventures: Compass plans group biking events and also rents bikes — it will transport bike rentals to Duthie or other trailheads.

Crank Sisters: This all-female riding group plans group rides, training classes and events.

Evergreen Mountain Bike Alliance: A nonprofit that offers camps, classes, trail guides and resources. In the fall, it hosts a "Take a Kid Mountain Biking Day" at Duthie; in June, the alliance holds its annual festival.

Evo: This outdoor retailer also has an online trail guide for Seattle-area mountain biking.

Sweetlines: Led by former professional mountain bike racer Kat Sweet, Sweetlines coaches a girls' junior racing team, and teaches classes and camps.

Wheely-fun trails

The Puget Sound area boasts a number of other trail systems and mountain bike parks that are geared to all levels.

Black Diamond Open Space: This 10-mile network of primarily flat, cross-country trails is good for beginners.

Raging River State Forest: A new 17-mile trail system in the North Bend area has trails for everyone.

Saint Edward State Park: Saint Ed's well-known trail system includes 25 miles of tracks, with trails and features of all kinds.

Soaring Eagle Regional Park: A square-mile network of twisty trails is in Sammamish, just a mile from Duthie.

Swan Creek Park: Located just a few miles from Tacoma, this park has 3 miles of trails, including a family-friendly cross-country trail.

Torguson Park: The 35,000-square-foot mountain bike park in Snoqualmie features an all-ages, all-abilities track, and a separate balance bike track for young children.

> ## More like this:
> ➤ **Beginning Bike Paths (Adventure 10)**
> ➤ **Epic Playgrounds (Adventure 12)**
> ➤ **Summer Splurges (Adventure 24)**

FALL

ADVENTURE

38.
Thrilling Indoor Pools

By Kali Sakai

Swimming — it wears 'em out. It's fun for babies, big kids and grown-ups alike. And with so many feature-packed, warm-water pools to choose from around Puget Sound, it's easy to indulge in serious water play all year long. Our winter tip: Find a pool with a hot tub close by so you can soak while the kids turn into fish. Our summer tip: Indoor pools tend to be less crowded in the summer.

People's Pool, Tacoma

COURTESY METRO PARKS TACOMA

FALL

ADVENTURE

IMPORTANT: Schedules change seasonally; check online. Also check height, age and skill restrictions for slides, deep water, hot tubs and public swims before you go. Buy multiple-visit passes and annual passes to help you save. Membership pools, such as Safe N Sound and Samena Swim & Recreation Club, are also a good option for swim lessons and swim practice.

Snohomish Aquatic Center

Snohomish

The biggest claim to fame for this 52,000-square-foot swim center is that it boasts the region's only FlowRider (surf-simulation machine). Kids also love the Splashtacular waterslide, recreational lap pool and lazy river. Little ones will have fun in the splash play area with buckets to dump water, stairs to climb and two slides. Water is a balmy 84–86 degrees. A second pool offers lap swimming and a diving board.

NEARBY BONUS: While in Snohomish, check out the charming downtown, with its antique stores, bakeries and Centennial Trail for biking or walking.

FINE PRINT: *$5–$6, younger than 2 free, $20/family; $15 for a FlowRider pass. Snohomish Aquatic Center, 516 Maple Ave., Snohomish. 360-568-8030. sno.wednet.edu*

Lynnwood Recreation Center
Lynnwood

This super-popular swim spot is actually three pools: a lap pool (with diving boards), a recreation pool (with two water slides, sprayers, lazy river, wobbly walkway, swirl pool, fountains and shallow play area) and a warm-water therapy pool (88 degrees). There are also two — yes, two — hot tubs: the family-friendly option situated next to the recreation pool, and the adult-only tub next to the lap pool.

GOOD TO KNOW: You can book swim session tickets online as early as two weeks in advance, which guarantees a spot. If you plan to go often, invest in an annual pass.

FINE PRINT: *$5.25–$5.75, ages younger than 2 free, $20/family. Lynnwood Recreation Center, 18900 44th Ave. W., Lynnwood. 425-670-5732.* lynnwood.wa.gov

North Shore Lagoon Pool, McMenamins Anderson School
Bothell

Located in the McMenamins hotel complex in downtown Bothell, this full-size saltwater pool doesn't have slides, lazy rivers or diving boards. What it does have is plenty of very warm, shallow water (88–90 degrees), a Hawaiian-inspired ambiance and an expansive schedule: It's open for non-hotel guests 9 a.m.–11 p.m. every day. The pool is in a glassed-in, greenhouse-like building with open windows; on cold days the steam can obscure the lifeguard's vision and the pool sometimes closes.

NEARBY BONUS: After your swim, get snacks and drinks at the tiki-themed North Shore Lagoon Pub restaurant on the second floor. Kids will love the corner booth at the back, which almost hangs over the pool.

FINE PRINT: *$6–$8, kids 3 and younger free; Bothell residents free. McMenamins Anderson School, 18607 Bothell Way N.E., Bothell. 425-219-4359.* mcmenamins.com

Mountlake Terrace Recreation Pavilion
Mountlake Terrace

This warm-water wonderland (87–88 degrees) is one of the region's best tot pools, with a large shallow-water leisure pool area whose beach-like entry is perfect for littles. You'll also find a lazy river, basketball hoops, inner tubes and pool toys. A hot tub and sauna are a short distance from the pool.

GOOD TO KNOW: Arrive at least 30 minutes before a swim session on weekends. Look for discounted "Happy Hour" one-hour sessions.

FINE PRINT: *$4.50–$5.50, $2.25 Happy Hour swim, $15/family. Mountlake Terrace Recre-*

ation Pavilion, 5303 228th St. S.W., Mountlake Terrace. 425-776-9173. cityofmlt.com

Rainier Beach Pool

South Seattle

The jewel of Seattle's public pools, Rainier Beach community pool is a gleaming space with a leisure pool (with exceptionally warm water at 93 degrees), a lap pool, slides, lazy river, spray and play park, sauna, steam room, spa and diving board. It also has an ADA lift and family changing rooms.

NEARBY BONUS: The pool is part of a community center complex, which includes the excellent Rainier Beach Playfield.

FINE PRINT: $3.75–$5.50, ages younger than 1 free; monthly and multiple-visit passes available. Rainier Beach Pool, 8825 Rainier Ave. S., Seattle. 206-386-1925. seattle.gov

Bellevue Aquatic Center

Bellevue

There are two pools here. Young kids and kids with disabilities will feel at home in the 91-degree therapy pool, which has a ramped entry. Kids ready for some thrills will head to the 82-degree Blue Lagoon lap pool, with a slide and diving board.

GOOD TO KNOW: Discount swim runs Monday–Saturday before 10 a.m., and Wednesdays 7–8 p.m. ($5.50 per person).

FINE PRINT: $6–$7. Bellevue Aquatic Center, 601 143rd Ave. N.E., Bellevue. 425-452-4444. parks.bellevuewa.gov

Federal Way Community Center Pool

Federal Way

The biggest draw to Federal Way's pool complex, one of the largest in the state, is the two-story tube waterslide. More timid youngsters will also love the lazy river, with its whirlpool feature, and the 2-foot-deep area with an interactive play structure and water sprayers. There is also a hot tub (for ages 6 and older, accompanied by an adult) and a six-lane lap pool.

GOOD TO KNOW: Another attraction in the community center is a 27-foot climbing pinnacle with eight belay stations; rent gear for $3 and try it. (Kids need to weigh at least 30 lbs.)

FINE PRINT: $5–$8, 2 and younger free. Federal Way Community Center, 876 S. 333rd St., Federal Way. 253-835-6900. itallhappenshere.org/swim.html

FALL

ADVENTURE

People's Pool

Tacoma

Located in the Hilltop neighborhood, Tacoma's newest pool is a balmy 85 degrees. For toddlers, it has stair-step access to an indoor spray pad area just for them. Kids ready for more thrills will enjoy the lazy river (no tubes), floating pads for walk-on water play and poolside basketball hoops.

GOOD TO KNOW: On the first Saturday of the month, the first recreational swim of the day is free.

FINE PRINT: *$3–$4, 4 and younger free. People's Pool, 1602 MLK Jr. Way, Tacoma. 253-404-3915.* metroparkstacoma.org

Bainbridge Island Aquatic Center

Bainbridge Island

Heading to Bainbridge? Consider stopping for a swim at its epic recreation pool (85 degrees) to get some thrills on the tube slide, frog-shaped slide, lazy river, diving boards and double rope swing (!). There is also a dedicated tot pool with sloped beach entry and a play area for ages 6 and younger. Grown-ups can do some self-care in the steam room, dry sauna and hot tub.

GOOD TO KNOW: Sign up for "Float and Float" Movie Night, when kids can watch a movie while eating ice cream floats in a separate room or floating on an inner tube in the pool ($7 per person).

FINE PRINT: *$5.50–$6.50. Bainbridge Island Aquatic Center, 8521 Madison Ave., Bainbridge Island. 206-842-2302.* biaquatics.org

More like this:
- ➤ **Shady Summer Hikes (Adventure 18)**
- ➤ **Super Spray Parks (Adventure 26)**
- ➤ **Diveworthy Outdoor Pools (Adventure 27)**

JENNIFER HURLBURT/MYMOMMAHEART.COM

Yurting at Grayland Beach State Park

39.

Yurts 101

By Emily Grosvenor

If camping with kids seems like one of those untenable dreams — just another activity to put off — it's time to discover "yurting."

It seems wrong to use "yurt" as a verb, considering what a passive experience it is. There is no pitching a yurt, no work needed beyond driving up to your prebooked dwelling, turning the lock and throwing your sleeping bags down on the beds: Yurts usually sleep up to six in a combo of bunk beds and futon couches.

Yurts originated as circular dwellings used by the nomadic peoples of central Asia roughly 3,000 years ago. In the Pacific Northwest, they have found a strong following among families, who value them for their high level of comfort, thin-walled access to the great outdoors and affordability. Renting a yurt is more expensive than tent camping but cheaper than a cabin.

The yurt's round structure is created by forming a latticework of wooden wall sections and strapping material such as cloth or canvas over the top and sides. A skylight in the middle of the roof lets in sunlight and moonlight. You can rent yurts at state parks, as well as at private resorts and properties that rent yurts to visitors. Here are top yurt spots.

Kayak Point County Park

Stanwood

Just 60 minutes northwest of Seattle, Kayak Point is home to a village of 10 yurts, a great home base for exploring the 3,300-foot shoreline of Port Susan. The yurts sleep as many as eight people, and some have a view and deck. Walk down the bluff to the shore to enjoy activities such as fishing, windsurfing, picnicking, hiking and boating; access to a saltwater beach and pier makes it a fisherman's heaven. Bring your crab pot. There is also a playground.

NEARBY BONUS: Not far from Kayak Point, just off Interstate 5, stop by the Hibulb Cultural Center to explore its exhibits on Tulalip culture, including a longhouse, canoe gallery and natural history preserve.

FINE PRINT: *$45–$85/night, depending on yurt size and season; there's always a two-night minimum stay. The park also has 30 campsites. Book via the Snohomish County website or call 360-652-7992. Kayak Point County Park, 15711 Marine Dr., Stanwood. snohomishcountywa.gov*

YURT SMARTS

Bring a blanket: If your children need absolute dark to go to sleep, bring something to cover the skylight.

Bring your camp stove: As with tent camping, you'll need to set up your cooking station outside.

Early birds win: You can make yurt reservations at Washington state parks as far in advance as nine months; and prices are cheaper in the off-season.

Go private: If state park yurt sites are booked already, try finding one on a private property instead through sites such as Airbnb.

Plan for pets: Most yurt sites are pet-friendly, but require an additional fee per night.

Kanaskat-Palmer State Park

Ravensdale

North of Mount Rainier National Park, this 320-acre camping park, set on a low plateau, is a favorite for exploring the Green River Gorge. Boat and raft launches provide access to the river for expert kayakers and rafters, while 2 miles of shore set the stage for wandering in the woods, fishing and exploration. Yurts sleep as many as five, with bunk beds that sleep three and a queen-size futon.

GOOD TO KNOW: Wander the trails along the river, but keep kids close, as the Green River has serious white water.

FALL
ESCAPES

FINE PRINT: $40–$59/night, depending on season. Book online, or call 888-226-7688. Kanaskat-Palmer State Park, 32101 Cumberland-Kanaskat Rd., Ravensdale. parks.state.wa.us/427/kanaskat-palmer-state-park

Grayland Beach State Park ····→
Grayland

It's a short walk from your cozy yurt at Grayland to 7,449 feet of Pacific Ocean beach, where you can fly kites, beachcomb, bird-watch and stoke bonfires to your heart's content. Razor clamming is also a popular activity, if you time your trip right.

GOOD TO KNOW: Grayland (along with Cape Disappointment) is one of the most popular yurting spots in Washington state, so book as early as you can. Several of the yurts are pet-friendly. There is also a large campground.

FINE PRINT: $59–$89/night, depending on season. Grayland State Park, 925 Cranberry Beach Rd., Grayland. Book online, or call 888-226-7688. Two-hour, 20-minute drive from Seattle. parks.state.wa.us/515/grayland-beach

Cape Disappointment State Park ····→
Ilwaco

You can't match the combination of scenery and history at poorly named Cape Disappointment. The 1,882-acre camping park on the Long Beach Peninsula offers dramatic vistas of steep cliffs overlooking the spot where the Columbia River meets the Pacific Ocean. Draws include long stretches of sandy beaches and seaside forests, 7 miles of trails, a historic coastal fort and two lighthouses. A highlight is the Lewis and Clark Interpretive Center, which tells the story of the famous expedition, which reached the Pacific Ocean here in 1805.

GOOD TO KNOW: The 14 yurts are walking distance from the beach; there are also three cabins to rent and a large campground.

FINE PRINT: $59–$89/night, depending on the season. Book online or call 888-226-7688. Cape Disappointment State Park, 244 Robert Gray Dr., Ilwaco. Three-hour, 15-minute drive from Seattle. parks.state.wa.us/486/cape-disappointment

FALL

ESCAPES

More like this:
➤ One-of-a-Kind Getaways (Adventure 14)
➤ Last-Minute Campgrounds (Adventure 28)
➤ Volcano Escapes (Adventure 29)

40.
San Juans on a Shoestring

By Lauren Braden

Have you given up on the San Juan Islands because of ferry lines and skyrocketing overnight rates? Not so fast. If you haven't visited in a while, let me assure you: Lopez Island has not suddenly transformed into Nantucket. Our gorgeous San Juans are as laid-back and charming as ever, especially if you know when to go and where to find the best deals. Here's a pocket guide.

Lopez Island

Just a 45-minute ferry hop from Anacortes are the quiet coves and driftwood-strewn beaches of friendly Lopez Island. The flattest of the main islands, Lopez has quiet country roads that crisscross family farms and peaceful pastures and seem to be made for riding — bicycles, that is. You can even walk your bikes onto the ferry in Anacortes and leave the family car behind. The island's only settlement is tiny Lopez Village, consisting of a few short streets with cafes and a grocery store. Most of the berry farms, public beaches and restaurants are scattered around the island.

WHAT TO DO: Explore tide pools at Shark Reef Sanctuary. Visitors who make the 10-minute walk to this quiet stretch of rocky shoreline are almost always rewarded with the sight of harbor seals lounging lazily on the rocks. You can also rent kayaks or take a guided paddle with Lopez Island Sea Kayak and Bicycle, located on Fisherman Bay. When you're ready to refuel, get your caffeine fix where the locals get theirs — at the funky shack (with a wrap-around porch) known as Isabel's Espresso. In the heart of Lopez, Haven Kitchen and Bar serves local, healthy, delicious food with a casual, welcoming atmosphere.

WHERE TO STAY: Lopez has just a few lodging options, all of which are homey and affordable. Lopez Islander Resort is a no-frills place tailor-made for families. There are boat rentals on-site, as well as a restaurant, gym and swimming pool. Families with tents will love both the forested and waterfront campsites at Spencer Spit State Park. Another find is Odlin County Park, located 1 mile from the ferry terminal, with waterfront campsites and beach access.

FINE PRINT: From $99/night at Lopez Islander Resort, 2864 Fisherman Bay Rd., Lopez Island. 360-468-2233. lopezfun.com. From $25/night at Spencer Spit State Park, 521 A. Bakerview Road, Lopez Island. 888-226-7688. parks.state.wa.us. Campsites from $21/night at Odlin County Park, 148 Odlin Park Rd., Lopez Island. 360-378-8420. sanjuanco.com

Orcas Island

The largest of the San Juan Islands, Orcas is about 60 square miles, but you can cover the main roads by car in just a few hours. That is, unless you pull over every time you see a sign that reads "Berries" or "Pottery." This pastoral island is a patchwork of farmland, pockets of forest and small island villages. Orcas comes up short on public beach access, although this con is made up for by a very big pro: the massive Moran State Park, with its two freshwater lakes and very own mountain.

WHAT TO DO: Ramble up a lush forested hill at Turtleback Mountain, or circle Mountain Lake at Moran State Park (Discover Pass required). Much of the island is made up of small, family-run farms, and you'll find that many of them are open (with alpacas ready to be petted) on summer weekends, selling eggs, fruit and pottery. The Orcas Island Farmers Market brings all these farms together on Saturdays, May–September. Hike (or drive) to the top of Mount Constitution to get a view of the surrounding straits, which you have to see to believe.

WHERE TO STAY: The Golden Tree Inn and Hostel, located in a restored Victorian farmhouse in Eastsound, has two private rooms, plus a hot tub, sauna and bicycle rentals. Doe Bay Resort, an old standby on the island's far eastern shore, has cabins, yurts and campsites, as well as an on-site cafe. Outlook Inn is in downtown Eastsound and offers a variety of choices for families. Rosario Resort and Spa has harborside rooms and kitchen suites with spacious decks located right on the shores of Cascade Bay. Nearby Moran State Park boasts the cheapest sleeps on Orcas: lakefront campsites just steps from a swimming beach and hiking trails.

FINE PRINT: From $65/night at The Golden Tree Inn and Hostel, 1159 North Beach Rd., Eastsound. 360-317-8693. goldentreehostel.com. From $155/night for a four-person cabin at Doe Bay Resort & Retreat, 107 Doe Bay Rd., Olga. 360-376-2291. doebay.com. From $150/night at the Outlook Inn, 171 Main St., Eastsound. 360-376-2200. outlookinn.com. From $119/night at Rosario Resort and Spa, 1400 Rosario Rd., Eastsound. 360-483-5048. Campsites from $30/night at Moran State Park, Olga Rd., Olga; book online at parks.state.wa.us or call 888-226-7688.

SAVING ON THE SAN JUANS

Count to tent: The cheapest sleep is found in your camping tent.

Ditch the car: Consider options that allow you to leave your car behind.

Get cookin': Book accommodations that have a kitchen so that you can cook your own meals; and pack fixings for picnics to stretch your dollars — dine on an ocean bluff with a view.

Go off-season: Wait for the off-season for deals on lodging.

Just ask: If you are staying at the same place for three or more nights, ask for a discount.

San Juan Island

San Juan Island is the easiest of the islands to visit without a car (remember that tip?). Disembark the ferry and you're smack-dab in the middle of Friday Harbor, a town with bustling restaurants, good hotels and indie boutiques. Bring your car if you wish to explore the island's unique rural beauty beyond Friday Harbor, which includes a pretty lavender farm and some awesome coastal parks. Or get around via San Juan Transit.

WHAT TO DO: Kids will love exploring the tide pools and interpretive nature trails at San Juan Island National Historical Park. On the island's west shore, Lime Kiln State Park is known as a great spot to see passing orca whales (more plentiful in summer), and it also features 1.6 miles of hiking trails through a hillside forested with madrone trees. Kids will learn all about orcas at The Whale Museum in Friday Harbor. If they're itching for more adventure, kids 8 and older can take a trip with the San Juan Zip Tour.

WHERE TO STAY: The best value for families is to book a hotel-style room at the Discovery Inn. Or book a room or suite with kitchenette at Earthbox Inn, a refurbished motor inn in downtown Friday Harbor with an on-site spa and indoor pool. In Roche Harbor, Lakedale Resort offers a family glamping option: wood-floored canvas tent cabins scattered in the woods along a freshwater lake. Book early for a campsite at San Juan County Park.

FINE PRINT: From $119/night at the Discovery Inn, 1016 Guard St., Friday Harbor. 360-378-2000. discoveryinn.com. From $180 at Earthbox Inn & Spa, 410 Spring St., Friday Harbor. 360-387-4000. earthboxinn.com. From $179/night at Lakedale Resort, 4313 Roche Harbor Rd., Friday Harbor. 800-617-2267. lakedale.com. From $34/night at San Juan County Park, 15 San Juan Park Rd., Friday Harbor. Book online at sanjuanco.com.

Guemes Island

Haven't heard of Guemes Island? Neither have most travelers bound for the San Juans. Besides leisurely walks on pebble beaches and playing board games on the cabin porch, there's not much to do on this rural island, and that's the point. Bring the bikes, though, for the island's quiet roads are perfect for family bike rides.

WHAT TO DO: Hike up the 1-mile trail to the top of Guemes Mountain for incredible views of nearby islands, straits, the Skagit River Delta and jagged peaks of the North Cascades. Got your GPS? Guemes is a geocaching hot spot. The Guemes Island Resort (see below) has kayaks available for guests. Guemes Island General Store is located at the ferry dock and is the place to stop for supplies, groceries, ice cream and cold beverages. It also houses the island's only restaurant/pub.

WHERE TO STAY: Lodging is limited but good — stay at the island's only resort or rent a vacation home. The family-friendly Guemes Island Resort hails from the 1940s and faces a stunning view across Samish Bay to snow-capped Mount Baker. Choose from a range of cabins and houses (some with hot tubs), as well as five heated yurts.

FINE PRINT: Take the Guemes Island Ferry (operated by Skagit County), a small car/passenger ferry that leaves from Anacortes and crosses the water in just five minutes. From $90/night at Guemes Island Resort, 4268 Guemes Island Rd., Anacortes. 800-965-6643. guemesislandresort.com

FALL

ESCAPES

More like this:
- ➤ One-of-a-Kind Getaways (Adventure 14)
- ➤ Walk-On Ferry Tales (Adventure 23)
- ➤ Volcano Escapes (Adventure 29)

WANDER LIST:
Jumpin' Play Spaces

The Seattle metropolitan area experiences an average of 152 rainy days a year. Drizzle, of course, doesn't stop us (right?), but there are those days when it's just too wet or windy to get outside. Here's a field guide to the great indoors with kids.

A NOTE: In any season, hanging with young kids can be isolating. Find yourself a meet-up group: In addition to PEPS, which is focused on new parents, check out resources such as Families of Color Seattle, MOPS International or form your own group with the help of your community Facebook group or listserv.

Aquariums: Touch tidal life and ogle octopuses at Seattle Aquarium; or spy on sharks in the underwater tunnel of Point Defiance Zoo & Aquarium's 35,000-square-foot Pacific Seas exhibit. Also, Poulsbo's SEA Discovery Center and MaST in Des Moines (open seasonally) are free aquariums with plenty to see.

Bounce and jump: Check out epic jumping spots, such as the 53,000-square-foot Flying Circus in Tukwila or Arena Sports' gigantic facility in Mill Creek. For the younger set, spots such as the free Ballard Playspace and WiggleWorks Kids get the, er, wiggles out.

Community centers: More than 20 Seattle community centers offer free drop-in play sessions designed for kids ages 5 and younger, complete with balls, trikes, scooters, push bikes and other entertainment. Many other regional community centers have indoor play of all kinds for kids of all ages.

Coworking centers: Coworking spaces that include child care are popping up. Try The Inc. (with two locations in Seattle), Roo's World of Discovery in Kirkland (also a play space) and others. Find more at *parentmap.com/childcare*.

Dance: So many options! Beyond formal ballet and tap classes, kids can try break dancing (try Anna Banana Freeze's Mini Breaks classes in Seattle's Chinatown–International District); square dancing (try a Family Dance at Phinney Neighborhood Center), Hawaiian dancing and much more.

Drop-in child care and gyms: Drop and shop (or work) at centers such as Woodinville's The Nest, or Adventure Kids Playcare in Bellevue and Issaquah. Athletic clubs can be a great source of reasonably priced child care for an hour or two.

Game stores: Unplug with board games at spots like Blue Highway Games in Queen Anne and Meeples Games in West Seattle; you can also borrow a game from most stores' lending library to try it out before buying. Other hot spots include Uncle's Games (Bellevue, Redmond, Tacoma), Games and Gizmos (Redmond) and Mox Boarding House (Ballard, Bellevue).

Home Depot: You can't leave your kid at Home Depot, but you can sign them up for a free DIY kids workshop, which will help them do projects such as building a frame or constructing a bird feeder.

IKEA: Yes, Virginia, you can shop for furniture and entertain your kids at the same time. Drop them off at Småland, or let them visit the activity stations in the showroom. *parentmap.com/ikea*

Indoor skate parks: All Together Skatepark in Fremont and Bellevue Indoor Skate Park help kids learn how to shred all year long.

Kaleidoscope Play & Learn: During these free play sessions around the Sound, kids can take part in early-learning-focused play activities while you meet new friends and hear about support programs in your neighborhood.

Libraries: Story times, audio books, classes, homework help, science kits, digital downloads, personal recommendations: See p. 200 for one-of-a-kind libraries to visit.

Maker spots: Many local art centers — such as Seattle ReCreative and Tacoma's Tinkertopia — offer drop-in sessions that are perfect for preschoolers and older. And even young kids can throw some paint and end up with a gift at a paint-your-own pottery spot.

COURTESY
READING
WITH ROVER

FALL

WANDER LIST

Malls: Malls are one-stop shops for family fun, from free play areas (in almost every mall) to international food (Crossroads, Westfield Southcenter) to covered playgrounds (University Village). Bonus: These malls typically have excellent family bathrooms and nursing/pumping rooms.

Museums: Kids' museums are a no-brainer for high-energy, interactive play, but museums of the history, art and science varieties also boast kid attractions.

Nature centers: Beautifully designed environmental centers, such as those at Bellevue's Lewis Creek Park, the Cedar River Watershed and Mercer Slough as well as the Tacoma Nature Center, are often empty midweek and have space for kids to play and learn. (Always check hours.)

Pet stores: Never underestimate the power of an hour at Petco to watch the fish, ferrets and dwarf hamsters. Just be prepared to say no to adding to your critter collection.

Playful cafes: Finding a cafe or low-key restaurant with solid espresso options, good snacks and a train table or play area is the Holy Grail for parents. Find a huge list at *parentmap.com/cafes.*

Tumble on: High-flying indoor playtime at spots such as Seattle Gymnastics Academy guarantees a huge nap later that day. Older kids may want to try parkour, an up-and-coming sport where kids learn to run, jump and climb over obstacles, at classes offered by the likes of Parkour Visions, MoveFree Academy and other organizations.

Unusual story times: Tugboat story time, multilingual story time, story time with theater, story time with chocolate, story time with nature exploration: You can find all that and more around Seattle. *parentmap.com/storytimes*

Zoos: Climb, jump and learn at Woodland Park Zoo's Zoomazium; wander and wonder at Point Defiance Zoo & Aquarium. And don't forget Pacific Science Center's gloriously warm Tropical Butterfly House.

FALL

WANDER
LIST

WINTER

Banish the darkness. Find a new holiday light extravaganza, or perhaps a quiet solstice walk. Play in the snow. Or pull out the ultimate getaway: a hotel with an epic pool.

MEGAN LEE

WINTER

41.
Screaming-Fun Sledding Hills

By Gemma Alexander

Whether you live in Seattle or Duvall, you can get to the mountains in an hour or less. In the winter, that means snow. Our kids take this stunning fact for granted, but we adults know just how special it is to have nearby snow in our otherwise temperate climate. And sledding is the most accessible winter activity: All you need is a slope, snow and a sled.

IMPORTANT: Dress warmly and bring a dry change of clothes for little ones. Adhesive hand and foot warmers can be a great tool for keeping fingers and toes toasty.

Summit Tubing Park
Snoqualmie Pass

Just off Interstate 90 at exit 53, The Summit at Snoqualmie's tubing center is hugely popular with kids and grown-ups, and it delivers exhausted, joyful kids. You can either walk back to the top of the hill or ride your tube back up on the "magic carpet."

SAFETY FIRST

Driving up to the snow requires extra prep and planning. Always check road conditions before heading out (Washington State Department of Transportation is a good source); and bring chains as well as a car emergency kit, extra snacks and water.

The Summit recommends that children be at least 3 years old before tubing, but does not restrict admission for families with younger children who want to try. Tip: Children less than 42 inches tall can ride double with a parent. Personal sledding devices are prohibited.

WARM-UP TIP: There is a small cafe with restrooms on-site, or, for more seating and options, the Silver Fir Day Lodge is nearby (though a bit of a walk).

FINE PRINT: *Open seasonally, Friday–Sunday, and daily during winter break and other school closures. $22–$28/two-hour session, $5 for children ages 5 and younger (sharing a tube with an adult). Book sessions online to guarantee a spot. The Summit at Snoqualmie, 1001 State Route 906, Snoqualmie Pass. 425-434-6791.* summitatsnoqualmie.com

Hyak Sno-Park
Snoqualmie Pass

Bring your speedy plastic sleds to this groomed sledding hill located off I-90 at exit 54, near Snoqualmie East. Hyak is a Washington State Parks snow-play area and is not affiliated with The Summit at Snoqualmie ski resort. The area is groomed as often as five times a week (depending on conditions) and has amenities including heated restrooms (!) but is not supervised by rangers or snow patrol. You can also go snowshoeing or cross-country skiing on the groomed trail.

GOOD TO KNOW: Hyak Sno-Park fills up fast, so go early or late in the day, or on weekdays, to avoid crowds.

FINE PRINT: *Open seasonally; call 509-656-2230 for updates on conditions. Hyak Sno-Park, I-90 at Exit 54, Snoqualmie Pass. 509-656-2230. No admission fee, but you need a daily Sno-Park permit and Discover Pass; or a seasonal Sno-Park permit plus Special Groomed Trails Permit sticker, without a Discover Pass. There is an electronic pay station at the lot.* snowrec.org/sno-parks-c20nd

Suncadia Tubing Hill
Cle Elum

If you want a more low-key tubing experience, Suncadia might be your answer. Located about 30 minutes east of Snoqualmie Pass — on I-90 at exit 80 — this grand resort offers a number of wintry activities, including a smaller tubing hill (with rope tow) about a half

WINTER

NATURE

mile from the main Suncadia lodge. There is also a small ice skating rink and cross-country skiing trails when there is enough snow (you can rent equipment at Suncadia).

WARM-UP TIP: Next to the sledding hill, Swiftwater Cellars offers eats and wine tasting for the grown-ups. You can also head to the main Suncadia Lodge for coffee and cocoa at the in-lodge coffee stand.

FINE PRINT: Open seasonally; check website for hours. Kids must be at least 3 years old and 36 inches or taller to tube and must ride in their own tube. $20/two-hour session. Suncadia Resort, 3600 Suncadia Trail, Cle Elum. 509-649-6461. suncadiaresort.com

Lt. Michael Adams Tubing Park, Ski Hill ····➔

Leavenworth

Just 2 miles outside of Leavenworth, Ski Hill is a small, friendly ski area with two downhill runs and a 100-foot tubing hill named for a West Point graduate killed in Iraq in 2004. The recommended ages for tubing is 8 and older, though kids as young as 4 are welcome. All must tube independently. You can take one free ride prior to purchasing a ticket to make sure you'll enjoy it. You can also bring your own sled to the nearby golf course in a designated area, and there are 26 kilometers of cross-country skiing/snowshoe trails in four areas around Leavenworth.

WARM-UP TIP: Food, beverages and warmth are available at the historic Ski Hill Lodge, and all of Leavenworth's Bavarian fun is just 2 miles away.

FINE PRINT: Open seasonally; check website for hours. $20 for six runs, with inner tube provided. $15–$19 for Alpine lift ticket, ages 5 and younger free; $34 for "Play All Day" pass,

MORE SNOW-PLAY SPOTS

Cool cross-country: At a fraction of the cost of downhill skiing, cross-country skiing (aka Nordic skiing) provides thrills and great exercise. Try The Summit at Snoqualmie's Junior Nordic program.

Downhill deals: At Mount Baker and Stevens Pass ski areas, fifth-graders ski for free; at Crystal Mountain ski area, kids 10 and younger ski free. Kids 6 and younger ski for free (or close to free) at most resorts.

Hurricane Ridge: If you're up for the trek, the small ski area in Olympic National Park also boasts a tubing hill.

Mount Baker: Bellingham-area snow bunnies sled at a number of informal spots off Mount Baker Highway, including Highwood Lake, near one of the Mt. Baker Ski Area's day lodges.

Snoqualmie Pass snowshoe tours: On winter Saturdays, the U.S. Forest Service leads 90-minute "Kids in the Snow" walks, which are easy, affordable and informative.

which includes Alpine and Nordic lift passes and a six-session tubing session. $5 for golf course sledding. 10701 Ski Hill Dr., Leavenworth. 509-548-6975. Two-hour, 30-minute drive from Seattle. skileavenworth.com

Mount Rainier National Park ┈→

Ashford

You can sled in spectacular Mount Rainier National Park in one place: the designated snow-play area at Paradise, near the Jackson Visitor Center. Access Paradise through the Nisqually entrance to the park. Bring plastic sledding devices to this ungroomed area, supervised by park rangers; wooden toboggans and sleds with metal runners are prohibited. You can also take free guided snowshoe walks from Jackson Visitor Center on weekends; the center has a snack bar, restrooms and is a good place to warm up.

GOOD TO KNOW: If the national park is closed because of conditions, Ashford County Park (a few miles outside of the national park) is a free and fun place to sled, with plenty of hills and easy parking.

FINE PRINT: *The Paradise snow-play area opens in late December (depending on snow), then is open on weekends and daily during school breaks. Sledding is free, but national park entrance fee required. Henry M. Jackson Memorial Visitor Center, Mount Rainier National Park. At least a three-hour drive from Seattle.* visitrainier.com

More like this:
> ➤ **Mountain Biking Thrills (Adventure 37)**
> ➤ **Swimming Pool Getaways (Adventure 52)**
> ➤ **Winning Winter Tours (Adventure 51)**

42.
Secret Urban Hikes

By Bryony Angell

When my son was a preschooler, I wanted to introduce him to hiking, but I knew he wasn't ready for long trails (or drives). We began exploring the wealth of tucked-away wild areas in the Lake Washington region. We discovered some jewels, from short wetland walks to a 1-mile hike with significant elevation gain. These short trails are part of

WINTER

NATURE

ELISA MURRAY

Licorice Fern Natural Area

official open space in and around Seattle; each offers different ecosystems to explore and different nature memories to treasure. Bonus: Since they're in urban areas, these trails are accessible all winter.

Licorice Fern Natural Area   FREE

Pinehurst, Seattle
Licorice Fern is one of several Thornton Creek natural areas in North Seattle that is being lovingly restored with the help of a neighborhood group. It offers a quiet creekside stroll, with logs and benches to sit on and listen to the water. This watershed is where I brought my son when he was still an infant, to experience the sounds and sights of nature on a small scale while still close to home. Look for pileated woodpeckers or evidence of beavers.

GOOD TO KNOW: Stay on marked trails and remember that this is a residential area as well as a sanctuary for wildlife. The closest retail area (and restrooms) is the large Safeway grocery store at the intersection of N.E. 125th St. and 15th Ave. N.E. in the Pinehurst neighborhood.

FINE PRINT: Less than 0.5-mile of trails. Enter the greenspace at the end of N.E. 130th St.,

WINTER

NATURE

a few blocks west of 15th Ave. N.E. Park on 12th Ave. N.E., in Seattle, and walk down to the entrance. Find more information on the Friends of Licorice Fern Facebook page (facebook. com/lfnafriuends).

Llandover Woods   FREE

Northwest Seattle

Just south of Shoreline, Llandover Woods feels like a secret forest at the edge of the city. Deep, heavily wooded ravines make this park seem like stepping into the mountains. The 0.6-mile-long loop trail is wide and well maintained, and the twitter of golden-crowned kinglets' song high in the conifers might be the only sound you hear other than your footfalls. It's also possible to extend the walk by passing through the neighborhood in one big loop.

GOOD TO KNOW: Find the closest public restrooms at the retail area of N.E. 145th St. and Greenwood, or head to the fantastic Central Market nearby in Shoreline for a pit stop and snacks (and groceries).

FINE PRINT: Shorter loop is 0.6 mile. The park entrance is at N.E. 145th St. and Third Ave. N.W., Seattle, where there is ample parking. seattle.gov/parks

Madrona Woods   FREE

Madrona, Seattle

This greenbelt above Madrona Park and Beach in the Madrona neighborhood of Seattle offers a quiet retreat from the sound of cars on Lake Washington Boulevard. Maintained by the dedicated Friends of Madrona Woods, the 9-acre forest features trails, a daylighted Madrona Creek and waterfall, and the novelty of a weathered 1940s-era Ford sedan lodged into the hillside. The trails are hilly, with reinforced plank stairs, and branch off across the slope to emerge into the neighborhood or the lakeside park below.

NEARBY BONUS: Madrona's cute shopping district is close by, with kid-friendly attractions such as Molly Moon's Homemade Ice Cream and Cupcake Royale.

FINE PRINT: Madrona Woods has several access entries on 38th Ave. and E. Spring St. in Seattle, as well as a crosswalk from the Madrona Beach Park below. Park on the street. madronawoods.org

Lakeridge Park   FREE

Rainier Beach, Seattle

Lakeridge Park, a 35-acre wooded canyon in the Rainier Beach area, might be the most overlooked gem of the Seattle parks system. Once called Deadhorse Canyon, the area

WINTER

NATURE

has a gravel trail that runs a half mile round-trip along the west side of the canyon over-looking Taylor Creek below. The trail ascends quickly, and soon you are looking across the ravine, feeling like you are at bird's-eye height. The drop-off can be intimidating, but the trail is wide and even, and our boys loved running across the well-fortified, hand-railed wooden bridge that spanned rougher terrain.

NEARBY BONUS: Adjacent to Lakeridge Park, on Rainier Ave. S., Lakeridge Playfield has a playground and a ball field (and restrooms).

FINE PRINT: Up to 0.5 mile round-trip. The trailhead is at a bend in the road where 68th Ave. S. becomes Holyoke Ave. S., just a block up from Rainier Ave. S. There is a pullout for three cars, and a kiosk and Seattle Parks and Recreation sign. seattle.gov/parks

O.O. Denny Park   FREE
Kirkland

Just up the road from better-known Saint Edward State Park, O.O. Denny Park is a 46-acre greenspace along Lake Washington that encompasses the Denny Creek water-shed area. Park in the lot across the street from the lakefront area, and find a trailhead at the south end that leads to a short loop trail. Interpretive signage at the halfway mark explains the restoration and history of the area. As you descend through tall trees, look for a 600-year-old Douglas fir tree nicknamed Sylvia, the biggest tree in King County. As you loop back down by Denny Creek, kids will have fun playing "hot lava" on the wood pavers on muddier sections of the trail.

NEARBY BONUS: After the hike, cross the road to the Lake Washington section of O.O. Denny Park for a lakeside picnic and playground time (and bathrooms). Find more trails at nearby Big Finn Hill Park.

FINE PRINT: Approximately 1.25-mile loop, around 200 feet elevation gain. Find trail map at alltrails.com. O.O. Denny Park, 12032 Holmes Point Dr. N.E., Kirkland. kirklandwa.gov

More like this:
- ➤ Roaring Waterfall Hikes (Adventure 1)
- ➤ Spring Hikes, Warm-Up Included (Adventure 6)
- ➤ Stairway Walks (Adventure 9)

WINTER

NATURE

43.
Family Birding Takes Flight

By Bryony Angell

Want to lure your kids outside with a hobby that includes scavenger-hunt-like fun, multisensory exploration, breathtaking scenery and a few bragging rights? Try birding, also called bird-watching, an age-old pastime that's gaining seriously cool cred among the younger generation.

Winter is the ideal season to take up birding. The cold months of the year in the Pacific Northwest mean the shedding of tree leaves and the fluttering arrival of many avian visitors. The result is world-class birding in our region from November to early May. Getting started is as easy as stepping out your door.

WINTER

NATURE

In your backyard

"My favorite place to watch birds is my backyard," says 9-year-old Avi Charlton of the Wedgwood neighborhood of Seattle. Avi's interest in birds began when his dad accidentally mowed over a dark-eyed junco's nest while doing yardwork. "It wasn't sad," he says. "Two nestlings escaped, and the mom bird was scolding my dad!"

He has since put up feeders, collected a library of field guides and participated in Seattle Audubon's summer Nature Camp.

"The staff recognizes him now whenever we visit the shop!" says his mom, Gabby Charlton. "Birding has become part of our family's life, thanks to Avi."

Your family can get started as easily as Avi did. First, buy a field guide to local birds and a pair of binoculars, which will greatly enhance your time in the field. Next, put up a bird feeder. Black oil sunflower seeds will attract chickadees, finches and grosbeaks. A suet cage will bring woodpeckers and bushtits, and a hummingbird feeder will draw Anna's hummingbirds to your house all year. A bird bath will attract every bird imaginable.

Put stickers or bright, dangling ribbon on the window glass near feeders, to prevent your avian friends from striking the window when coming to feed. Encourage kids to watch birds from a respectful distance.

Birding around Seattle and the Eastside

To explore more, find a class or walk put on by local Audubon chapters or other nature organizations (see sidebar), or head to a park.

Marymoor Park is King County's largest and most visited park, and it has diverse habitats for bird viewing. (Birds reliably flock to three habitat features — water, tree canopy and a food source — and Marymoor has acres of all three.)

The best areas for birds in Marymoor are along the Sammamish River and in the community garden. Wander the bird-named loop trails that lead to the river, and look for hawks, belted kingfishers, waterfowl and songbirds. Keep your eyes aloft and ears pricked.

Apply the same birding principles to any park near you. Try the Seward Park peninsula in South Seattle for waterfowl on the lake and barred owl sightings in the wooded interior. Golden Gardens Park in northwest Seattle is ideal for seeing seabirds just offshore, and belted kingfishers and great blue herons at the north end of the park.

Skagit treasures: eagles, snow geese and swans

River deltas are prime birding locations, and the world-famous Skagit Valley delivers every winter: Swans and snow geese, which look like patches of snow amid miles of open farmland, come from Alaska and northern Canada to feed on waste grain, roots and seed. Eagles gather to feed on spawning salmon along the Skagit River. The Skagit Eagle Festival, held every year in January, plans activities and events to celebrate this seasonal migration.

A good place to see the Skagit's treasures is to park at the end of Rawlins Road on Fir Island (between Conway and La Conner in the Skagit Wildlife Area; no Discover Pass required) and hike along the dike, keeping an eye out for low-flying raptors hunting voles. This is one of my favorite spots for seeing bald eagles, short-eared owls and ravens, and sometimes a flock of snow geese. Dress for mud and cold.

BONUS: Spend a weekend exploring the Skagit and stay overnight in charming La Conner. Stop in tiny Edison for pastries at the Breadfarm bakery and pick up a loaf or two for the drive home.

Nisqually magic

Another river delta rich with bird life is the Billy Frank Jr. Nisqually National Wildlife Refuge (NWR), a short hop off Interstate 5 between Tacoma and Olympia. Unlike the sprawling Skagit, the Nisqually NWR packs a complete ecosystem within an easily traversable (and wheelchair-accessible) system of boardwalk and earthen-dike trails, a flat, easy and beautiful hike. Start at the visitor center to pick up a bird list and map.

The best time to see birds at Nisqually is within two hours on either side of high tide, so check the tides before your visit.

WAYS TO WING IT

Apps: Apps, such as Merlin Bird ID, can be a great way to engage kids in birding in real time. Check the Cornell Lab of Ornithology online for suggestions.

Bird counts: Families can become citizen scientists by participating in Audubon's Great Backyard Bird Count (held over Presidents Day weekend every year) or similar efforts.

"BirdNote": Learn about birds in two-minute snippets by listening to "BirdNote," a daily radio program available online, by podcast or on local stations.

Bird walks: Many Puget Sound-area nature organizations (such as local chapters of Audubon) hold free or affordable family bird walks.

Books: Invaluable resources include the American Birding Association's "A Birder's Guide to Washington" and "Sibley Birds West: Field Guide to Birds of Western America."

WINTER

NATURE

Sandhill cranes in Othello

Every year in late March, thousands of sandhill cranes — a species that stands more than 4 feet tall — visit the area around the agricultural town of Othello, Washington, from their breeding grounds in northern Canada. Each March, Othello partners with the Washington Department of Fish and Wildlife for a three-day celebration of the cranes, the family-friendly Othello Sandhill Crane Festival. Go for the day or spend the night to explore the area after the festival.

BONUS: The nearby Columbia National Wildlife Refuge is a stunning place to hike or picnic. If you're lucky, you might catch sight of a marmot peeking over a cliff.

Shorebirds in Grays Harbor

For another spectacular migration experience, head to Bowerman Basin in the Grays Harbor National Wildlife Refuge on the Washington coast in late April or early May to see migrating shorebirds by the thousands (and the peregrine falcons that hunt them). Park at the Bowerman airfield (itself a novelty for kids) and walk along the boardwalk to the end viewing platform, where you'll see plovers, sandpipers, dowitchers, red knots and dunlins converging on the mudflats. The undulating sight of so many birds in flight is unforgettable.

BONUS: Make a weekend of it by staying on the coast at places in Ocean Shores, the town of Copalis Beach (try Iron Springs Resort) or Seabrook's beachside village.

> ## More like this:
> ➤ **Oh, Baby Animals! (Adventure 3)**
> ➤ **Secret Gardens (Adventure 5)**
> ➤ **See Salmon Run (Adventure 31)**

44.
Holiday Magic on the Cheap

By Kris Collingridge

Not feeling flush this holiday season? Not to worry — some of Seattle's most magical and venerable holiday traditions are free or almost free. Another bonus: Most of

Westlake Park Holiday Carousel

these events are unscheduled. From late November through December (and beyond, in some cases), you can drop by whenever the mood strikes you (or naptime doesn't loom).

Swansons Nursery FREE

North Ballard, Seattle

Two reindeer, Santa, a model train: It's all at Swansons Nursery in North Ballard from mid-November until just before Christmas, and it's a low-key outing that you can take anytime. Browse Swansons' displays of gorgeous — and pricey — greenery, ornaments and bulbs at your own risk. There's also an amazing holiday train setup, a fish pond and more, and Santa shows up for photo sessions on select days between Thanksgiving and Christmas.

GOOD TO KNOW: You can stop by for a "Meet the Reindeer" session and take a selfie.

FINE PRINT: *The festival starts with a two-day opening event in mid-November, and the Christmas critters are on display daily through Dec. 24. Swansons Nursery, 9701 15th Ave. N.W., Seattle. 206-782-243.* swansonsnursery.com

Westlake Park Holiday Carousel

Downtown Seattle

Head downtown to Westlake Park to take a spin on the holiday carousel and support a good cause. There is a $3 suggested donation per ride, with proceeds going to Treehouse, an organization dedicated to helping foster kids, as well as the Downtown Seattle Association. You can also drop off a toy for a foster kid while you are there.

WINTER

CULTURE

NEARBY BONUS: Stop at nearby Macy's to see its holiday window displays; or by Pacific Place to see its 6 p.m. nightly snow flurries.

FINE PRINT: The carousel usually runs from the day after Thanksgiving to Jan. 1. $3/ride. Check the website for details. Westlake Park, 401 Pine St., Seattle. downtownseattle.org

Gingerbread Village   FREE
Downtown Seattle

Every year, the Sheraton Seattle hosts a show of stunning gingerbread creations created by chef-architect pairs who team up on a certain theme ("Star Wars" and "Harry Potter" have been among recent ones). Expect jaw-dropping amounts of candy and sugar on display in creative and immaculately realized creations.

GOOD TO KNOW: Since the Gingerbread Village is open late into the evening every day, this is a good outing to combine with a downtown holiday show or event.

FINE PRINT: Usually open daily from late November through Jan. 1. Free, though the event is a fundraiser for the Juvenile Diabetes Research Foundation and donations are encouraged. Location has varied from the Seattle Sheraton; check the website. gingerbreadvillage.org

Fairmont Olympic Hotel   FREE
Downtown Seattle

This stately Seattle hotel is alight with holiday festivities beginning in mid-November. The Festival of Trees is a magical collection of stunning themed Christmas trees on display in the Fairmont's lobby. The trees are for sale, and proceeds benefit Seattle Children's Hospital. Also at the Fairmont, the beloved Teddy Bear Suite is a winning stop, especially for young kids. The suite, decorated with a new design every year, is stuffed with teddy bears of every type.

GOOD TO KNOW: A new addition to the Fairmont's holiday line-up is an oversized gingerbread house.

FINE PRINT: The Festival of Trees runs from mid-November until a few days after Thanksgiving. The Teddy Bear Suite opens just before Thanksgiving and is open for viewing daily through Dec. 26, 10 a.m.–6 p.m. Free for viewing, although donations are suggested (proceeds go to Seattle Children's). 411 University St., Seattle. 206-621-1700. seattlefestivaloftrees.com

Christmas Ships viewing   FREE
Multiple locations around Puget Sound

The classic Northwest Christmas adventure: Bundle up, stash a flashlight in your pocket and head to a Puget Sound or Lake Washington beach for live choral music from the best groups around, broadcast by the brightly lit Argosy Christmas Ship and its decorated "follow boats." You can pay to ride the ships, but it's free (and more fun, in this cheapskate's opinion) to watch from shore.

GOOD TO KNOW: Some communities hold festive bonfires on Christmas Ship nights. Check the schedule for locations.

FINE PRINT: From the day after Thanksgiving through Dec. 23 at more than 60 beaches around the Sound. Schedule released in the fall of each year. argosycruises.com

Winterfest FREE
Seattle Center
Starting on the Friday after Thanksgiving, Seattle Center's winter celebration is a cash-strapped family's best friend. Opening weekend is particularly fun, with the unveiling of the elaborate model train village on display in the Armory, ice sculpting and numerous free performances in the Armory all weekend.

NEARBY BONUS: Slide over to Fisher Pavilion for skating on the small but fun Winterfest ice rink; if you arrive on a weekday morning, you might have it to yourself.

FINE PRINT: Winterfest runs from the day after Thanksgiving through Dec. 31 each year. All activities free except ice skating. Seattle Center Armory, 304 Harrison St., Seattle. seattlecenter.com/winterfest

MORE HO-HO-HOLIDAY FUN

Fantasy Lights: The largest drive-through holiday lights show in the Northwest features hundreds of holiday scenes on a 2-mile route along Spanaway Lake.

The Lights of Christmas: This huge holiday lights festival at Warm Beach in Stanwood has more than a million lights on display and plenty of other attractions.

WildLights: Woodland Park Zoo's annual holiday lights show features wild scenes illuminated by more than 600,000 LED lights, plus endless "snowball" fights at the Snowmazium.

ZooLights: Point Defiance Zoo & Aquarium's beloved tradition includes camels, a carousel and favorite light displays such as the green-and-purple flame tree.

WINTER

CULTURE

Garden d'Lights

Bellevue

The always lovely Bellevue Botanical Garden dresses up for the holidays in hundreds of thousands of colored lights twisted into fanciful flower and garden shapes, which are showcased in a magnificent, nightly light show. Kids especially love the smoking dragon. The garden can get more crowded as Christmas approaches; if avoiding the crush is your priority, visit early in the evening or the season.

GOOD TO KNOW: Every year, a number of free-admission nights are planned; check the schedule on the website.

FINE PRINT: *Open nightly from the Saturday after Thanksgiving through Dec. 30 (including Dec. 25) from 4:30 to 9 p.m. $5, ages 10 and younger free; reserve tickets online to avoid lines. Bellevue Botanical Garden, 2001 Main St., Bellevue. 425-452-6844. gardendlights.org*

Snowflake Lane   FREE

Bellevue

The lavish music and light show called Snowflake Lane — complete with live toy soldiers — holds court nightly at Bellevue Square between Thanksgiving and Christmas. It's a free and thrilling holiday parade of falling snow, lights, live drummer boys and Jingle Belles, costumed characters, princesses and Santa.

NEARBY BONUS: Prior to the show, take a spin at the covered Magic Season Ice Arena at Downtown Bellevue Park (be sure to include playtime at the awesome Inspiration Playground).

FINE PRINT: *Performed at 7 p.m. nightly on the sidewalks around Bellevue Square from the Friday after Thanksgiving through Dec. 24. Free. Find the show on the sidewalks between Bellevue Square and Lincoln Square from N.E. Fourth to N.E. Eighth streets, Bellevue. snowflakelane.com*

Clam Lights   FREE

Renton

You can't get any more old-school Seattle than this. The paths at Gene Coulon Memorial Park, at the south end of Lake Washington, are decorated with holiday lights — and yes, there are clams. Kids can run or walk the entire 1-mile loop, and an Ivar's and Kidd Valley are right there to provide sustenance.

GOOD TO KNOW: Opening-night festivities (usually the first Friday in December) include live music performances, a Christmas Ship stop and a community sing-along.

FINE PRINT: Lit nightly from opening night through Jan. 1, 5–9 p.m. Gene Coulon Park, 1201 Lake Washington Blvd. N., Renton. rentonwa.gov/clamlights

More like this:

➤ **Kid-Friendly Indie Bookstores (Adventure 7)**
➤ **Crafty Museum Spaces (Adventure 34)**
➤ **Cool Kids' Museums (Adventure 49)**

JERAMEY JANNENE/URBANMILWAUKEE.COM

45.
Quirky Landmarks

By Gemma Alexander

As construction booms, many longtime residents have become concerned that Seattle will lose its quirky character. My family has taken solace from an unusual source: the Amazon Spheres. Amid a sea of high rises, those greenhouse domes prove that Seattle hasn't completely abandoned its love of the eccentric. We may have lost The Blob on

Queen Anne, but Seattle has plenty of oddities left for those who know where to look. (Note: For Spheres tips, see p. 90.)

Fremont Troll   FREE
Fremont, Seattle

Every child familiar with fairy tales knows that trolls live under bridges. Fortunately, the Fremont Troll underneath the north end of the Aurora Bridge doesn't eat billy goats or people. The ironic self-portrait of artist Steve Badanes is quite happy eating bugs (of the Volkswagen variety). It used to be possible to hang out with the troll by yourself, but nowadays it's crawling with people at all hours of the day and night.

NEARBY BONUS: While you're in the neighborhood, check out Fremont's other public art pieces, such as the oft-decorated "Waiting for the Interurban" and Lenin statues. Use the walking guide at *fremont.com* to help you find them all.

FINE PRINT: Underneath the Aurora Bridge on Troll Avenue N. at the intersection of N. 36th Street, Seattle. Find restrooms at the nearby Fremont Public Library. fremont.com

Gum Wall   FREE
Downtown Seattle

This famous, always-gross landmark originated in the 1990s, when clubbers standing in line for shows in Post Alley used the walls to dispose of their gum. In 2015, the city cleaned up the wall — removing 2,350 pounds of chewed gum — but visitors quickly restored the landmark to its sticky glory. Today, it's as good a photo op as ever.

GOOD TO KNOW: If you're inclined to make a personal contribution to the wall, nearby Ghost Alley Espresso sells gum.

FINE PRINT: Gum Wall, 1428 Post Alley, Seattle. facebook.com/thegumwall

Hat 'n' Boots   FREE
Georgetown, Seattle

No Seattle landmark list would be complete without the Hat 'n' Boots, a 22-foot-high set of cowboy boots, and 44-foot-wide orange hat that dominate Oxbow Park in Seattle's Georgetown neighborhood. Seattle artist Lewis Nasmyth originally designed the structures to house a gas station in Georgetown. In the 1950s, it was the most successful roadside attraction in Washington state, but its kitschy appeal wasn't enough to draw customers off the newly completed Interstate 5 in the 1960s. Eventually, the beloved boots (and the hat) were saved when the City of Seattle recognized it as a historic landmark and moved it to Oxbow Park.

NEARBY BONUS: Oxbow Park has a small play structure. Or head to the terrific playground at Georgetown Playfield, a half-mile away, before filling up at nearby Flying Squirrel Pizza Company.

FINE PRINT: Oxbow Park, 6430 Corson Ave. S., Seattle. seattle.gov/parks

Lakeview Cemetery   FREE
Capitol Hill, Seattle

Lakeview Cemetery has been a pilgrimage site for martial arts and film fans for decades. So many people visit the graves of the groundbreaking artist, philosopher and actor Bruce Lee, and his son, Brandon, that the cemetery provides a map on its website. Pay your respects and then honor Lee's legacy of advocacy for Asian-Americans with a visit to the Wing Luke Museum, located in Chinatown-International District.

NEARBY BONUS: Just a few blocks away from the cemetery, find another sweet and unusual landmark, the Seattle Wishing Tree (at E. Galer St. and 21st Ave. E.)., where passers-by can write wishes or notes of gratitude and read others' words (a fun task for beginning readers).

FINE PRINT: Lakeview Cemetery, 1554 15th Ave. E., Seattle.
lakeviewcemeteryassociation.com/popup_lee_map.php

Henry Murals   FREE
Multiple locations, Seattle

In about 2008, a series of whimsical murals started appearing around Seattle's Ballard neighborhood. Each quixotic painting was populated by surreal animal characters and signed "Henry." Artist Ryan Henry Ward exploded on the Seattle scene through sheer persistence. At times homeless and working for free in the early days, he has now sold more than 2,000 canvases, yet he still makes murals. You'll find more than 200 Henry murals around Seattle, with the highest concentration near his studio in Ballard. Start your search for Henrys with the goldfish house at Nickerson Street by the Fremont Bridge, and end at Naked City Brewery in Greenwood, which also sports a Henry.

GOOD TO KNOW: Once you know about Henry murals, you'll spot them all over town, but if you like to be efficient, use the online Henry map to find them faster.

FINE PRINT: Multiple locations, Seattle. ryanhenryward.com

Museum of History and Industry
Lake Union Park, Seattle

Much of Seattle's funky past has been paved over, making it impossible to see past favorite landmarks "in the wild." But the Museum of History and Industry (MOHAI), at

WINTER

CULTURE

Lake Union Park, has saved some of the best artifacts for display. You can see the Toe Truck with its 11.5-foot-tall, cab-mounted, bright pink toes; the original neon "R" that marked the Rainier Brewery for 50 years; and other locally significant objects.

NEARBY BONUS: The Center for Wooden Boats is also worth a visit while you're at Lake Union Park.

FINE PRINT: Open daily. $19.95 adult, kids 14 and younger free; free on first Thursday. 860 Terry Ave. N., Seattle. 206-324-1126. mohai.org

Dick's Drive-In
Multiple locations, Seattle
Dick's Drive-In was serving Seattle inexpensive and addictive late-night burgers when McDonald's was still just an idea. It's never tried to expand beyond our region, and it's kept its prices low — Dick's is still a place kids can afford with their own money.

GOOD TO KNOW: Pay respects to the original Seattle shop on N. 45th St. in Wallingford, or visit the Broadway location (on Capitol Hill), which was name-checked by Sir Mix-a-lot and filmed by Macklemore for one of his videos.

FINE PRINT: Open daily. Multiple locations. ddir.com

> ## More like this:
> ➤ **Stairway Walks (Adventure 9)**
> ➤ **Live Like a Tourist (Adventure 21)**
> ➤ **Hidden-Gem Playgrounds With a View (Adventure 25)**

46.
Global Bakeries

By JiaYing Grygiel

A bakery visit is an indulgence that won't break the bank, and — considering how international the Puget Sound region's bakery scene has become — kids might also learn something about a different culture. To sweeten the deal, we've paired each bakery with a nearby outing. Sugar in, sugar out — right?

Kiki Bakery

North Seattle, Redmond

At Kiki Bakery, you're free to linger as long as you like over the selection of Taiwanese pastries. Consider the taro mochi bun or a green tea and red bean bun. The hard-to-find pineapple cakes are worth searching for. Don't let the name of the pork floss bun scare you. It's a savory bread topped with dried, shredded pork. Pork floss, or rousong, is a staple for Chinese kids, just like mac and cheese is for kids in the U.S.

NEARBY BONUS: Kiki Bakery's Aurora location is next to the Asian Food Center, where you can pick up tropical produce such as dragon fruit and longans. Then take your kids to the free "zoo" next door — the PetSmart store.

FINE PRINT: Open daily. Kiki Bakery has two Seattle-area locations: 13200 Aurora Ave., Suite E, Seattle, 206-617-7688; 15230 24th St., Suite O, Redmond. 425-728-8056. kikibakery.com

Cafe Besalu

Ballard, Seattle

Even on a weekday morning, this tiny bakery bustles with happy carb-seekers of all types, from a dozing newborn and her family to a hipster couple with a little dog. Crunch into a Besalu flaky croissant dabbed with nectarine jam and summer explodes in your mouth. Cafe Besalu is famous for its croissants, but my oldest child's favorite is the ginger biscuit, with just a tingle of spice and a whole lot of sugar crystals on top.

NEARBY BONUS: Ballard Playspace, just a mile away, is a free indoor play mecca inside a neighborhood church.

FINE PRINT: *Open daily. Cafe Besalu, 5909 24th Ave. N.W., Seattle. 206-789-1463.* cafebesalu.com

Hello Robin Bakery

Capitol Hill, Seattle

Robin Wehl Martin, who opened her cheerful blue and white bakery in 2013 with a nudge from her friend, Molly Moon Neitzel, has built a sizable following. The baking happens on a big kitchen island in the center of the room; just pull up a stool to watch. You'll find a dozen or so kinds of cookies a day, including regular flavors and seasonal specials, as well as ice cream sammies made with a scoop of Molly Moon's ice cream. A walk-up Molly Moon's window is open seasonally.

NEARBY BONUS: Just a short walk down 19th Avenue is Miller Community Center, a neighborhood hub with a playground, a free and well-stocked toddler gym and, in the summer, a spray park.

FINE PRINT: *Open daily. Hello Robin, 522 19th Ave. E., Seattle. 206-735-7970.* hellorobincookies.com

Despi Delite Bakery

Beacon Hill, Seattle; Everett

Two words: purple pastries. At Despi Delite Bakery in Seattle's Beacon Hill neighborhood, you'll find ube (purple yam) — the star of many Filipino desserts — marbled in a loaf, sprinkled with shredded cheese and sugar in the ensaymada, and tucked inside sweet rolls. Another irresistible pick is the pan de coco, a hamburger-size sweet bun stuffed with coconut.

NEARBY BONUS: Despi Delite Bakery is one block from the Beacon Hill light rail station and just two blocks from the Beacon Hill branch of the Seattle Public Library.

FINE PRINT: *Open daily, except Monday (for the Seattle location). Despi Delite Bakery, 2701 15th Ave. S., Seattle. 206-325-2114. 3713 Broadway, Everett. 425-249-2295.* despidelitebakery.com

Yummy House

Chinatown–International District, Seattle

Get a taste for Hong Kong–style desserts, which are light and not too sweet, at this beloved bakery that sits kitty-corner from Asian specialty supermarket Uwajimaya in the International District. Our go-to celebratory cake is the fresh mango. Yummy House also makes buns that are big and bready; crowd-pleasers are the red bean bun, lotus seed bun and taro bun.

NEARBY BONUS: Just a few blocks away, the Donnie Chin International Children's Park features a bronze dragon created by artist Gerard Tsutakawa, as well as other sculptures kids can climb, and a play structure.

FINE PRINT: Open daily. Yummy House, 522 Sixth Ave. S., Seattle. 206-340-8838. facebook.com/yummyhousebakery

The Salvadorean Bakery
White Center
This bakery/restaurant/grocery store carries an impressive array of goods from Latin American countries as well as Mexican pastries. Try the empanada de guayaba, which is like a (better) Pop-Tart filled with guava jam, minus the frosting. Look for special seasonal breads, such as Day of the Dead bread.

NEARBY BONUS: A bicycle playground is a short drive away, at Dick Thurnau Memorial Park, so bring along wheels for the kids.

FINE PRINT: Open daily. Salvadorean Bakery, 1719 S.W. Roxbury St., Seattle. 206-762-4064. thesalvadoreanbakery.com

85°C Bakery Cafe
Federal Way, Lynnwood, Tukwila
This wildly popular Hong Kong–based chain of Taiwanese bakeries is famous for fabulous fresh pastries at modest prices — most items are less than $3. It opened its first outlet at Westfield Southcenter in 2017, and followed with branches at Alderwood Mall and Federal Way's Pavilion Centre. The menu includes 50 varieties of pastries that are baked hourly (many varieties of brioche, puff pastry and cheese strudel), as well as bread, cakes and drinks. Look for Coffee Monday deals: A cuppa for 85 cents.

GOOD TO KNOW: This place is famous for its lines, so time your visit accordingly.

FINE PRINT: Multiple locations; find addresses and hours on website. 85cbakerycafe.com

> ## More like this:
> ➤ **Hidden Seattle Center (Adventure 20)**
> ➤ **Sweet Ice Cream Spots (Adventure 22)**
> ➤ **Destination Libraries (Adventure 48)**

WINTER

CULTURE

COURTESY THE MUSEUM OF FLIGHT

Museum of Flight

47.

Geektastic Outings

By Kali Sakai

We live in a metropolitan area peppered with high-tech, biotech, aerospace and gaming companies, and our climate is often conducive to hunkering down indoors. Is it any wonder geekery thrives around Seattle? The opportunities to have a blast with your young nerd in training increase every year.

Living Computer Museum and Labs

SoDo, Seattle

Opened in 2016, the Living Computer Museum is a temple of retro geekdom. This 15,000-square-foot facility houses a Paul Allen–assembled collection of 60-odd vintage computers that have been meticulously restored and are still functional. You can show your kids what it was like to "boot" a computer and use floppy disks; they can also experiment with writing computer programming in BASIC, play vintage computer games and try a teletype.

WINTER

CULTURE

NEARBY BONUS: Kids can play at another retro-geek mecca, the Seattle Pinball Museum, in the Chinatown–International District just 1.5 miles away.

FINE PRINT: Closed Monday–Tuesday. $14–$16, ages 5 and younger free; free first Thursday (and open late). Living Computer Museum and Labs, 2245 First Ave. S., Seattle. 206-342-2020. livingcomputers.org

Museum of Popular Culture (MoPop)
Seattle Center

Originally created to showcase music, this iconic museum was developed by Paul Allen and designed by famed architect Frank Gehry, who took inspiration from the shape of a smashed guitar. Now the museum also explores the culture and history of popular culture, from gaming to comics and movies. Geeks will especially love its collection of science fiction memorabilia, which includes "Star Wars" items such as Darth Vader's light saber. You can also rock out in the Sound Lab and explore temporary exhibits.

NEARBY BONUS: Climb and swing at the adventurous (and free) Artists at Play playground, right next to MoPop at Seattle Center. For lunch, try the Collections Café at Chihuly Garden and Glass.

FINE PRINT: Open daily. $19–$28, free 4 and younger; online discount. MoPop, 325 Fifth Ave. N., Seattle. 206-770-2700. mopop.org

The Museum of Flight
SoDo, Seattle

Explore aeronautical history and the triumph of human persistence at one of the largest private air and space museums in the world. Start with the Aviation Pavilion, a 3-acre covered outside gallery featuring 19 rare commercial and military airplanes. Get up close and personal with the world's fastest aircraft, the Blackbird spy plane, in the Great Gallery. In the Kid's Flight Zone, pilots in training can test a hang-gliding simulator, explore aircraft instrumentation and see working models of engines. Exciting flight simulator experiences are also available.

GOOD TO KNOW: Space fans 10 and older should be sure to get tickets ahead of time for the space shuttle trainer tour.

FINE PRINT: Open daily. $14–$22, ages 4 and younger free; online discount; half-price admission after 3 p.m. Monday–Friday; free first Thursday from 5–9 p.m. The Museum of Flight, 9404 E. Marginal Way S., Seattle. 206-764-5700. museumofflight.org

WINTER

CULTURE

Cinerama
Downtown Seattle

Seattle's Cinerama, renovated in the late 1990s and again in 2010, balances a lush, nostalgic, mid-century movie theater ambiance with state-of-the-art digital 3-D technology. Visit other worlds under the starry-sky ceiling, which is illuminated during previews in this 808-seat piece of history. For extra fun, munch on your chocolate popcorn and Full Tilt ice cream in the lobby as you gawk at sci-fi movie memorabilia on loan from the Paul G. Allen collection.

NEARBY BONUS: Around the corner, Tom Douglas' Cantina Leña serves modern Mexican food.

CON ARTISTS

Emerald City Comic Con (held in March every year) is the most well known of the "cons" but there are plenty of other family-friendly conventions that provide opportunities to cosplay (dress up as your favorite character) and meet experts in the gaming, comics and film industries. Other top cons include Sakura-Con (anime) in April, PAX Prime (gaming) in August/September, and BrickCon (Lego) and GeekGirlCon in October.

FINE PRINT: *Open daily. Tickets start at $15. Cinerama, 2100 Fourth Ave. S., Seattle. 206-448-6680.* cinerama.com

Comic book shops
Multiple locations

As a cornerstone of geekdom, the comic book shop is sacred. Make a pilgrimage to the mecca known as Golden Age Collectables (the oldest comic shop in the U.S.), located in the heart of Pike Place Market. It sells a wide selection of comics, collectible merchandise and toys. Other shops to explore include Arcane Comics and More (Shoreline), Alter Ego Comics and Collectibles (Bellevue), Corner Comics (Kirkland) and Fantasium Comics and Games (Federal Way). A promising newcomer on the scene is Fremont's Outsider Comics and Geek Boutique, a physical space dedicated to bringing together individuals (such as women, minorities and LGBTQ groups) who identify with geek culture, but have traditionally not been well served by comic shops.

GOOD TO KNOW: One of the best days to check out a new comics store (if you're okay with crowds) is Free Comic Book Day, held the first Saturday of each May.

FINE PRINT: *Golden Age Collectables is located on a lower level of Pike Place Market, Seattle.* goldenagecollectables.com. *Check websites of other comic stories for their hours and locations.*

WINTER

CULTURE

Gaming centers
Various locations

From role-playing games (RPG) to board games to video games and beyond, Seattle has many places to play and meet other game lovers. Start with downtown Seattle video arcade wonderland, GameWorks. Or unplug with a new board game at Blue Highway Games (Queen Anne), Meeples Games (West Seattle) or super family-friendly Mox Boarding House (Ballard or Bellevue). Check out Mox's attached restaurants and a designated kids' room in the Ballard location. Other hot gaming spots include Uncle's Games (Bellevue, Redmond) and Games and Gizmos (Kirkland).

GOOD TO KNOW: At many of the board game stores, you can choose a game from the lending library to test-drive it before buying.

FINE PRINT: *See businesses' websites for addresses and hours of operation.*

Seattle CoderDojo   FREE

Are your geeks in training looking to develop new skills? Kids 8–17 can learn how to write computer code and develop websites, apps, programs and games from an army of computer science professional volunteers through the group CoderDojo, which has branches around the world. To participate, kids will need to bring a Wi-Fi-enabled laptop running Windows, OS X (Mac) or Linux with at least two hours of battery life. Check the website for specifics.

GOOD TO KNOW: If you don't have a laptop, CoderDojo usually has a limited supply of loaners on hand.

FINE PRINT: *Free. CoderDojo is usually held 2–4 p.m. on Sundays at an Amazon location, but the program goes on hiatus over the summer. Check the website.* seattlecoderdojo.com

More like this:
- ➤ **Pinball, Putt-Putt and More Old-School Fun (Adventure 8)**
- ➤ **For Love of Legos (Adventure 36)**
- ➤ **Quirky Landmarks (Adventure 45)**

WINTER

CULTURE

JIAYING GRYGIEL

Suzzallo Library

48.
Destination Libraries

By JiaYing Grygiel

Libraries used to be places where you went to check out a book or ask a question at the reference desk. Now, libraries are all that and much more, with a huge roster of activities, programs, services and attractions that make some branches bona fide tourist destinations. The Seattle area's showstopping libraries include one that is shaped like a boat, one that has a rooftop garden, and even a library built over a river.

The best part? Everything is still free.

Ballard Branch, Seattle Public Library
Ballard, Seattle

The Ballard branch is the Chia Pet of the Seattle library system. On top of its roof is 4 inches of soil planted with more than 18,000 Northwest native plants. To see for yourself, ask library staff to take you upstairs to look around, or use a periscope on the main level to check out the roof; look for the periscope's two unmarked slits in the wall, just to the right as you walk through the branch's main entrance. Another attraction at this library, one of the busiest in the city, is a kids' section that includes Magna-Tiles and big Legos.

WINTER

CULTURE

NEARBY BONUS: Within a three-block radius, you can pick your poison: Cupcake Royale, Clover (toy store), Secret Garden Books and Sweet Mickey's candy shop. We love getting the extra-large bowl of pho beef noodle soup from Pho Than Brothers on Market Street.

FINE PRINT: Open daily. Ballard branch, 5614 22nd Ave. N.W., Seattle. 206-684-4089. spl.org/hours-and-locations/ballard-branch

Suzzallo Library
University District, Seattle

Everyone calls it the "Harry Potter room." With its Gothic details, vaulted ceilings, stained-glass windows and ornate bookcases, the Reading Room at the University of Washington's Suzzallo Library does look like the stuff of fiction. The University of Washington is a public institution, so anyone can visit the library and use the materials on-site. Note: The Reading Room is a self-identified "silent zone," so prep kids ahead of time. Just outside the Reading Room is one of the world's biggest books, a photo book about Bhutan.

NEARBY BONUS: The campus is also home to two museums that are good for kids: the Henry Art Gallery (free on Sundays); and the Burke Museum (free on the first Thursday of the month), which covers natural history and culture. If you have a dinosaur fan, the Burke's playroom is a must.

FINE PRINT: Open daily. Suzzallo Library, University of Washington, 4000 15th Ave. N.E., Seattle. lib.washington.edu

Elisabeth C. Miller Library
Laurelhurst, Seattle

It's the library no one knows about, and the nicest people work there. The Miller Library, located at the UW Center for Urban Horticulture, is a horticulture library. Once a month, the library hosts a children's story time, followed by an art activity. And yes, it has a children's section, a sunny nook with more than 700 kids' books. Topics are wide-ranging, from bees to seeds. Anyone can register to check out books at the Miller Library. There is even a free parking lot.

NEARBY BONUS: After book time, a hike is in order. Explore the five display gardens at the Center for Urban Horticulture campus, and find a trail at the 74-acre Union Bay Natural area, where 200 species of birds have been spotted. The Yesler Swamp boardwalk trail is popular with bird-watchers.

FINE PRINT: Open daily, except Sunday. UW Center for Urban Horticulture, 501 N.E. 41st St., Seattle. 206-543-0415. depts.washington.edu/hortlib

WINTER

CULTURE

Central Library, Seattle Public Library

Seattle

The Central Library, which opened in 2004 to a collective gasp from the architecture community, is an iconic building at the heart of the Seattle library system, and its hot-pink children's section is so vast, it's practically like its own branch. But don't stop there: Take the elevator up to the 10th floor to find a dizzying lookout point, from which you can peer all the way down to the lobby. On the fourth floor, the walls, ceilings and floors are all painted trippy shades of deep pink and red.

NEARBY BONUS: Two blocks from the library is Columbia Center, where you can get a 360-degree view of the city from the observation deck on the 73rd floor. Or get off at the 40th floor and enjoy the (free) view from Starbucks.

FINE PRINT: *Open daily. Central Library, 1000 Fourth Ave., Seattle. 206-386-4636. spl.org/hours-and-locations/central-library*

Beacon Hill Branch, Seattle Public Library

Beacon Hill, Seattle

This branch is known for welcoming everyone, especially the immigrants and refugees who live in the diverse Beacon Hill neighborhood, and the architecture of the building echoes that warmth. The library is shaped like a giant ship, and stepping inside is like walking into the belly of an overturned boat. Wood and stone materials keep the vibe cozy, and big windows flood the interior with light.

NEARBY BONUS: Arrive at the library by Link light rail; there's a stop just across the street. Find sweet snacks at Despi Delite Bakery; and there are epic play structures at Jefferson Park, less than a mile south of the library.

FINE PRINT: *Open daily. Beacon Hill branch, 2821 Beacon Ave. S., Seattle. 206-684-4711. spl.org/hours-and-locations/beacon-hill-branch*

Sammamish Library

Sammamish

Find a book and settle into a comfy seat by the fireplace. You might feel like you are at a fancy lodge — one that happens to be stuffed with books. The Sammamish Library is modern, light and bright, with walls of windows and yes, a glass-enclosed gas fireplace. The children's area is partially corralled by a row of bookcases, helpful if your children tend to be escape artists.

NEARBY BONUS: Pack your swim stuff. Next door to the library is a YMCA with a family swimming pool that has a two-story waterslide, lazy river and a shallow wading area.

WINTER

CULTURE

It's also on the edge of a 25-acre, two-level park called Sammamish Commons, which includes a skate park, playground, swings, sand pit and spray park.

FINE PRINT: *Open daily. Sammamish Library, 825 228th Ave. S.E., Sammamish. 425-392-3130*. kcls.org/locations/1534

Bellevue Library

Bellevue

The biggest library in the King County Library System, the Bellevue branch also has the largest staff (six children's librarians alone). Sometimes, size does matter. The building is modern and inviting, with a grand staircase, skylights and big windows. The children's section is located on the first floor; look for the story time room's special child-size entrance. Creative older kids will want to spend time in the IdeaX Makerspace, a workspace outfitted with art kits, sewing machines, a Cricut cutting machine, sound-recording equipment and more to help kids and adults create. (Check the library schedule for drop-in sessions and workshops.)

NEARBY BONUS: It's easy to pair a visit to the Bellevue Library with playtime at KidsQuest Children's Museum, located next door. But be warned that the library's large parking lot is for patrons only.

FINE PRINT: *Open daily. Bellevue Library, 1111 110th Ave. N.E., Bellevue. 425-450-1765.* kcls.org/locations/1492

Renton Library

Renton

The most distinctive feature of the King County Library System's Renton branch is that it's built over the Cedar River. The library rests on 12 giant columns on an 80-foot bridge. You can sit by the floor-to-ceiling windows with a book and watch the mallards paddling in the river. Stop by the library during Renton River Days in July to watch rubber ducks float downstream, and in early fall to see salmon making their annual migration.

NEARBY BONUS: The library sits on the edge of Liberty Park, which has a playground, baseball field and skate park. It's also next to the Cedar River Trail, terrific for biking and walking.

FINE PRINT: *Open daily. Renton Library, 100 Mill Ave. S., Renton. 425-226-6043.* kcls.org/locations/1556

More like this:
- ➤ **Kid-Friendly Indie Bookstores (Adventure 7)**
- ➤ **Walk-On Ferry Tales (Adventure 23)**
- ➤ **Crafty Museum Spaces (Adventure 34)**

WINTER

CULTURE

KidsQuest Children's Museum

49.
Cool Kids' Museums

By Elisa Murray

If your children can happily play indoors at home for hours, you might dismiss the concept of a children's museum. But spend an afternoon at, say, KidsQuest Children's Museum in Bellevue or Imagine Children's Museum in Everett, and you'll soon become a convert to the variety of unplugged, hands-on play experiences that they offer. And bring friends: You might get a chance for a real conversation as your child deeply engages on driving a fire truck or exploring the physics of balls and ramps.

DOUBLE BONUS: As the Puget Sound area is blessed with a kids' museum in almost every corner, you can easily combine a museum mini adventure with other attractions.

Note: Check museum websites to find out about the specific programs they offer, from special hours for children with autism or sensory issues to camps and classes.

Imagine Children's Museum
Everett

Snohomish County residents would love you to not know about their beloved, three-story museum in downtown Everett. Kids can act on a stage, drive trains on the

WINTER

ADVENTURE

Monte Cristo mining railway, study X-rays in the vet clinic, build in the construction zone and even dig for dino bones in its 9,000-square-foot Tall Timbers Rooftop Adventure outdoor space. Head to the lower level to create in the art studio or eat your snacks. Every third Sunday, Imagine Children's Museum offers a free-admission "Sensory Time" program on Sunday from 9 to 11 a.m.

NEARBY BONUS: Combine with a visit to epic Forest Park, Schack Art Center (across the street from the museum) and (in the summer) Jetty Island.

FINE PRINT: Open daily except Monday. $12, younger than 12 months free; half-price every Thursday 3–5 p.m.; free admission every third Friday 5:30–9 p.m. Imagine Children's Museum, 1502 Wall St., Everett. 425-258-1006, ext. 1000. imaginecm.org

Seattle Children's Museum
Seattle Center

If you haven't stopped by this venerable institution, located in the lower level of the Seattle Center Armory, recently, it's time for another look. Seattle Children's Museum has been busy updating exhibits and adding cultural programming, from a renovated theater to new building equipment for the Dunn Lumber exhibit. The Global Village exhibit is being revamped, and there are regular pop-up cultural events.

NEARBY BONUS: Upstairs in the Armory, find free Festál cultural festivals almost every weekend.

FINE PRINT: Open daily. $10.50–$11.50, younger than 12 months free; the last hour of the day (4–5 p.m.) is discounted admission. Every first Saturday, it opens its doors early for a "sensory hour," for kids with autism. Seattle Children's Museum, 305 Harrison St., Seattle. 206-441-1768. thechildrensmuseum.org

KidsQuest Children's Museum
Bellevue

KidsQuest Children's Museum's spacious home in downtown Bellevue stars huge windows, beautifully designed exhibits and an adventurous, two-story ropes-and-ladders climber in the atrium. Kids of all ages will love cranking boxes up and down conveyor belts in the On the Go gallery; building with real tools next door in the Recycled Rebuild room; or conducting physics experiments in the Water lab. Other highlights include lots of seating for grown-ups and an outdoor area with "loose parts" for kids to build with.

NEARBY BONUS: Combine your trip with a visit to the Bellevue downtown library next door (but don't park there!) or Bellevue Downtown Park and its fantastic playground.

WINTER ADVENTURE

FINE PRINT: Open Tuesday–Sunday; open late on Friday. $11.50–$12.50, younger than 12 months free. You can reserve museum passes through King County library's museum pass program. KidsQuest Children's Museum, 1116 108th Ave. N.E., Bellevue. 425-637-8100. kidsquestmuseum.org

Kids Discovery Museum
Bainbridge Island

Location, location. Just a short walk from the Winslow Ferry Terminal on Bainbridge Island, the small but awesome Kids Discovery Museum (KiDiMu) works well as part of a day trip to the island. And for some families, the museum's small size — 5,000 square feet — will be a draw, as it's easier to keep track of multiple kids. Kids always love the pirate tree house, the huge Light Wall and the electric car. Older kids will be drawn to the second floor's "Motion Madness" exhibit. Sensory Sundays is KiDiMu's monthly program that supports children with autism.

NEARBY BONUS: Bainbridge brims with nature and cultural fun, from the always-free Bainbridge Island Art Museum (next door to KiDiMu) to the lovely, wild Bloedel Reserve.

FINE PRINT: Open Tuesday–Sunday. $7–$8, younger than 12 months free; free first Thursday. Kids Discovery Museum, 301 Ravine Lane N.E., Bainbridge Island. 206-855-4650. kidimu.org

Children's Museum of Tacoma
Tacoma

Since it opened in 2012, Children's Museum of Tacoma has offered pay-what-you-wish admission, which means that you can stop off for an hour without worrying about whether you've gotten your money's worth. The museum is built around four play scapes (Woods, Water, Invention and Voyager), and favorite activities include the wood-cabin tunnel, water table, marine vessel with tower, air pipes, lit Lego table and art studio (called Becka's Studio).

NEARBY BONUS: Children's Museum of Tacoma partners with Tacoma Art Museum (TAM) on an innovative program: Families create an art project related to a TAM exhibit, and then can visit TAM with a free Family Explorer Pass to see the actual exhibit.

FINE PRINT: Open daily, except Monday, when it's members only. Admission is pay what you wish. Children's Museum of Tacoma, 1501 Pacific Ave., Tacoma. 253-627-6031. playtacoma.org

Hands On Children's Museum
Olympia

My son's eyes still light up whenever I mention "that museum in Olympia." At 28,000 square feet, it really does seem to have it all: an "emergency" area with fire truck, helicopter and cop car; a tugboat; a climber/slide to the third floor; a scream room where kids can measure their decibels; and a maker space. Step outside and you'll find another half-acre of creative fun, including a driftwood building area and a trike track.

NEARBY BONUS: In the summer, a reclaimed-water stream runs in front of the museum, where kids can splash and wade without paying an admission charge. The free-admission WET Science Center (designed for older kids) is across the street.

FINE PRINT: *Open daily. $11.95–$13.95, ages younger than 2 free (ticket still required); free every first Friday, 5–9 p.m. Hands On Children's Museum, 414 Jefferson St. N.E., Olympia. 360-956-0818.* hocm.org

More like this:
- ➤ **Summer Splurges (Adventure 24)**
- ➤ **Crafty Museum Spaces (Adventure 34)**
- ➤ **Swimming Pool Getaways (Adventure 52)**

50.
Rainy-Day Playgrounds

By Linnea Westerlind

As the mom of three very energetic boys, I've learned the hard way that, rain or shine, we have to get out of the house every morning before 9 a.m. Though it can be tough to leave, once we're active — whether hiking on a trail with good tree cover or watching a storm roll in on a beach — it's always exhilarating. These play spots offer plenty of wet-day thrills, as well as a nearby warm-up spot.

Richmond Beach Saltwater Park   FREE
Shoreline
Everyone likes this stunning park in Shoreline, but families with dogs feel like they've found nirvana, at least in the winter: From Nov. 1 to March 15, this Shoreline park includes an off-leash area right on the beach. Play fetch with your pup, dig in the sand and explore the driftwood forts. Watch the whitecaps from a shelter on the beach or head to another shelter at the ship-inspired playground above the beach.

WINTER

ADVENTURE

Miner's Corner County Park   FREE

Bothell

This spacious Bothell park, designed for kids of all abilities, has been wildly popular ever since it opened in 2013. A flat, paved half-mile path — perfect for beginning bikers — meanders around the park. The three-story climbing structure has a long wheelchair-accessible ramp (reputedly one of the tallest of its kind in the world). Rock-climbing features, bridges, a fire pole and a long spiral slide add to the excitement. And a sand and water garden, fed by rainfall and runoff, invites kids to explore and get muddy.

WARM-UP TIP: Tall trees provide rain protection over an area next to the playground, which has logs and stumps that my kids have been known to turn into a parkour course. If it starts to pour, duck under the large covered structure. Just 2.5 miles away, Crystal Creek Cafe serves breakfast, lunch and dinner in a kid-friendly atmosphere,

FINE PRINT: Miner's Corner County Park, 22903 45th Ave. S.E., Bothell. snohomish.org/explore/detail/miners-corner-park

Blyth Park   FREE

Bothell

Adjacent to the Sammamish River Trail in Bothell, Blyth Park is a 40-acre park that's popular with picnickers. The two covered picnic shelters are just steps away from the playground if the rain becomes steady. The playground has two climbing structures with slides and a little suspension bridge. An interesting structure made of old tires is also a fun place to climb, and kids can look for boats on the river.

WARM-UP TIP: In nearby downtown Bothell, Social Grounds Coffee & Tea Co. sells espresso, pastries, sandwiches and salads.

FINE PRINT: Blyth Park, 16950 W. Riverside Dr., Bothell. ci.bothell.wa.us

SUPER SENSORY PLAYGROUNDS

Miner's Corner and Seattle Children's Play-Garden are examples of a trend in playground design to serve kids of all abilities. These "sensory playgrounds" are designed to be fully accessible for kids with physical limitations, and inclusive and safe for kids on the autism spectrum, with many sensory options for children who seek them. And they typically offer plenty of adventure as well. Find a list at *parentmap.com/sensory*.

Seattle Children's PlayGarden   FREE
Mount Baker, Seattle

This wonderful park, whose playground was updated in 2018, is designed for kids of all abilities. It's fairly small and fully fenced, so parents and caregivers can let little ones explore without worrying about losing them. Kids will find gardens, a large sand area, a tree fort, a boat, farm animals, multi-person swings, balancing structures, a "garden truck" for kids to climb in and much more. Note: The park is also the grounds for a preschool, but is open to the public (check hours on the website). Make sure the gate is securely shut after entering and exiting the park.

WARM-UP TIP: Visit Northwest African American Museum, housed in the historic Colman School building just a half-block from the park (open Wednesday–Sunday).

FINE PRINT: Check online for public hours. Seattle Children's PlayGarden, 1745 24th Ave. S., Seattle. 206-325-5576. childrensplaygarden.org

Mount Baker Park   FREE
Mount Baker, Seattle

A newer tree-house-style playground, with bridges, slides and tricky ladders, is the star attraction at this forested South Seattle park, which stretches a third of a mile down to Lake Washington. Two structures suit older and younger kids alike with slides, instruments and a suspension bridge; and the zipline is one of the city's best, with a fast ride and a thrilling bump at the end. A paved path winds around the park and down to the waterfront under good tree cover.

WINTER

ADVENTURE

WARM-UP TIP: Around the corner from the playground, the adorable, vintage-themed Feed Store serves pour-over coffee, smoothies, fresh produce and other nibbles. Kids love the old-fashioned, coin-operated pony ride.

FINE PRINT: Mount Baker Park, 2521 Lake Park Dr. S., Seattle. seattle.gov/parks

Santos Rodriguez Memorial Park   FREE
Beacon Hill, Seattle

This fully-fenced playground, located in the front yard of Beacon Hill's historic El Centro De La Raza, opened in 2014 to the delight of local families. Kids love the colorful climbing structures, which have little roofs on the tops of each platform, the mosaic art that serves as steppingstones and the demonstration garden. Duck under the covered shelter if rain hits. Note: The playground was named to honor a 12-year-old Mexican-American boy killed by a Dallas police officer in 1973. Look for the small plaque.

WARM-UP TIP: Beacon Hill cafes and eateries are steps away; and you may find food trucks on Plaza Roberto Maestas, a wonderful public space that's next to El Centro and across from the Link light rail station.

FINE PRINT: The playground is closed during child care center hours at El Centro. 2524 16th Ave. S, Seattle. 206-329-9442. elcentrodelaraza.org

Pioneer Park   FREE
Mercer Island

Enjoy a hike along flat trails under a thick tree canopy in the middle of Mercer Island at Pioneer Park. Cedars and other evergreens will keep you mostly dry as you explore this 113-acre natural area. Pioneer Park has three quadrants totaling about 6 miles of trails. In two of the sections, dogs are allowed to go off-leash, so keep an eye out if your kids are nervous around dogs.

NEARBY BONUS: Need to bribe the kids with playground time? Deane's Children's Park (also known as Dragon Park) is a half-mile north, with a large covered area for picnicking.

FINE PRINT: Pioneer Park, Island Crest Way and S.E. 68th St., Mercer Island. mercergov.org/Page.asp?NavID=1116

Lewis Creek Park   FREE
Bellevue

This park in the Cougar Mountain area of south Bellevue feels like a true urban wilderness adventure. If the weather is turning into a deluge, start at the beautifully designed

WINTER

ADVENTURE

visitor center, which offers kids' puzzles, comfortable seats and huge windows that look out over the wetlands. Pick up a scavenger-hunt sheet to take outside on the half-mile loop trail; and consider signing up for one of the center's awesome nature programs.

WARM-UP TIP: Next to the center, find two play areas that both have large sail-like covers that protect from both rain and sun.

FINE PRINT: Visitor center open Wednesday–Sunday. Lewis Creek Park, 5808 Lakemont Blvd. S.E., Bellevue. parks.bellevuewa.gov

Lake Meridian Park   FREE
Kent

The good news about visiting this lakefront park in the off-season is that kids may have its fabulous playground to themselves. The brightly colored, imaginative play equipment (most of which is wheelchair-accessible) includes fun, fast slides and a pirate-ship-like structure that inspires imaginative play. If necessary, take cover in the huge covered shelter nearby.

GOOD TO KNOW: Kids will also enjoy digging at the long, sandy beachfront, or walk out on the dock for access to year-round fishing. Kid-friendly MOD Pizza is about a mile west.

FINE PRINT: Lake Meridian Park, 14800 S.E. 272nd St., Kent. kentwa.gov

Point Defiance Park   FREE
Tacoma

Tacoma's epic park has enough play options to occupy kids for a week, and with several covered shelters to pop under and heavy tree cover, it's great for unpredictable weather. Climb and slide at the playground, get sandy at Owen Beach, hike through old-growth forest on the Inside Loop Trail or fish at the marina's pier. If you have more time, visit the critters and sharks at Point Defiance Zoo & Aquarium.

WARM-UP TIP: The marina, located inside the park, offers snacks and sandwiches. Or warm up at the cozy Antique Sandwich Co., three blocks south.

FINE PRINT: Point Defiance Park, 5400 N. Pearl St., Tacoma. metroparkstacoma.org/point-defiance-park

More like this:
➤ **Spring Hikes, Warm-Up Included (Adventure 6)**
➤ **Stairway Walks (Adventure 9)**
➤ **Epic Playgrounds (Adventure 12)**

WINTER

ADVENTURE

51.
Winning Winter Tours

By Gemma Alexander

When it comes to fun, summer gets most of the love. But families don't have to resign themselves to the relentless school-year routine. These off-the-beaten-path experiences will keep you — and your holiday visitors — entertained through the darkest months. Bonus: Most are educational.

Sunday Ice Cream Cruise
South Lake Union, Seattle

Surprise: This kid-friendly, surprisingly affordable Lake Union tour is open year-round. Departing from Lake Union Park, the cruise leaves on the hour between 11 a.m. and 3 p.m. each Sunday, even in winter. On the lighthearted 45-minute, narrated tour, you'll see Lake Union's floating homes, take a peek at Dale Chihuly's glass studio and get a new perspective of Gas Works Park. Take note: Reservations and credit cards are not accepted.

GOOD TO KNOW: It's short, there's no walking, and food is available, making this tour appropriate for all ages. You can even bring your dog.

FINE PRINT: $8–$12 for cruise, kids 4 and younger $3; ice cream and hot drinks $2–$4. Walk on; no reservations. Lake Union Park, 860 Terry Ave. N., Seattle. 206-713-8446. seattleferryservice.com

Fire station tours
Multiple locations, Seattle

Did you know that Seattle's fire stations are open to residents for free tours upon request? Station tours last approximately 20 minutes and include viewing the fire engine and firefighting equipment, as well as talking to the firefighters about their job. Other local cities, including Renton, Kent and Everett, also have tour programs for fire stations. Check your city's website or call your city hall.

FREE SELF-GUIDED TOURS

Appy walking: GPSmyCity offers 17 different self-guided tours you can download from its website. *gpsmycity.com*

Neighborhood walks: Get to know your neighborhood's arboreal nature with free Tree Walks maps. *seattle.gov/trees/treewalks.htm*

Pike Place Market: Download one of four pocket guides from the Market's website (the "Kids and Families Guide" is the obvious choice). *pikeplacemarket.org/tours-market*

Pressed-penny walk: Do your kids love the pressed-penny machines found at many hotels and attractions? Create your own itinerary at *pennycollector.com.*

STQRY: This app offers guides to local museums and historic sites, as well as neighborhood art guides. *stqry.com*

GOOD TO KNOW: Preschools and daycare programs can take part in the Seattle Fire Department's Smart Kids! Safe Kids! Injury Prevention Program.

FINE PRINT: To request a tour (or a school visit), fill out a form on the seattle.gov page about firefighter tours (or contact your city).

Ballard Locks Tour
Ballard, Seattle

Unlike salmon, you can pass through the Hiram M. Chittenden (Ballard) Locks any time of year on a locks cruise. This two-hour, narrated Argosy cruise takes you around Elliott Bay and Lake Union (where you'll see houseboats and bridges). But the highlight is the slow-motion tension of passing through the narrow locks of the Lake Washington Ship Canal, a thrill for any age.

NEARBY BONUS: Take in more waterfront thrills near Pier 55, including the Seattle

WINTER

ADVENTUR

Aquarium, and continue the water theme by eating at Ivar's Acres of Clams.

FINE PRINT: Schedule changes seasonally; check and book online. $19.50–$47.50, ages 3 and younger free. Several options available for boarding and returning. argosycruises.com

Stadium Tours
SoDo, Seattle
Bring your Hawks superfans for a 90-minute tour of CenturyLink Field offered Friday–Sunday (three tours daily) through the winter. Tickets must be purchased in person. If baseball is your game, take a "behind the seams" tour of Safeco Field and gain access to areas such as the press box, the owners' suite, the field, dugouts, Visitors' Clubhouse and All-Star Club.

GOOD TO KNOW: Team spirit has no age limit, but these tours involve a lot of walking, so plan accordingly.

FINE PRINT: CenturyLink tours: $8–$14, ages 4 and younger free. Tickets must be purchased in person at one of several locations. 800 Occidental Ave. S., Seattle. 206-381-7555. centurylinkfield.com. *Safeco tours: $10–$12; buy tickets online. Tours depart from the Mariners Team Store, First Ave. S. side of Safeco Field, Seattle. 206-346-4241.* mlb.com/mariners/ballpark/tours

Wolf Haven International
Tenino
Add some wildness to your winter by making a reservation for a 50-minute guided tour of the internationally recognized sanctuary of Wolf Haven in Tenino. The tour takes visitors through the public portion of the sanctuary, which provides the opportunity (but not a guarantee) of sighting wolves at home in a naturalistic habitat. A bonus: With thicker winter coats and a higher activity level in the winter, wolves may be easier to spot.

NEARBY BONUS: Make a weekend of it by staying in a cabin at Offut Lake Resort, just a mile away.

FINE PRINT: $7.50–$13, ages 3 and younger free. Visits must be reserved. 3111 Offut Lake Rd. S.E., Tenino. 360-264-4695, 800-448-9653. wolfhaven.org

More like this:
- ➤ **Stairway Walks (Adventure 9)**
- ➤ **Live Like a Tourist (Adventure 21)**
- ➤ **Quirky Landmarks (Adventure 45)**

WINTER

ADVENTURE

Alderbrook Resort & Spa

52.
Swimming Pool Getaways

By Lauren Braden

Seasoned parents know that a hotel pool is a perk that can make a vacation for a kid. But here's a radical idea: What if the steamy hotel pool is the destination? All of these hotel options boast terrific pools where children are welcome (though a few pools may have restricted hours; check when you book). And they're all less than a two-hour drive from Seattle.

Tips: Pack an extra suit and your own beach towels, just in case. Hotel pools rarely have lifeguards on duty, so keep a close eye on your kids in the pool.

Suncadia
Cle Elum

Surrounded by thousands of acres of ponderosa pine forest and snowcapped Cascade peaks, this deluxe 254-room lodge near Roslyn has plenty going for it, both inside (a grand lobby with fireplace and several cozy nooks, luxury guest rooms with soaker tubs and million-dollar views) and outside (hiking and biking trails, cross-country skiing and sledding in winter). Just a short walk from the lodge sits Suncadia's ultramodern swimming pool facility and fitness center, boasting a huge indoor pool with two adventurous waterslides, a hot tub, steam room and cedar sauna, plus two heated, steamy outdoor

WINTER

ESCAPES

BIG THRILLS AT GREAT WOLF LODGE

At Grand Mound's Great Wolf Lodge, the hotel is all pool, of course — a 56,000-square-foot indoor water park featuring thrilling rides, such as the Howlin' Tornado and a zero-depth-entry wave pool with 3-foot swells. Stay in one of the themed rooms, and be sure to maximize your stay: You can use the pool as early as 1 p.m. on the day of check-in, and play until closing on the day you leave. Your PTA membership gets you a discount; also look for Groupon coupons and specials on the website. *greatwolf.com/grand-mound*

pools. Note: Unless you book a special package, there's an additional resort fee for access to pool and fitness facilities.

GOOD TO KNOW: In December, Suncadia plans a range of holiday activities, including Santa sightings, "elf tuck-ins," ice skating and more. Check the resort's website for details.

FINE PRINT: From $175/night (plus resort fee). Suncadia Resort, 3600 Suncadia Trail, Cle Elum. 509-649-6461. suncadiaresort.com

McMenamins Anderson School

Bothell

Your kids may recoil at the thought of going to "school" for a weekend getaway, but rest assured there's nothing academic about splashing around in a huge indoor pool ringed with tropical plants. Converted from an Art Deco junior high school building into McMenamins' offbeat hotel, the Anderson School seems tailor-made for near-home weekend getaways. After a few hours in the ultrawarm saltwater pool, kids can play a few rounds of shuffleboard or pinball at The Woodshop pub and game room (there are three restaurants in all!).

NEARBY BONUS: Catch a first-run flick at the on-site movie theater; there's almost always a kid-friendly choice.

FINE PRINT: From $195/night. McMenamins Anderson School, 18607 Bothell Way N.E., Bothell. 425-398-0122. mcmenamins.com/anderson-school

Hotel Bellevue

Bellevue

Attached to the exclusive Bellevue Athletic Club, this posh hotel gives guests full use of the luxurious club's many fitness facilities, including its two beautiful Olympic-size indoor pools set at different temperatures (there's an outdoor heated pool as well) and two-tiered hot tubs. Also complimentary is the use of the fitness facility's indoor tennis courts, multiple cardio rooms, racquetball courts, Pilates studio, climbing gym and more. In addition, there's a full-service spa, four restaurants and a professionally staffed child-care room.

GOOD TO KNOW: Though it's several blocks from downtown shopping, the hotel provides two chauffeured town cars available for guests, who pay gratuity only. Look for discounted web specials as winter sets in.

FINE PRINT: From $175/night. Hotel Bellevue, 11200 S.E. Sixth St., Bellevue. 800-579-1110. bellevueclubhotel.com

Alderbrook Resort & Spa
Union

Hood Canal is shaped like an arm, and right at its "elbow" sits the tiny and picturesque town of Union. Once the vacation destination for the families of wealthy Seattle lumber barons, Union retains its appeal as a nearby, scenic getaway, thanks in large part to the refurbished Craftsman-style Alderbrook Resort & Spa. Alderbrook's large lobby is anchored by a huge stone fireplace and supported by peeled-log architecture, creating a cozy, rustic ambiance. Guest rooms are modern and deluxe and there are also several cute cottages with kitchenettes. And what a pool! It's huge, heated and glass-enclosed, so you can look directly out to Hood Canal while you swim. Or watch kids swim as you hit the whirlpool jets in the large, kidney-shaped hot tub that is next to the pool.

GOOD TO KNOW: There is also a steam room, sauna, fitness center, and an on-site spa.

FINE PRINT: From $222/night (but look for specials). Alderbrook Resort, 10 E. Alderbrook Dr., Union. 360-898-2100. alderbrookresort.com

More like this:
➤ **One-of-a-Kind Getaways (Adventure 14)**
➤ **Diveworthy Outdoor Pools (Adventure 27)**
➤ **Volcano Escapes (Adventure 29)**

WINTER

ESCAPES

Get Out and Do Good

Shake off the winter doldrums by starting a family volunteer habit that will last all year. In the process, you can help kids explore interests such as gardening, critters or cooking. Here's a starter list.

Create care kits: Buy basics in bulk for homeless people — energy bars, socks, hand wipes, lip balm — and get a group together to make care kits that you can hand out at street corners and bus stops. Kids can make cards to brighten somebody's day.

Drive for good: Turn your car into a do-good-mobile — and your kids into your deputy do-gooders — by picking up and delivering donations for organizations such as those listed below.

Empower teens: Older teens are eligible to volunteer independently for many types of causes. Check *parentmap.com/teenvolunteer* for ideas.

Foster an animal: Fostering an animal through organizations like PAWS or Seattle Humane can help children learn responsibility and build empathy and compassion. Families can also help raise money, donate needed items or participate in events like the annual PAWSwalk.

Garden for good: Want to flex your family's green thumb for a cause? Late winter is the perfect time to begin thinking about planting a giving garden or helping grow one in a local community garden.

Help the hungry: Kids and parents can work together to repackage bulk food at food banks and related nonprofits, such as Food Lifeline, Northwest Harvest or St. Leo Food Connection in Tacoma. Perks include getting to watch trucks and conveyor belts in action, and practicing counting skills.

Home-based help: With your kitchen table designated as your "doing-good HQ," you can write cards to veterans, sick children or seniors; decorate placemats for Meals on Wheels; or make care kits.

Host a student: Learn about another country firsthand by hosting an international student for a homestay. Check organizations such as EarthCorps, the Foundation for International Understanding Through Students (FIUTS) or AFS-USA.

Plant trees: It's hard to beat the earthy pleasure of planting trees, doing battle with invasive plants or cleaning up a beach. Find events run by the likes of Mountains to Sound Greenway, Nature Consortium and the Tacoma Nature Center.

Senior visits: Call up that nursing home down the road and see if you can bring the kids for a visit (extra points for budding musicians). Check senior centers, elderly day-care facilities, nursing homes and nonprofits such as North East Seattle Together (NEST), which helps seniors age in place.

Sort baby clothes and toys: Let your kids practice sorting skills by helping nonprofits organize incoming donations of children's clothes and material goods. Examples include WestSide Baby, Eastside Baby Corner, Hopelink and Treehouse, which runs a free store for kids in foster care.

Trail build: If your kids are comfortable with hiking, join a Washington Trails Association (WTA) work party to maintain trails in some of the most beautiful spots in the region.

More online: Online tools abound for helping you find a volunteer match. Try Doing Good Together; GenerationOn; Learning to Give; or Do Something, a useful resource for older kids and teens.

WINTER

WANDER LIST

Checklist for Year-Round Fun

When you're raising humans, the days can seem long, but the years are short. So, you've got to plan carefully to hit some of the Puget Sound area's best annual events while your kids are still young.

Here's your mini bucket list of cool holidays, festivals and more. You won't find biggies like Easter and Halloween, but you will find Star Wars Reads, National Coffee Day and the Skagit Tulip Festival. (Find more on ParentMap's online calendar at *parentmap.com/calendar.*)

IMPORTANT: Check festival dates and venues, and then go forth and have fun!

JANUARY

Polar bear plunges: Take an exhilarating New Year's Day dip in locations ranging from Matthews Beach in Seattle to Gene Coulon Memorial Beach Park in Renton.

Bald Eagle Festival: View wintering bald eagles along the Skagit River. The festival includes story times, science activities and other kid fun.

Dr. Martin Luther King, Jr. March: Give your kids a taste of history by joining this annual march in Seattle on the Saturday before MLK Day.

Children's Film Festival Seattle: Detox from Disney at this one-of-a-kind Seattle festival featuring films from around the world.

Monkeyshines: Tacoma's Lunar New Year guerrilla-art event is a citywide treasure hunt for glass art.

FEBRUARY

Lunar New Year: Find enthralling firecrackers, lion dances, dumplings and quieter cultural fun at local festivals. Depending on the lunar calendar, it's celebrated in January or February.

Kids 'n' Critters: The annual winter festival at Northwest Trek is a great bargain: As many as four kids are admitted for free with each paying adult.

MARCH

First viewing at Seattle Japanese Garden: Held on the first Sunday in March, this event includes a Shinto blessing and kid-friendly performances.

Holi: Known as the "festival of colors," this Indian Hindu holiday is celebrated at Lake Sammamish State Park and other Eastside locales.

Pi Day: Bake a pie for the neighbors, look for pie deals and try to explain 3.14 to your kids.

St. Patrick's Day Parade: Marching bands, bagpipes and dancers parade down Fourth Avenue in downtown Seattle.

Emerald City Comic Con: Bust out that Star Wars costume and get tickets as early as you can for this cosplay extravaganza.

APRIL

Sheep shearing at Kelsey Creek Farm: Annual fun fest at Bellevue's urban farm celebrates the Eastside's rural heritage.

Tulip Festival: Visiting Skagit Valley's Technicolor fields is a fun family tradition and usually lasts through the month of April.

Procession of the Species: Olympia's annual Earth Day procession is one of the region's best annual parades.

Washington State Spring Fair: This more low-key version of the September giant features rides, entertainment, monster trucks and animals.

Daffodil Festival: The South Sound celebrates spring with this grand street parade.

MAY

Free Comic Book Day: On the first Saturday in May, pick up, yes, a free comic book at local shops.

Opening Day of boating season: Also on the first Saturday in May, a parade of decorated boats travels through Seattle's Montlake Cut to mark the start of boating season.

May the Fourth (be with you): Yet another reason to throw on your Chewbacca or Boba Fett costume.

Bike to School Day: Get your wheels in gear. It's also Bike Everywhere Month.

Syttende Mai: On May 17 every year, Ballard flies its Scandinavian colors high with this popular and historic parade and assorted other events (fjord horses!).

Northwest Folklife: This vast, affordable Memorial Day festival at Seattle Center (admission is by donation) always includes an incredible lineup of music and dance.

JUNE

Free fishing weekend: On the first weekend after the first Monday in June, Washington state doesn't require fishing licenses (or a Discover Pass).

Vashon Sheepdog Classic: This herding competition is one of the most attended on the West Coast.

Evergreen Mountain Bike Festival: Take guided rides, try demos and watch amazing jumps at the Eastside's Duthie Hill Park.

Fremont Solstice Parade & Fair: This famous artsy, quirky festival stars a free-spirited parade (naked bikers!), art cars, dog parade and kids' activities.

Black Arts Festival: Explore the cultural roots of African-American culture through performances, music, hands-on activities and food.

Pride Month and PrideFest: A fantastic and flamboyant parade, drag queen story time and much more.

JULY

Seafair: Starting in July and spilling into August, Seattle's old-timey maritime festival is a series of events, parades and street fairs.

BAM Artsfair: The largest juried arts and crafts fair in the Northwest, held at Bellevue Arts Museum and Bellevue Square, also includes the amazing Kidsfair.

King County Fair: The Enumclaw fair is inexpensive and old-fashioned, with free entertainment, rides and farm animals.

Ethnic Fest: An annual celebration of Pierce County's cultural diversity is held at Wright Park in late July.

Canoe Journey: In late July, tribes join together for an epic paddle to celebrate and preserve Coast Salish culture.

AUGUST

National Night Out: The first Tuesday of August is an excuse to block off your street and get to know your neighbors.

Evergreen State Fair: The fair in Monroe revs into action with animals on display, midway rides and the rodeo.

Salmon viewing at Ballard Locks: From mid-June to October (best viewing in August), the fish ladder at the locks offers a spectacular view into the life cycle of our iconic fish.

SEPTEMBER

National Coffee Day: This made-up holiday is an excuse for cafes to offer discounts and perfect for moms and dads with a caffeine habit.

Washington State Fair: Bring on the deep-fried Snickers! Also find carnival rides, animals, a rodeo, monster truck jams and lots more entertainment.

Bremerton Blackberry Festival: Blackberry treats, fun runs, fly-ins and more family fun on the Bremerton boardwalk over Labor Day weekend.

OCTOBER

Issaquah Salmon Days Festival: Take a look at salmon swimming upstream to spawn, then stick around for a parade and kids' activities.

Star Wars Reads Day: Typically held on a Saturday in October, this newish, unofficial holiday is celebrated at local libraries, bookstores and museums.

BrickCon: Got Lego lovers? This Seattle Center festival, with displays and group builds, has everything.

GeekGirlCon: Support girls and women in geek culture, and share facts and fandom at this two-day convention.

Oktoberfest Northwest: At the Puyallup Fairgrounds, parents can sip the region's newest brews, while kids go on rides and taste at the "root bier" garden.

NOVEMBER

Day of the Dead: Honor your family's dearly departed at events at spots such as Seattle Center, Tacoma Art Museum, Phinney Neighborhood Center and, farther afield, Tieton.

Yulefest: Check out the new Nordic Museum and find Scandinavian crafts, traditional foods and straw ornaments for gift giving.

Winterfest: Beginning on the Friday after Thanksgiving, Seattle Center's awesome (and mostly free) holiday fest stars a miniature train layout, ice carving and even an ice rink.

Magic Season in Bellevue: Snowflake Lane, Garden d'Lights and the Magic Season ice arena are three reasons Bellevue shines so bright in holiday fun.

DECEMBER

Pathway of Lights: Seattle's Green Lake hosts the Pathway of Lights walk sometime near the solstice, which can be a magical way of reconnecting during the holidays over magical lights.

Christmas Lighting Festival: This annual festival is reason no. 600 to go to the faux-Bavarian town of Leavenworth.

Model Train Festival: The Washington State History Museum celebrates all things choo-choo at this December festival (with Santa in attendance on select days).

Christmas Ship Festival: Gather on a dark beach for live music broadcasting to shore from decorated ships, and (if you're lucky) a bonfire.

Tacoma First Night: This huge indoor/outdoor festival on Dec. 31 features dozens of exciting performances, including giant puppets and fire dancers.

Resources for Further Adventuring

BOOKS

"Best Hikes with Kids: Western Washington" by Susan Elderkin: The long-awaited update to Joan Burton's classic guide includes 125 family hikes, from berry-picking walks to peak-bagging treks. (Mountaineers Books)

"By the Shore" by Nancy Blakey: A seasonal guide to coastal adventures, including squid jigging, making your own sea salt, beach hikes and stand-up paddleboarding. (Sasquatch Books)

"Curious Kids Nature Guide" by Fiona Cohen: Filled with full-color, scientifically accurate illustrations about the Pacific Northwest, this book teaches kids about some of the most intriguing flora, fauna and natural phenomena of the region. (Sasquatch Books)

"Discovering Seattle Parks" by Linnea Westerlind: First, Westerlind, a mom of three, visited each of Seattle's 426 city parks. Then she wrote the ultimate guide to them. (Mountaineers Books)

"Northwest Kid Trips" by Lora Shinn: This book guides family travelers through four vibrant cities, with a goal of maximum fun with minimal hassle. (ParentMap)

"Seattle Stairway Walks" by Jake and Cathy Jaramillo: There are 600 publicly accessible stairways in Seattle that thread through the city's hills, bluffs and canyons. With this book, the Jaramillos guide you through the best of them. (Mountaineers Books)

"Seattle Walks: Discovering History and Nature in the City" by David Williams: A natural historian, Williams shares the best walks in one of the most walkable cities in the United States. (University of Washington Press)

"Swimming Holes of Washington" by Shane Robinson and Anna Katz: This lavishly illustrated, full-color guide shares the goods on 70 prime swimming holes, most of them in nature. (Mountaineers Books)

WEBSITES, BLOGS, APPS

Adventure Awaits: The recreation blog and storytelling site for Washington State Parks has all kinds of adventure photos and trip tips for exploring state parks. *adventureawaits.com*

Atlas Obscura: This global community of explorers curates "a comprehensive database of the world's most wondrous places and foods," including many in Seattle. *atlasobscura.com/things-to-do/seattle-washington*

Cascade Bicycle Club: Get bike and safety tips, and sign up for camps and classes. *cascade.org*

Evergreen Mountain Bike Alliance: A nonprofit promoting mountain biking and offering a huge trail guide, camps, clinics and annual festivals. *evergreenmtb.org*

Families of Color Seattle: This Seattle nonprofit supports families of color in many ways, including parenting groups, resource sharing and events. *focseattle.org*

Hike it Baby: If you've got tots and want hiking/walking partners, your first stop should be *hikeitbaby.com*, an almost-free platform that helps hiking parents connect.

Mamava mobile app: Got milk? This app locates (and unlocks) Mamava lactation pods for you, and also maps out other reader-reviewed nursing and pumping locations. *mamava.com/mobile-app*

Moms Pump Here: Another great resource for nursing and pumping moms, the website and app offer access to its community-driven nursing locator that maps 7,000 lactation spots around the U.S. *momspumphere.com*

National Park Service: Plan your next trip to a national park, and learn about the National Park Service's "Every Kid in a Park" program, which gives fourth-graders and their families free admission to national parks. *nps.gov*

Northwest TripFinder: Written by ParentMap travel blogger Lauren Braden, this blog is a deep resource for offbeat getaways around the Northwest that are fun, affordable and easy to plan. *nwtripfinder.com*

PEPS: A nonprofit that supports parents through its neighborhood-based parent groups and other resources. *peps.org*

Rain or Shine Guides: Two Seattle moms share their favorite places around Seattle in a lighthearted, visual style. *rainorshineguides.com*

Sounds Fun Mom: The best resource around on family fun in the South Sound area, by ParentMap writer Maegen Blue. *soundsfunmom.com*

The Hiker Mama: ParentMap writer Jennifer Johnson hikes all around western Washington with her two children and shares her reviews and tips on her blog. *thehikermama.com*

Thrifty NW Mom: Jen Dotson founded the website in January 2009 as a way to share "her love of a good deal and frugal ways with family and friends." *thriftynorthwestmom.com*

Utrip: This intuitive online travel planner lets you easily build personal itineraries to plan the ultimate family vacation in the Seattle area (and far beyond). *utrip.com/plan-travel/united-states/seattle*

Washington Department of Fish and Wildlife: The best source around for information on how and where to fish, crab, shellfish, hunt and more in Washington state. *wdfw.wa.gov*

Washington Trails Association: The nonprofit's website is the best online hiking guide in Washington state, providing trip reports, hiking guides and loads of resources for safe hiking. *wta.org*

Index

EDITOR'S NOTE: This is a limited index of attractions and places mentioned in "52 Seattle Adventures With Kids." It does not include every location noted, only those that were listed as attractions (eg., Bellingham, San Juan Island).

Who's Who

Want to know more about the writers behind the adventures? Read on! You can also find more of their work at *parentmap.com*.

Gemma Alexander is a freelance writer who blogs about the arts at *gemmadeealexander.com* and who also spends too much time on Twitter. In their quest to visit all 27 Seattle Public Library branches, she and her two daughters have gotten to know Seattle pretty well.

Nancy Schatz Alton is a Seattle-based freelance writer, writing teacher and author of two holistic health care guides, "The Healthy Back Book" and "The Healthy Knees Book." Find out more at *withinthewords.com*.

Bryony Angell is a Seattleite, born and raised, and has a deep love for the tall trees and rocky beaches of the Pacific Northwest. She's raising two kids to love birds and hug trees for the next generation.

Maegen Blue is the founder and editor of *SoundsFunMom.com*, a blog for South Sound families. She lives in Puyallup with her husband and two boys.

Lauren Braden is a Pacific Northwest writer who focuses on outdoor recreation and local travel. Her favorite season to explore is autumn, when fall foraging and colorful foliage lure her family out of town almost every weekend. She blogs at *nwtripfinder.com*.

April Chan is a journalist who previously served as editor for several area Patch community news sites and as online editor for *The Olympian*. A kid tip from Chan: Don't mow the lawn. Tall grass harbors tons of neat critters and wildflowers for the kiddos to observe, and the TV stays off!

Nancy Chaney is ParentMap's Out + About editor. Although a Washington native, she hates rain and lives for playing outside with her family during the Seattle summer.

Fiona Cohen lives, writes and grows tomatoes in Seattle. She is the author of "Curious Kids Nature Guide" (Sasquatch Books). Her favorite season is summer, and her favorite place to be in the summer is out of the city.

Kris Collingridge is a former editor for ParentMap, and, to her amazement, the mother of two grown children. She only goes on vacation in the fall, winter or spring, because she can't bear to miss one day of Puget Sound's gorgeous summers.

Annie Fanning, a Seattle-based writer and copy editor, believes that parents should continually teach their children that the best things in life are free. Wish her luck during her daughters' teenage years.

Emily Grosvenor is the editor of *Oregon Home* magazine, the author of the math picture book, "Tessalation!," and a freelance writer.

JiaYing Grygiel is a writer and photographer who loves exploring Seattle with her two little boys. Her favorite things are freebies and bargains, overcast days and yummy things to eat.

Allison Holm is a Seattle native, mom of three and coffee enthusiast who is always on the lookout for the next "great idea." She is working on her first chapter book for kids. Find out more at *allisonholm.squarespace.com*.

Jennifer Johnson is an Edmonds-based writer and naturalist who has chronicled her hiking adventures with her two children on *thehikermama.com*. Her family motto is: "Be (over)prepared!"

Jennifer Kakutani is working on her forthcoming memoir, titled "Thoughts No Mother Should Have," about her recovery from postpartum depression. It's the story of how one mother's determination was tested when disturbing thoughts about her baby interrupted her plans to become a blissed-out, placenta-nibbling earth mama.

Kate Missine is a Sammamish-based writer, foodie and girly girl raising two wild boys. She lived in Canada and sunny Cali before returning to the Pacific Northwest, where she rediscovered a love for its drizzly fall, cloudy skies and little rain boots.

Elisa Murray, who edited "52 Seattle Adventures With Kids" and wrote many of its chapters, is a Seattle-based freelance writer, former editor at ParentMap and mom to one cool kid. True story: She got a dog just to get out of the house more. It worked (at least for her).

Kali Sakai is a Seattle-based freelance writer and advocate who explores parenting, media, geekery and social policy. She is also a shark-loving, multi-ethnic Washingtonian who lives in Ballard with her family and pet fish. Find more of her stories on *evidentlyblog.com*.

E. Ashley Steel, Ph.D., studies rivers and loves statistics. Together with her husband, Bill Richards, she co-wrote "Family on the Loose: The Art of Traveling with Kids" and "100 Tips for Traveling With Kids in Europe."

Linnea Westerlind is the author of "Discovering Seattle Parks" (Mountaineers Books) and the creator of *yearofseattleparks.com*. She has been known to use old Halloween candy to get her three kids to hike longer.

Acknowledgments

My family of origin moved six times by the time I was 12 years old, from Tulsa to Chicago to Marshfield, Massachusetts. So I came by my mobile spirit both by nature and nurture. I am grateful to my two sisters and my mother, who were my original adventure partners, and to my father and dear stepmother, who introduced me to the joys of global travel.

The nuclear family that I've since built — husband, son and dog — are more home-oriented than me, so I owe them a debt for letting me nudge them on all kinds of explorations of forest, sea and city. Thank you, John, Isaac and Lucy. You are my preferred partners in all everyday adventures.

I am grateful to everyone associated with ParentMap during the time that I've worked there (and since, too!) for encouraging my editorial pursuits and sharing their ideas. I can't begin to name everyone, but want to call out current and former ParentMap staff members Tara Buchan, Lindsey Carter, Diana Cherry, Rory Graves, Sonja Hanson, Emily Johnson, Patty Lindley, Nicole Persun, Natalie Singer-Velush and Elisa Taylor. I am particularly indebted to those ParentMappers who directly worked on this book. Beth Kramer and Nancy Chaney, thanks for all your ideas, feedback and edits. I also thank fact-checking intern extraordinaire Lillian Prime and terrific proofreader Jill Walters. Sunny Parsons, having you as copy editor immeasurably improved the quality of the words here. Amy Chinn, your design work made those words come alive. Alayne Sulkin, you made it all happen!

Finally, this book wouldn't have happened without the wonderful writers who contributed to "52 Adventures" (see "Who's Who"). Thank you for letting me take your pieces and sew them into this quilt of a project.

—*Elisa Murray*

CPSIA information can be obtained
at www.ICGtesting.com
Printed in the USA
BVHW072309211218
535918BV00004B/4/P

9 780990 430667